THEY
WILL
BE
HEARD

Books by Jonathan Daniels

Clash of Angels
A Southerner Discovers the South
A Southerner Discovers New England
Tar Heels: A Portrait of North Carolina
Frontier on the Potomac
The Man of Independence
The End of Innocence
The Forest Is the Future
Prince of Carpetbaggers
Mosby, Gray Ghost of the Confederacy
Stonewall Jackson
Robert E. Lee
October Recollections
The Devil's Backbone
They Will Be Heard

THEY WILL BE HEARD

America's Crusading Newspaper Editors

by Jonathan Daniels

McGraw-Hill Book Company

New York　　Toronto　　London

They Will Be Heard

First Edition

15331

To my friends

Barry Bingham
Hodding Carter
Ralph McGill
*Gallant captains in
the continuing American Crusade*

Contents

I will be *as harsh as truth,*
and as uncompromising as justice.
On this subject I do not wish to think,
or speak, or write with moderation....
I am in earnest—
I will not equivocate—
I will not excuse—
I will not retreat a single inch—
and I will be heard.

—*William Lloyd Garrison*

THEY
WILL
BE
HEARD

1

"By the Ears
for a Groat"

"Messieurs printers," young John Adams addressed a communication to the *Boston Gazette* in August 1765.

"Be not intimidated," he enjoined them, "nor suffer yourselves to be wheedled out of your liberty by any pretenses of politeness, delicacy or decency. These, as they are often used, are but three names for hypocrisy, chicanery and cowardice."

That communication dressed the lion, already roaring, in the skin of the lamb afraid to bleat. Actually, the press needed no goading. The Stamp Act, by directly taxing newspapers, touched its most sensitive nerve. Its screams carried anger and excite-

1

ment to tavern and dockyard, wharf and shop. And in the same
month Adams wrote to the *Gazette,* a Boston mob demolished the
mansion of a responsible royal official with a savage thorough-
ness seldom duplicated.

John Adams always solemnly deplored violence. As President
of the United States he so revised his views about freedom of the
press as to seem its chief enemy, when editors were fined and
imprisoned under the Alien and Sedition laws. Such change of
view is not exceptional. Thomas Jefferson, whom angry editors
helped displace Adams in the White House, has been regarded as
a sort of parent of press freedom in America. But he learned, as
had Adams, that in the case of crusading editors one man's patriot can be another man's poisoner.

Jefferson put in his records a report of a Cabinet meeting on
August 2, 1791, in Philadelphia, when President George Washington was as inflamed as the summer heat outside. The mosqui-
toes, soon to bring yellow fever from the steaming stagnant
places about the handsome town, had no sharper stings for
Washington than the press.

The great Chief Magistrate, wrote Jefferson, "got into one of
those passions when he cannot command himself, ran on much on
the personal abuse which had been bestowed on him." Such had
been the malevolent attacks, Washington cried, that he had re-
pented only once not having retired at the end of his first term
"& that was every minute since." "By God," he would rather
be in his grave than in his present situation. He would rather be
on his farm than be made emperor of the world, and yet they
were charging him with wanting to be king. He saw "an impudent design to insult him."

Mr. Jefferson was not sympathetic that day. Washington
emerges from his description of the occasion as a furious old man
lapsing from his high tone into querulous complaint against editorial abuse. The editor Washington regarded as a rascal Jefferson considered a savior. Conservative editors, led by Alexander
Hamilton, were already calling the followers of Jefferson "Jacobins" who would bring the dangerous radicalism of revolutionary France into the infant Republic. But Jefferson felt that the
editor of Washington's ire was one whose "paper saved

our constitution which was galloping fast into monarchy" with the whip applied by Hamilton's conservative editorial and other companions.

Jefferson had already led the demand for the addition to the Constitution of a Bill of Rights, including stipulation of freedom of the press. He never retreated from his faith in that freedom which could serve the furies as well as the facts. He said "Were it left to me to decide whether we should have a government without newspapers, or newspapers without government, I should not hesitate a moment to prefer the latter."

That statement has been better remembered by journalists than some other views expressed on the subject by the red-headed Virginia President and political philosopher. As he himself advanced toward the Executive Mansion he was called atheist, adulterer, and red-handed revolutionary by editors solemnly and venomously certain that they were serving the public safety. And while friendly editors answered the abuse in kind, Jefferson was not so much the philosopher that he did not upon occasion become as irate as Washington had been. Indeed, during his second term, he piled the whole press into an expression of distaste: "The man who never looks into a newspaper is better informed than he who reads them; inasmuch as he who knows nothing is nearer to truth than he whose mind is filled with falsehoods & errors."

Other Presidents have found outspoken or merely sharp-penned editors hard to bear. So have many rogues. Editorial onslaughts have hit the just and the unjust, causing pain to each. Yet, as Mr. Jefferson ruefully admitted to the end of his life, the violence, malevolence, venom of some could not be dispensed with lest the nation lose the courage, the criticism, the everlasting evangelism in public affairs of others. And high and low, on the left and the right, all the exuberant editors have regarded themselves as crusaders. They have been apt to regard their articulate opposites in other offices as the wicked deserving their damnation. But combative journalists have kept their chief contempt for the quiescent in the craft.

All such editors clamoring for causes come down to us in American history as crusaders. The word *crusade* has almost been monopolized by journalists, although an occasional politician or general turned politician picks it up for his own purposes. But editors have not generally looked like crusaders in armor; in the early days of the printer as editor he wore instead a smeared apron to keep ink stains off his pants. Sometimes he fashioned a paper hat to protect his hair. It was no visored helmet, though one might have helped when some readers answered his pen with their canes. Careless costume became almost a uniform in some shabby sanctums. Other editors looked, in the dress of dandies, like river-boat gamblers. Some in spirit were. And there were those who wore elaborate shirts suitable for stuffing.

All crusaders, both among the pious pilgrims journeying to Jerusalem and in the press on its self-appointed errands, have been at least as marked by roughness as by holy purposes. The sword was never neatly separated from the Cross. In many editorial sanctums the pistol lay beside the pen—or ready in a desk drawer beneath it. In others, pacifists were the most furious men. Some editors wrote with bottles of liquor beside bottles of ink, yet some of the most intoxicated were teetotalers.

Early editorial crusades in America were for the right to crusade itself. Printers confronted Puritans whose eagerness for religious freedom for themselves did not include such right for others and certainly did not contemplate the extension of any liberties to the press. Kindred views about the impertinence of printers were held by Cavalier governors. In Virginia in 1671, Sir William Berkeley, who governed that colony for thirty-eight years, summed up the official view of the time in a classic statement.

"I thank God," he said, "we have not free schools nor printing; and I hope we shall not have these hundred years. For learning has brought disobedience and heresy and sects into the world; and printing has divulged them and libels against the government. God keep us from both."

The hundred years he hoped for were scarcely over when the newspaper crusade was for American independence, led in clamorous fashion by editors who had a first, cash interest in the Stamp Acts. Editors cheered the revolution on; others sailed off with the Tories; some managed to be sharp-spoken on both sides as Patriots and Redcoats alternately occupied their towns.

The Alien and Sedition laws made the battles between the Democrats (then called Republicans) and the Federalists a self-protective cause of the press as well. Editors pilloried Andrew Jackson while other editors helped bring his frightening equalitarian frontier democracy to the national capital. Equally angry editors fought for and against slavery. Abraham Lincoln was lambasted—and not merely by the Southern editors who called him an ape on a manure pile. And some editors in the South seemed to add their voices to the Yankee chorus about hanging Jeff Davis on a sour apple tree.

Beyond civil war some editors waved the bloody shirt while others called for the closing of the bloody chasm. They damned the Money Power and warned of the godless grasping of Labor. Furiously they opposed violence. They caricatured other crusaders. And some saved Cuba by providing an almost private war for their circulation departments. They clamored to keep America out of world war and for America to make Democracy safe in the world. Isolationists and interventionists have had their eager champions in the press. And from the Bastille to the Bolsheviks there has been a jeremiad journalism hailing revolution and hating it. The yellow press has often been most insistently red, white, and blue.

In their diverse fashions editors have both recorded history and made it. Their stories fall into no neat chronological pattern; the labors and belaborings of journalists do not fall into precise periods. Their papers came from their presses day by day and week by week. Yesterday's papers were often and quickly only like fallen leaves in the recurrent autumns of old issues and new causes. Contents and contributors overlap in time. But the papers and their makers overlooked nothing in native directions, dreams, and disappointments. They wrote the diary of a diverse nation—of its separate sections and large and small communities. They cleaned up cities and states, driving crooks from state house and courthouse, and on some other occasions shamed cities—and defamed good men in them. They faced sacrifice for conviction and in some cases were not above blackmail.

Statesmen in their shirtsleeves, advisors and agitators of Presidents, dreamers and drunks, poets and panderers, mild-man-
nered men and marauders, martyrs brave or merely bluster-
ing, patriots and turncoats, crusading editors have been as diverse as the whole American scene and American company they
scolded. Many were ready—and required—to sacrifice their lives
for a cause. And in the American press the salvation of the
people has not always been inseparable from the desire to sell
papers.

Merely to list the journalistic crusaders would require a direc-
tory and in it their addresses would be important in indicating
the continental geography in which they were generated. Even
to define them is difficult. There is a distinction between crusading writers and crusading editors. Tom Paine—whom Theodore
Roosevelt, in galloping misunderstanding of history, called "a
dirty little atheist"—was essentially a pamphleteer. And most
of those the same Roosevelt called *muckrakers*—Lincoln Steffens
and Ida Tarbell, among others—wrote for the magazines and the
book publishers. Rather than editors, modern columnists, amplified by syndication, are like the regular contributors to early
papers who often signed their pieces with Latin names. Across
history there have been writers working in terms of the uninterrupted exposé of Drew Pearson and the scream-pitched scorn of
Westbrook Pegler. There have always been quieter commentators
like Walter Lippmann and perceptive interpretive reporters like
James Reston. Richard Harding Davis was only one glamorous
swashbuckler with words. Like other reporters, Irvin S. Cobb
could work in crime and comedy. Such men cannot be included
in the company of crusading editors. And it is certainly not easy
to choose which editors to include in a sampling of the story of
them all.

The problem is the wealth of subject matter and the complex
character of those who made it. The first editors were printers as
well, and capitalists even if their investments were only handkerchiefs full of type. Sometimes crusading editors have been
publishers, even though that term has come generally to connote
plush gentlemen more concerned with revenues than with raids
on wrongdoers. But the platoon of fighters here arrayed was

chosen to suggest in time, geography, and personality a sample
of the men whose hostilities and hopes have marked America
with ink on the unrolling reel of its national story.

It is not easy to find the first of the crusading American editors. *First* has always been a matter of furious debate in the
competitive and combative press—from first in history to first
with the news. The honor of printing the first American newspaper, regarded as more dubious then than now, belongs to Benjamin Harris of Boston. He produced there the first issue of his
Publick Occurrences Both Forreign and Domestick on September 25, 1690. In a sense Harris was crusading. His announced
purpose was to expose false rumors. He was ready, he said, to
publish the names of all the liars who started them. The liars, if
any, in Boston were safe. The first issue of *Publick Occurrences*
was the last. In "high resentment" the Governor and Council
promptly suppressed the unlicensed sheet. Earlier, in London,
Harris, as printer of a "seditious pamphlet," had been made to
stand in the pillory and pay a fine by a judge who declared that
he was a wretch who would "set us all by the ears for a groat."
Such fury for fourpence is a charge which has rung around the
ears of crusading editors ever since.

Then there was James Franklin, older brother of the greater
printer, Benjamin. He began his protest obliquely against civil
and religious authorities in the *New-England Courant* in 1721 by
a campaign against smallpox vaccination, which was approved by
such powerful Puritans as Increase and Cotton Mather. He was
wrong. Toward the end of the century another newspaper crusader in Philadelphia, William Cobbett, whose furious pen became well known on both sides of the Atlantic, attacked the
copious bleeding of yellow fever sufferers by eminent doctors. He
was right. But a libel verdict against him broke him all the same.
The roar is not always the measure of the righteousness. Good
causes come to catastrophe, some bad ones are durable. The vitality of the American press from colonial complaint to contemporary controversy rises chiefly from the fact that there never has
been an American cause without editors, confident that they
were crusading, on both sides.

Also, there has never been a time when such editors were not

under the scrutiny of and subject to attack by citizens, subscribers, politicians, and often by street mobs. Perhaps their
story is best begun with the lament of Cotton Mather about the
printed impertinences of James Franklin: "A wickedness never
parallel'd any where upon the Face of the Earth!" Two centuries and two decades later complaint came from the self-
described curmudgeon, Harold L. Ickes, Secretary of the Interior in the Franklin Roosevelt Cabinet. He spoke of "the hounds
of the Baskervilles that the publishers lost no time in loosing
upon me." All understood then that it would take as brave a
hound to bite Ickes as it required to snap at the heels of Cotton
Mather.

But the pursuit of editors is quite as constant as the editors
after the malefactors of their own choice and description. Sometimes in the conclaves of one or the other of the great political
parties, hoots and cheers have risen highest at angry mention of
the "one-party press," depending upon which party at which
time seemed to be getting editorial preference. Then the rafters
only rang with the long echoes of the alternative cries of Jeffersonians and Hamiltonians, the outrage of both colonial governors
and tax-sensitive colonial subjects.

Now anonymity grows. Electronics and syndication sometimes
seem to obscure the crusading editor behind the better-known
voices of commentators and columnists (*calumnists* to Mr.
Ickes). The press appears more and more a business, less and less
a vehicle of verbal violence. Competition and combativeness both
seem muted in an opulent society. In a computer age the pen—
even the typewriter—may seem as obsolete as the pistol. Actually, little changes. The pattern of the past is the continuity of
the future. Lacking their monumental dimensions, there will always be Washingtons to wince and rant at abuse and Jeffersons
who hold to their faith in freedom despite freedom's faults. And
there will always be men, word-armed and word-ready, in the
tradition of crusading American editors. Impertinent often,
pugnacious always, unintimidated by power, uncaptured by con-
formity, they will be at every barricade of American battling.
The meaning of this land will be lost when their spirit is gone.

2

Songs for the Hangman

On paper emblazoned *God Save the King,* His Excellency William Cosby, Captain General and Governour in Chief of the Provinces of New-York, New-Jersey, and Territories thereupon depending in America, Vice-Admiral of the same, and Colonel in His Majesty's Army, on November 6, 1734, issued his proclamation:

Whereas Ill-minded and Disaffected persons have lately dispersed in the City of New-York, and divers other Places, several Scandalous and Seditious Libels, but more particularly two Printed Scandalous Songs or Ballads, highly de-

9

faming the Administration of His Majesty's Government in this Province, tending greatly to inflame the Minds of His Majesty's good Subjects, and to disturb the Public Peace. . . .

THEREFORE, Governor Cosby offered £20 reward to "the person or persons who shall discover the Author or Authors of the two Scandalous Songs or Ballads." He was eager for "the Discovery of the Offenders, that they might, by Law, receive a Punishment adequate to their Guilt and Crime."

The crime was clear. The verses of the song had been written in celebration of the election of officials in New York who did not bow to the whims of His Excellency. One ("To the tune of To you fair Ladies now on land") ran:

> To you good lads that dare oppose
>   all lawless power and might,
> You are the theme that we have chose
>   and to your praise we write:
> You dar'd to show your faces brave
> In spight of every abject slave;
>   with a fa la la. . . .

It went on for four stanzas, including the patriotic injunction:

> Stand up and save your Country dear,
> In spight of usquebaugh and beer;
>   with a fa la la. . . .

So they arrested John Peter Zenger, from whose press the verses undoubtedly came. Zenger was an ink-stained printer, who spoke English with the heavy accent of a Palatine peasant. The typesetting, capitalization, and spelling in the printed songs were unquestionably his. The gay insubordination probably came from his "authors" or contributors. Still John Peter Zenger, printer of the *New-York Weekly Journal*, went to jail to become the head of the procession of crusading American editors who have sometimes enlightened and always enlivened this land.

Around his print shop and his name in the colony of New York in 1735 was established the right—at least the idea—of a

free press not only in America but in the world. He seemed an
unlikely man for such a mission. Zenger's people were those Palatines who were left starving after a French army laid waste the
valley of the Rhine in the spring of 1707. And upon wasted
fields, uprooted vineyards, and torn orchards came a winter so
cold, it was said, that the farmers could not coax a flame out of
the firewood into the open air. Starving, they snatched at the
proposal of Queen Anne that they go to America to settle the
land and make tar out of the pine trees to break the Swedish
monopoly in naval stores.

The warm offer led to a terrible pilgrimage. Thousands of the
Rhenish refugees squatting in London on the way attracted the
curiosity, then the annoyance, and finally the anger of British
mobs fearing competition for their jobs. At last, they sailed on
what they first called the "Wonder Fleet." The 2800 passengers
packed in ten vessels constituted the single largest emigration to
America during the colonial period. The ships became a pest
fleet, rotten with typhus. Zenger's father died with more than
300 others on the voyage. But the Palatines who survived practically doubled the population of New York, a city of rich English
and Dutch merchants, of mechanics and seamen, and a squalid
populace including hundreds of black slaves.

Many of the Palatines moved up the Hudson to make tar in
the pine forests for the British fleet. They were cheated in the
process by settlers who had come earlier and taken vast tracts of
land. Young Zenger was luckier. At fourteen he was apprenticed
to William Bradford, the famous early printer who had moved
to New York after troubles with Quaker censorship in Philadelphia. Now, approaching his fifties, Bradford was more willing
to be subservient as royal printer. He published no newspaper
then. If he had, he would probably have taken scant notice of the
sensational news in the tough and elegant town in which he
taught the Palatine apprentice his trade.

Popular Governor Robert Hunter and his rich colonial chief
justice, Lewis Morris, wrote and published a lively play, the first
known to have been produced in America, which put the people
into "a laughing humor." Still, the year after young Zenger
went to work for Bradford, fear stalked the town when a party

of Negro slaves staged a revolt in an orchard near Maiden Lane
and murdered a dozen whites. Twenty-one slaves were shot,
hanged, or burned at the stake.

Young Zenger set type. He bedaubed himself as he inked the
forms with a wool-filled sheepskin ball. Then, at a wooden press
not much improved since Gutenberg had invented movable-type
printing more than two centuries before, he gave the strong pull
which pressed the paper against the inked type. A good man—
perhaps an eager boy—could make 200 impressions or "pulls"
an hour. Evidently this boy satisfied Bradford. At the end of his
apprenticeship he went wandering. His marriage to a girl in
Philadelphia did not last long, though it brought him a son.
Apparently, however, he had money enough to do printing on his
own in Maryland. A new print shop could be equipped for £75 to
£100. But, despite a printing contract from the Maryland Assembly, Zenger came back to New York. There in 1722 he married Anna Catherina Maulin, who was to become the kind of wife
his vicissitudes in printing were to require.

The next year he was made a freeman of the city. William
Bradford took him into partnership in 1725, the year Bradford
issued New York's first newspaper, the *New-York Gazette*. Zenger's partnership in that enterprise lasted hardly longer than
his first marriage. At the end of a year, he moved out and set up
his own "struggling little business" on Smith Street (that portion of the present William Street lying between Maiden Lane
and Pearl Street).

There was nothing exciting at the time about Zenger's printing, much of which was in Dutch. His most notable product was
the first arithmetic text printed in the colony. Then sometime in
the early fall of 1733 rich, aristocratic, combative James Alexander talked with him. Alexander wanted neither textbook nor
handbill nor tract. He wanted a newspaper to oppose the new
royal governor, William Cosby. With Alexander in that enterprise were William Smith, an able young lawyer, and Lewis
Morris, no longer in a happy playwriting mood.

Starting a newspaper in New York was a daring venture for a
small printer. Not many of the 10,000 people in the town, which
ran only as far north as Cortlandt and Frankford streets, were

readers of anything. More preferred to shoot quail in the brush
along Broadway. Furthermore, Zenger's old partner Bradford
was providing a paper. Perhaps it was, as Zenger scornfully said
later, filled with "dry, senseless Stuff, and fulsome Pane-
gyrics." Nevertheless, behind it was the financial security of the
royal printing contract—and the royal governor's pleasure.

Zenger was thirty-six. Anna Catherina was filling his house
with children. The probability is that he talked the proposal over
with her. The shop needed business. Printing a paper would
provide it. It seems certain, according to the printer's biographer Livingston Rutherfurd, "that he went into the newspaper
scheme from a commercial point of view only." There is no
question that his rich backers went into the business to "expose" Cosby. Alexander even expressed that intention to former
Governor Hunter when he sent him the first copy, which
appeared on November 5, 1733. As citizens quickly realized and
as historians report, "an independent and truculent spirit was
infused into New York journalism."

They were truculent times, and behind him John Peter Zenger
had independent men. James Alexander, who has been called the
de facto editor of the *Weekly Journal,* was born heir to the title
of the Earl of Stirling. He had served as a Jacobite in the confused and blundering rebellion of 1715. Fortunately for him
when the defeated Scots were scurrying to safety, John, Duke of
Argyle, who had smashed the revolt, was an hereditary friend of
Alexander's family. He may have aided young James' escape.
Apparently, through the Duke's assistance and on the basis of
his own training as an engineer officer, Alexander was established in security in America within months after the revolt was
over.

He was appointed surveyor-general of the Province of New
Jersey and later of New York. Soon after his arrival in America
he married the shrewd and lively widow of a prosperous New
York merchant named Provoost. She not only presented Alexander with five children; with much success, she also continued
her first husband's mercantile business. Alexander studied law
and came to be regarded as the foremost lawyer in New Jersey.
Important posts, including places on the Councils of New Jersey

and New York, then under the same governor, came his way.
Just as he had not hesitated to support the exiled Stuarts in
Scotland, in America he remained ready to oppose what he re-
garded arbitrary autocratic power. And in 1733, he believed that
strutting tyranny was embodied in the elegant person of new
Governor Cosby.

William Cosby was accustomed to taking what he wanted. He
felt that he had a right to be affronted by resistance. After all, he
came of a powerful Irish family. His haughty wife was Grace
Montagu, sister of the second Earl of Halifax. There had, indeed, been some little difficulty when, as Governor of the balmy
Mediterranean island of Minorca, Cosby had been charged with
extortion. That irritating incident was behind him. He expected
no such impertinence in that colder, more remote area when in
1731 he received his commission as Governor of New York and
the Jerseys.

Governor Cosby moved without haste to his new post. There
were problems of concern to the colony to which he gave his
attention in London. But he was in a hurry soon after he arrived
in August 1732 to fill his pockets. He appointed his son ''Billy''
to a sinecure as secretary of the Jerseys. He grasped real trouble,
however, when he demanded that the rich provincial gentleman
who had acted as governor in the interim before his arrival turn
over to him half of all he had gotten for his services. Seventy-
year-old Rip Van Dam, declined in words as staccato as his
name.

Possibly Cosby needed the money more than Van Dam did.
Lady Cosby was already intriguing then, the Governor's critics
said, to marry their daughter to Lord Augustus, son of the Duke
of Grafton. The manners and maneuvers in matchmaking and
other things in such exalted station were costly to maintain.

But old Dutch Van Dam knew the value of a guilder. Born in
the colony, he had made a fortune in stores, ships, and forests, in
supplying soldiers and building houses. Now he declined either
to give up his money or to be kicked off the Council, on which he
had served for thirty years. Instead he retained as lawyers William Smith and James Alexander. Smith had studied at both
Yale and the Inns of Court in London. He was a classical scholar

and had identified himself with the more radical group in provincial politics.

Alexander and Smith pursued the case with such zeal that, in
its aftermath, Lady Cosby was heard to say that "her highest
wish for Alexander and Smith was to see them strung up on the
gallows at the gate of the Fort." One of Cosby's loyal supporters on the Council charged that Alexander came near treason in
working the people up to the pitch of rebellion. The Governor's
critics did, indeed, tell the people that "if Mr. Van Dam had
suffered himself tamely to be devoured," how would a poor man
fare?

The two lawyers seemed to the Governor in sufficient rebellion
when they vigorously asserted Van Dam's cause. He saw sedition when Lewis Morris, as chief justice, declared illegal the
Executive's proceeding to wrench the money from Van Dam.
Promptly the furious Cosby removed Morris and named as chief
justice in his place James DeLancey, another rich aristocrat.
DeLancey, as a judge, had taken the Governor's side on the court
with Frederick Philipse, whose family had grown rich in trade—
including slaves and, it was charged, some complicity with the
pirate, Captain Kidd.

So the lines were drawn between the "court party" and the
popular cause. There were equally rich provincials on both sides.
But the court had its paper in Bradford's obsequious *Gazette*.
So Morris, Alexander, and Smith turned to John Peter Zenger.

They were not mistaken in their man. If he went into the
business for profit, he threw zeal into the bargain. Before the
first year of the paper's publication was over Zenger moved his
shop to Broad Street "near the Long Bridge." People took the
paper eagerly. Perhaps it was read for the contributions of Morris, Smith, and Alexander. Some articles clearly came from the
pen of men better educated than Zenger. They reprinted classics
on liberty and government which, in the context of the controversy, were pertinent to or impertinent about the conduct of
Cosby. Evidently precise legal minds were behind some of the
words in the small, four-page, rather poorly printed paper. But
Zenger was not only publicly responsible, he also personally
made the publication "the vehicle of invective and satire against

the governor and his adherents.'' He boldly declared that old
Bradford's *Gazette* was completely subservient to the Governor.
Such a statement by his old apprentice did not please Bradford.
Bradford's publication put the Governor's furious finger on the
German printer when it cried that the word *Zenger* should be
introduced into the language as a synonym for liar.

Much of the *Journal*'s satire was veiled just enough to amuse
its readers more. One such matter involved Cosby's attempt to
prevent the election of Morris to a seat in the Assembly from
Westchester County, where he had his great manor of Morris-
ania. The Governor sent the High Sheriff to disenfranchise some
of the former chief justice's supporters because they were
Quakers and would not take an oath. But Morris won. The *Journal* put its ridicule in a pretended advertisement for a strayed
animal:

> A Monkey of the larger Sort, about 4 Foot high, has lately
> broke his chain and run into the country.... Having got a
> Warr Saddle, Pistols and Sword, this whimsical Creature
> fancied himself a general; and taking a Paper in his Paw he
> muttered over it, what the far greatest part of the Company
> understood not....

Cosby did not miss the point. Neither did the laughing people.
The proclamation about the ''Scandalous Songs'' was nailed up
for all to see. And in this same fall of 1734 issues of the *Journal*
containing comic verses and other matter in a similar vein were
ordered by the Council ''to be burnt by the Hands of the common Hangman, or Whipper, near the Pillory....'' Popular resistance to the order showed itself among the magistrates. New
York aldermen told the public whipper not to obey it. At last,
the little blaze was set only by a Negro slave of the lampooned
sheriff. Cosby's anger rose higher than the fire. Zenger was
charged with libel and with inviting sedition. Bail was fixed so
high that he could not furnish it. Still, though he missed one
issue while held incommunicado, his paper continued to appear
every Monday thereafter. Instructions for its operation came,
the paper said on November 25, 1734, to John Peter's wife Anna
Catherina ''through the Hole of the Door of the Prison.''

Alexander and Smith appeared as Zenger's lawyers. When

the printer was brought to trial for criminal libel in April, the
attorneys questioned the commissions of Cosby's friendly
judges, DeLancey and Philipse. Promptly the judges disbarred
them. Zenger was packed off to jail again. The situation was
getting hot for lawyers as well as Zenger. Also tempers were
rising high in the town against Governor Cosby. Judge DeLancey was indulging in judicial understatement when he said earlier that Zenger's "sedatious Libels" against the Governor
"have gain'd some credit among the common People."

Those "common People" packed the courtroom when the case
finally came to trial on August 4, 1735. The judges in their red
robes and great wigs looked glum. They were surprised, as were
the excited people, when a white-haired lawyer from Philadelphia appeared for Zenger. He had, of course, been obtained by
Smith and Alexander, since New York lawyers were either an-
tagonistic or intimidated. Though unknown in New York, in
Pennsylvania Andrew Hamilton had been active in opposition to
the "encroachments" of governors. Symbolically for later generations, he was the man responsible for the site and the main
architectural features of the old Pennsylvania State House,
afterward known as Independence Hall.

He stood erect in the New York court, though he seemed to
have a hopeless case. At that time the libelous character of
printed statements was universally regarded as a question for
the judges. The jury's only function was to determine the fact
of publication. And Hamilton seemed to throw his chances away
at the outset by admitting that Zenger had printed the statements involved in the charges against him.

The Attorney General quickly called for a verdict for the
King. "Supposing the libels were true," he said, "they are not
the less libelous for that; nay, indeed, the law says their being
true is an aggravation of the crime."

"Not so neither, Mr. Attorney," Hamilton answered. "There
are two Words to that Bargain. I hope it is not our bare Printing
and Publishing a Paper, that will make it a Libel: You will have
something more to do, before you make my Client a Libeller; for
the Words themselves must be libellous, that is, *false, scandalous,
and seditious,* or else we are not guilty."

Chief Justice DeLancey brushed aside the proposition so

clearly contrary to the law as the courts had determined it before
that time.

Hamilton bowed. Denied argument to the court, he turned to
the jury. He appeared weary as he began. Indeed, he seemed to
dramatize himself as one laboring "under the Weight of many
Years, and am borne down with great Infirmities of Body." But,
his voice rising as he proceeded, it was clear that he suffered no
infirmities of mind. His words flowed. He brought old learning
to the support of a new doctrine of freedom. Afterward his
speech was spoken of as "the greatest oratorical triumph won in
the colonies" to that time.

Hamilton spoke of power to the jurors, most of whom were of
Dutch descent and did not like English power of any sort. It
justly might be compared, he said, "to a great River which,
while kept within its due Bounds is both Beautiful and Useful;
but when it overflows its Banks, it is then too impetuous to be
stemm'd, it bears down all before it and brings Destruction and
Desolation wherever it comes. If then this is the Nature of
Power, let us at least do our Duty, and like wise Men (who value
Freedom) use our utmost care to support Liberty, the only
Bulwark against lawless Power. . . ."

It is difficult now to understand why no objection rose from
the Attorney General or the court, but the situation was tense in
the courtroom and the town beyond it. Hamilton went on, still
putting history, learning, the power of his personality into
the speech:

"The question before the Court and you, Gentlemen of the
Jury, is not of small nor private Concern; it is not the Cause of a
poor Printer, nor of New-York alone, which you are now trying:
No! It may in its Consequence, affect every Freeman that lives
under a British Government on the main of *America*. It is the
best Cause. It is the Cause of Liberty . . . the liberty both of
exposing and opposing arbitrary Power by speaking and writing
Truth."

That was not the recognized law then; it was the law the jury
and the people wanted. It was the law the English-speaking
world was afterward to accept and cherish. But at this time even
Judge DeLancey seemed confused by the power of Hamilton's
appeal. His charge was brief. And the jury required little time

to come back with a "not guilty" verdict which was greeted with such resounding cheers that DeLancey threatened to send the jubilant to jail.

The joyful demonstrations continued outside the courtroom. Hamilton was toasted that evening at a lively celebration at the Black Horse Tavern. Smith and Alexander were there, and probably Lewis Morris and old Rip Van Dam, whose troubles had started it all. The inn that night resounded with the singing of those "Scandalous Songs" which had angered Cosby so much. It is easy enough to imagine the company, honoring Hamilton, raising its voice in the free singing of such a "seditious" ballad as:

> Come fill a bumper, fill it up,
>   unto our Aldermen;
> For common-council fill the cup,
>   and take it o'er again.
> While they with us resolve to stand
>   for liberty and law,
> We'll drink their healths with hat in hand,
>   Whoraa! whoraa! whoraa!

While the celebrants rejoiced, John Peter was still in jail. He was not a ballad singer. Before he got out next day, however, he was already preparing—no longer "through the Hole of the Door"—the complete verbatim account of the trial, which he published in his *Journal* and which was republished around the world.

Triumph was complete. Guns on the ships in the harbor saluted Hamilton as he sailed back to Philadelphia. The song-saluted aldermen of New York sent him the keys to the city in a golden box. Years of prosperity and honors were ahead for Alexander, Smith, and Morris. Smith went on to a long and successful career as a lawyer. Alexander was recalled to the Council of New York. His son William reclaimed the Stirling title and with that lordly British label served with distinction as Patriot general in the Revolutionary War. Morris became governor of the Province of New Jersey. His son was one of the signers of the Declaration of Independence.

John Peter Zenger never became rich. The hour of his celeb-

rity passed. He seemed forever in financial straits. He was made
public printer for the colony of New York in 1737 and was given
the same position in New Jersey the following year. He continued to publish his *Weekly Journal* until his death in 1746. Then
Anna Catherina took over. The paper survived in the hands of
members of his family until 1751.

The Zenger case drew long-lasting lines between those who
opposed arbitrary power and those who stood with Cosby's
court. When Independence and Revolution came, the families of
Tory Judges DeLancey and Philipse, who had stood with Governor Cosby against Lewis Morris in the Van Dam case, both left
America. For their confiscated properties the British government
paid them two of the largest compensation grants any Loyalists
received.

Only the Bradford name seems oddly placed in the Zenger
fight. Before he came to New York, old William of the *Gazette*
had undertaken to defend himself against libel on the same
grounds upon which Zenger won. As editor of the *American
Weekly Mercury*, his son Andrew tried the same defense in
Pennsylvania later. Both got off in confused courts, but only the
Zenger case set up the principle. Old William, hale and hearty,
outlived the younger Zenger. His grandson, William Bradford, as
editor of the Philadelphia *Weekly Advertiser* or *Pennsylvania
Journal*, became for history the "patriot printer" of the Revolution—a title which in justice he shares with others.

Governor Cosby, of course, was the great and permanent loser
in the Zenger case. Not long after his humiliating defeat in the
court, though only forty-five, he took to his bed, a sick man. In
less than a year he was dead. History has been no kinder to him
than the New Yorkers of his own time. He lacked statesmanship.
He was proud and avaricious. Perhaps he was as profane as his
enemies charged. His wife was ambitious, and it is doubtful that
the Zenger verdict quieted her proud and angry tongue. At least
she had rich and aristocratic relatives to whom she could
return.

Cosby, deflated and dying, seems entitled to more sympathy.
He wrote pathetically to his great patron, the Duke of New-

castle: "I am sorry to inform your Grace that ye example and spirit of the Boston people begins to spread among these colonys in a most prodigious manner. I had more trouble to manage these people than I could have imagined."

Seeking company in his misery, Cosby could turn to Massachusetts, which had had its serious quarrels between people and Crown, Puritans and governors. Not only were there proud men of influence in Boston, there was also, as in New York, an increasingly impatient populace. Before Cosby ran up against Rip Van Dam in New York, in a fight over the issue of paper money Governor Samuel Shute in Boston found the hostile Assembly composed of men of "Small Fortunes & Meane Education."

Even so, in 1735 the Boston press was relatively quiescent. That year James Franklin died in Rhode Island, to which he had retreated. After his quarrel over vaccination with the Puritan Mathers, he had gotten into active trouble with the governor for suggesting that there was dawdling in the suppression of pirates. The younger Franklin had moved to Philadelphia to make his fortune rather than his fame in the newspaper business.

Some idea of the generally noncombative quality of the Boston press in the period is given by pious Bartholomew Green of the Boston *News-Letter*. The Green name was as famous among New England printers as was that of Bradford in the Middle Colonies. As editor of the oldest continuously published newspaper in America, Bartholomew said that he intended to publish "those Transactions only, that have no Relation to any of our Quarrels, and may be equally entertaining to the greatest Adversaries." Many editors since have followed that pattern. At this time the *Boston Gazette*, also run by Green family members, was equally cautious and equally dull. Certainly it gave no indication that it was surviving to become a resounding herald of revolution.

When Cosby wrote his pitiful letter to Newcastle, the future incendiary editors of the *Gazette*, John Gill and Benjamin Edes, were infants across the river in Charlestown. Isaiah Thomas, who was to make a "Sedition Factory" of *The Massachusetts Spy*, had not even been born. Samuel Adams was a schoolboy, not thinking yet of the press as an instrument of radical revolt.

All was quiet around the Common. Cows grazed under the elms. Sam Adams' father was a deacon of Old South Church, a prosperous brewer, and so highly regarded in the community that when his boy reached Harvard he ranked fifth socially in a class of twenty-one.

The Puritan Cotton Mather, who had so often found the press a plague, was dead. His son had become a scapegrace. The last of the witches had long since been hung in Salem. In Boston ideas about this world and the next were changing rapidly. There too printers were inking the types which would produce and proclaim independence.

3

Trumpeters of Sedition

Newspapers had grown with the expanding colonies, which did not wish to be treated as overseas stepchildren. Onetime Boston apprentice Ben Franklin grew rich as operator of the *Pennsylvania Gazette*. An early developer of chain newspapers, he extended his business partnerships from Connecticut to Georgia, even to the West Indies. More publisher than crusader, he had been able to retire at forty-two in 1748 from "all care of the printing office." Among printers, Franklin was the plutocrat.

Other newspapers, including those in Boston, were prospering, too. The Fleets, father and sons, operated the popular *Evening-*

Post. Well off, too, were the several descendants of Samuel
Green, once the only printer in the English colonies: the Drapers
of the *News-Letter;* Timothy Green, Jr., of the *Post-Boy;* Samuel Kneeland of the *Boston Gazette.*

Boston printers at this point neither stirred great troubles nor
shared them. The town was growing rich behind its tall ships at
its long wharves. Its people were more interested in cargoes,
often smuggled, than in controversy. Carriages rolled through
the streets to and from mansions of rich merchants. The numbers
of the poor increased also, but there was work in the counting
houses, the shipyards, and the rope walks. But even in productive Boston, Samuel Kneeland in 1755 decided to give up his
Boston Gazette.

That year, without prodding from king or parliament, the
Massachusetts provincial assembly levied a halfpenny stamp tax
on newspapers. A little later a similar provincial tax was imposed on papers in New York. Printers cried discrimination. The
freedom of the press was menaced, they declared. But no public
outcry rose against these stamp acts. No mobs of Liberty Boys
raged in the streets. Printers grumbled but paid. Kneeland, however, figured that the tax reduced the probability of newspaper
profits. He had other properties. He was fifty-eight. He passed
the paper to younger men who did not think that that stamp tax
was a tyranny they could not tolerate.

Kneeland might have sold to his cousins, the Drapers of the
News-Letter or Green of the *Post-Boy.* He himself had acquired
the *Gazette* in an earlier newspaper merger. But John Draper,
printer of the *News-Letter,* was growing old, too. His son Richard was already a man of delicate health—though secure in his
support of the Governor and Council, as whose printer he succeeded his father. The Drapers were content in their substantial
brick house on Washington Street. If Kneeland had sold the
Gazette to the Drapers, or to Timothy Green, Jr., patriots in the
years ahead would have lacked its support. Instead he looked
closer home.

He liked his apprentice, young John Gill. A few months later
Gill married Kneeland's daughter Ann. Perhaps Ann spoke for
the paper. She was descended not only from old Samuel Green

but also, on her mother's side, from the Puritan Priscilla who spoke to and for John Alden. Gill's forebears in America had held military titles. While holding to his convictions, Gill preferred to confine his activities largely to the printing shop. He found as partner the more belligerent Benjamin Edes, who like himself was twenty-three. Ben had little education, but he could put words together to incite and persuade; he could bring men together in action. The preceding year he had married Martha Starr, and was now ready to settle down, work hard, and make the paper a success. Neither Martha, Ann, nor their men knew that they were settling into excitement.

Edes and Gill did better than Kneeland had expected. The provincial stamp act was repealed in 1757. In that year they were commissioned by the Boston selectmen to print the votes of the town in the *Boston Gazette*—a commission accompanied by a warning. If the *Gazette* continued to publish attacks on people's "religious principles," the city's officers said, the partners "must Expect no more favours from Us." Edes and Gill were not ready to be defiant. They had accumulated property worth protecting. Edes, whose home was to become a sort of annex to the *Gazette*'s great crusade, acquired a good house on Brattle Street just down the lane from the printing office. Then, as peace came after the war with the French and Indians in the back country, business slumped in the seaport city. Trade seemed even more stifled by British efforts to stop the smuggling all had regarded so long as respectable. Muttering grew at mother-country meddling. Then the Stamp Act came almost as an invitation to opposition from those who controlled the one medium of general communication.

Men had already been grumbling before the Stamp Act came. In the Green Dragon Tavern, near the ink-stained office of the *Gazette* on Queen Street, men resentful of stiffening royal rule gathered. In words stronger than their drinks, they denounced the British ministry and its Tory toadies in America. Now, as John Adams urged the printers not to be intimidated, more leaders gathered in the print shop. They needed a greater audience than could hear even the loud harangues of Samuel Adams, John's older, tougher cousin, or the flaming oratory of brilliant, erratic James Otis. Other less eminent but no less determined men came to the *Gazette* office. Edes, who welcomed the contributions of the great patriots, was also the Edes who was a member of the Loyall Nine, which directed many operations of the rough-and-ready semisecret Sons of Liberty.

The *Gazette* carried the words of revolutionary erudition. Its zeal was amplified by the roars of rougher elements in the streets. The paper cried at Sir Francis Bernard, the Governor, "Retreat or you are ruined." Otis, writing under a pseudonym, struck so sharply at Lieutenant Governor Thomas Hutchinson, whose house was smashed by a mob, that Bernard sought action against Edes and Gill for a "breach of privilege tending to overthrow all government." But the Council refused to go along, believing that they would only "be rescued by the mob." In England feeling grew that the Stamp Tax was not worth the fury it had stirred. Finally in May 1766 came word that so far as the printers were concerned the Stamp Act was repealed. No punishment was inflicted on those who had resisted. The newspapers crowed, none more loudly than the *Gazette*. The press had not only won its point, it had proved its power.

Patriot leadership recognized that. The dingy Queen Street office of the *Gazette* became more than ever their meeting place. The shop was often crowded with such men as Otis, the two Adamses, Josiah Quincy, and Joseph Warren. It was a "curious employment," John Adams said. With Edes and Gill they worked "cooking up paragraphs, articles, & occurences &c., working the political machine!" From the shop, by printed word and by direct action, the patriot party line was spread through Boston and the surrounding countryside.

Recognizing the power of the patriot press, loyal officials tried to meet it. The *Evening-Post* teetering in impartiality did not serve them. There was not much hope in the timorous Richard Draper of the *News-Letter*. He quailed when the *Gazette* sneered at him as a cat's paw in British pay as official printer. The *Post-Boy*, John Adams felt, was "harmless, dovelike, inoffensive." Even when the *News-Letter* and the *Post-Boy*, both favored with government printing, issued a joint supplement, one on Monday, one on Thursday, as the *Massachusetts Gazette*, it carried little weight. This publication, "Published by Authority," only won derision as the "Court Gazette" and the "Adam and Eve paper."

Clearly the government was going to need stauncher press support when the new tax-levying Townshend Acts, designed to prove Britain's tax power despite Stamp Act repeal, went into effect on November 20, 1767. The same month demand was made in parliament that Edes and Gill be brought to England for examination concerning the libels in their paper which stirred the Stamp Act resistance. The demand was shelved. Royal officials in the colonies would have to deal with such printers as they could. So to deal with them, John Mein, a successful Scots bookseller, was launched as publisher of the well-printed *Boston Chronicle* on December 21.

Though Mein's first interest seemed literary rather than political, he did not postpone collision with the *Boston Gazette* very long. Within a month he printed an article from an English paper which angered the patriots. "Americus" (whom Mein believed to be Otis) damned him in the *Gazette*. And when Gill declined to tell him the writer's name, the pugnacious Mein attacked him with a club. Patriots were outraged. Sam Adams as "Populus" in the *Gazette* called the assault a "Spanish-like Attempt" on the freedom of the press. Otis as prosecutor also insisted this was no private affair. In Boston courts Mein was lucky enough to get off with a fine.

Edes and Gill were even luckier. In February 1768, "A True Patriot" in the *Gazette* clearly referred to Governor Bernard when he wrote of "obstinate Perseverance in the Path of Malice." Some patriots were shocked by this article. When the Governor sought action against Edes and Gill in the Council, though the upper branch clucked its disapproval of the article, the popular branch rebuked the Governor, declaring that freedom of the press was the "great Bulwark of the Liberty of the People." Bernard got no further with the grand jury, and the true bill was withdrawn. The *Gazette,* of course, hailed that action as a victory for the people. Its writers would continue to "strip the serpents of their stings."

The paper published, to his surprise and before he wished it,

Bernard's plans to quarter red-coated British soldiers in Boston to quiet the town. In January 1769, Bernard desperately begged his superiors to seize Edes and Gill and make them identify their "treasonable and seditious" contributors. These two printers, the Governor said, were no mere Boston journeymen. Far beyond that city they were "the apparent Instruments of raising that Flame in America, which has given so much Trouble & is still like to give more to Great Britain & her Colonies." The Massachusetts Council declined to back the Governor. If there were subversive writers in the Colony, it said, there were fifty in England to one in Massachusetts.

While Bernard unsuccessfully sought help from home, the *Gazette* obtained confidential correspondence he had sent home about conditions in Massachusetts. In it harsh things were said about many individuals. Members of the Council itself demanded Bernard's removal, so he got recall, not help. He sailed from Boston on August 1. Once again the *Gazette* tasted victory. A flag was hoisted on the Liberty Tree. Bells rang. By way of farewell the *Gazette* declared that Bernard "has been a Scourge to this Province, a Curse to North-America, and a Plague to the whole Empire."

Soon afterward Otis, in the *Gazette,* labeled some of Bernard's remaining associates, who had mentioned him in the correspondence, liars. Next evening, in the British Coffee House (at the site of present 60 State Street) a British officer attacked Otis with a cutlass, slashing him across the skull. He was left wounded and bleeding on the tavern floor. This was, the *Gazette* reported, an "intended and nearly executed Assassination." The blow, many believed, finally brought on Otis' insanity.

Mounting anger turned attention to Mein again. He had declined to sign the nonimportation agreements against the Townshend Acts. He spoke his mind in increasing disagreement with the views expressed in the *Boston Gazette.* He went on to charge that some of those pushing the nonimportation agreements were themselves cheating. Worse, he sent off pamphlets to other colonies damaging to the reputations of the Boston patriots.

The *Gazette* was crammed with answers and denials. But, as

always in that newspaper war, words were not the only weapons
of the patriots. Mein was expelled from the Free American Fire
Company and hung in effigy on the Liberty Tree. Boycott
stiffened about his paper and his bookshop. Stealthy hands broke
his office windows. Filth was smeared upon his business signs. A
night crowd, which had tarred and feathered an informer who
had reported a cargo of smuggled wine, smashed Mein's office
doors to give him some of the same. After narrow escape there,
he began to go about armed. He still wrote in derision of
Hancock, Otis, and Samuel Adams. The rich Hancock was
"Johnny Dupe Esq.," Otis was "Muddlehead."

On October 28, 1769, one of Boston's mobs—"trained mobs"
British officials called them—attacked him on the street. In the
melee Mein wounded a soldier bystander. For once Bostonians
were outraged by an injury to a redcoat. Indignant citizens
swore out a warrant against Mein "for having put innocent
people in bodily fear." Innocent or not, Mein was in bodily
terror. He slipped to a ship in the harbor and fled to England,
where Bernard had gone. Patriots insisted that he was running
from private creditors as well as public clamor. In London he
was given £200 by a grateful king for his services. Attention in
Boston turned to the King's red-coated soldiers who remained.

"Town-born, turn out!"

That cry rose more and more often from the lusty boys in the
rope walks and the shipyards. The winter of 1769–1770 passed
uneasily. Clashes between town-born and redcoat increased before February passed. Insults were shouted at British soldiers.
Some were attacked on lonely streets. Anger and fear under-
standably grew among them. They challenged scorn-shouting
workmen to a boxing match, but the boys from the yards and the
shops used sticks instead of fists. They were met by cutlasses
from the camps.

On March 5, 1770, wary soldiers passing to their posts from
the main guard at the head of King Street (now State Street),
not far from the *Gazette* office, met a club-armed crowd which
refused to let them pass. In the confusion a soldier hit one particularly annoying boy with the butt of his musket. The alarm
bell called out more citizens. More soldiers joined their encircled

comrades. Musket shots rose above the clamor. Five civilians lay
dying in the snow.

History had its Boston Massacre and Ben Edes his best story.
He had a week in which to write it. Perhaps, as a modern Massachusetts historian has said, he helped fashion "folk heroes out of
street loafers and hoodlums." He began solemnly: "The Town
of Boston affords a recent and melancholy Demonstration of the
destructive Consequences of quartering Troops among citizens in
a Time of Peace." But words were not enough. At this time Gill
performed his only remembered public activity outside the
print shop by serving as a member of the committee to demand
the removal of the troops. In the shop Edes got help from his
comrade in the Sons of Liberty, the ingenious master of many
crafts, Paul Revere. Revere had already advertised in the
Gazette false teeth of his manufacture which, he claimed, were
not only ornamental but also actually useful in talking and eat-
ing. Now he added to the newspaper's bite by providing coffin-
shaped cartoons carrying the initials of the dead.

Strangely, the massacre did not feed the furies; in a sense it
sated them. John Adams and Josiah Quincy even helped defend
the soldiers. Other circumstances created a sort of intermission
in the rush toward independence. The troops were removed from
their camp in the town. The major part of the Townshend duties
were repealed. Merchants—who may or may not have been cheating under them—gladly abandoned the nonimportation agreements.

It was then that the *Gazette* and Sam Adams, as one of his
biographers has said, made their chief contribution to independence. Under a variety of pen names—Poplicola, Vindex,
Candidus, and the like—Adams labored to convince the people
that they were being lulled out of their liberties. He contrasted a
virtuous America with a degenerate Britain embodied in "an
abandoned, shameless Ministry, hirelings, pimps, parasites, pan-
ders, prostitutes and whores."

Hutchinson, Governor Bernard's successor, needed and
sought answers to such diatribes. He tried to build the courage
of the *News-Letter* and the *Post-Boy*, though the timid Draper

often begged off from printing his propaganda for fear of offending the town.

"The misfortune is," said the new Governor as he read the *Gazette* with growing bitterness, "that seven eighths of the people read none but this infamous paper."

There seemed little need for another patriot paper when young Isaiah Thomas established his *Massachusetts Spy* on July 17, 1770. It was to be at the outset "Open to all Parties, but Influenced by None" and was shaped to appeal to the mass readership of the mechanic class. Nevertheless, when his start was slow, he accepted a loan from a Tory. He printed loyalist contributions. Soon, however, it was evident that such impartiality would not be prolonged. Active around his shop was James Otis—"his eyes fishy and fiery"—who had already received the blow on his head. His eccentricity was becoming more marked. He shattered windows in the Old State House. He shot guns from his own windows. He talked interminably and unpleasantly. He was unhappy with his wife. But Otis gave Thomas a sort of wild, shrewd support.

Loyalist contributions disappeared from the *Spy*. It became the "Sedition Factory." It adopted as its emblem the "Join or Die" snake emblematic of the need for all the colonies to unite against oppression. Based on the superstition that a snake cut in pieces would come to life if put together before sunset, Benjamin Franklin had used the design to promote British colonial unity against the French in 1754. On Thomas' paper the snake was darting its tongue at a British dragon. Other patriot papers used the cartoon. James Rivington, best-hated of the Tory editors, ridiculed it in his *New-York Gazetteer* with the lines

> Ye Sons of Sedition, how comes it to pass,
> That America's typ'd by a SNAKE—in the grass.

Thomas was apparently easy to like or hate. Apprentice product of a small, sloppy Boston print shop, he had acquired no such stature as Edes and Gill when he set up his paper in Boston. He was only twenty-one. As a young tramp printer with a good opinion of himself, he had already gotten into trouble in Halifax, Nova Scotia, by opposing the Stamp Act. He found more lasting trouble when he worked in Charleston, S.C., on the *South Carolina and American General Gazette* (one of the many papers Ben Franklin helped establish). There he met Mary Dill, a girl from Bermuda.

Isaiah married her on Christmas Day, 1769; he was twenty, she was nineteen. Soon after marriage he discovered, he reported, that his wife "had had a bastard son years before and that she had been prostituted to the purposes of more than one." Considering Mary's past and young Isaiah's chagrin, the Charleston climate was not congenial; the move to embattled Boston seemed a good one. There he soon attracted the easy anger of Governor Hutchinson. Patriots lent him the money to pay off the mortgage on his paper held by a Tory. In 1771 by trick, bid, or both, Thomas humiliated the timid Tory Draper of the *News-Letter* by getting the contract to print the Latin theses of Harvard students which Draper had long and proudly printed. The *News-Letter* fumed at him as a "dunghill Journeyman Typographer."

Thomas crowed. He was not entirely happy in his shop or his house, however. In March 1772 he wrote a gentleman in his fretful Mary's native Bermuda about the possibilities for a printer in that island. His anti-British propaganda, aimed to stir others in too-quiet Boston, made him uneasy, too. He published a poem signed "A Bachelor" which told why young Boston men were shying away from marriage:

> Of late the red coat stranger, silver'd round,
> The gold tipt hilt, the black cockade abound . . .
> Still one more question! doleful as the first
> Remains!—'tis this!—this answer!—is it worse
> To marry red coats leaving, or a———!!!?
> Read this, and trouble bachelors no more.

Edes, John Gill, Samuel Adams, and others were less troubled in their own households than by the lack of troubles in the all-too-quiet town. Sometimes even soldiers walked the streets unsneered at. Hutchinson appeared much too content as he rolled

by in his coach. Royalists made a favorite joke about Edes. It
was about a Negro in the *Gazette* printing office where the editor
was complaining that news was scarce.

"Well, if you've nothing new, Massa Edes," the slave was
supposed to have said, "I s'pose you print the same dam' old
lie over again."

Then the tea came. As a result of continuing smuggling of
Dutch tea into the colonies, vast stores of East India Company
tea had piled up in English warehouses, so what may have
looked in London like a simple plan was devised. By substituting
a lower collectible duty for a higher uncollectible one at colonial
ports happy results were expected. The straitened East India
Company might be aided, surpluses disposed of, smuggling reduced, and British power to raise colonial revenues and thus
make colonial executives independent of popular control demonstrated. It was a neat plan for Britain. Boston could get cheaper
tea. But parliament's plan became the patriots' cup of tea and a
bitter brew for Britain.

The day the first of the tea ships arrived, November 29, 1773, a
great protest meeting was held in Faneuil Hall. It resolved that
the tea must be returned to the place from which it came. The
Gazette put the protest into print, but Ben Edes was playing a
role greater than that of printer alone. He and Gill recruited
armed patrols who day and night watched the ships to prevent
any attempt to unload. Edes himself served as a member of the
guard. As one of the Loyall Nine of the Sons of Liberty, he also
maintained communications from the top patriot politicians to
the rank and file. He helped recruit "fifty sober-minded Boston
working men." And on the day of climax, during mounting
demands that Governor Hutchinson let the ships be returned
unloaded, men began gathering in the afternoon at the Edes
house on Brattle Street at the end of the lane from the *Gazette*
office.

No tea was served. In a room adjoining the meeting place in
the house, Edes' son Peter, a boy in his teens, mixed punch for
the company in a china bowl. Whatever was in the punch, Edes'
men held it well—it was the town about them which seemed
intoxicated. Since early morning crowds from the city and the

countryside had filled and surrounded the Old South Meeting House. Through the December day they waited. Sam Adams and other spellbinders took turns addressing the turnout of 7000. Reports were brought back regularly to Edes' house. Night came. In the darkness the picked group of men moved down the lane from the printer's house to the printing office on Queen Street.

They brought with them—or found waiting for them there— the costumes of Mohawk Indians. They painted their faces and donned feathered headdresses. They knew their instructions. They waited for an arranged one-sentence signal Sam Adams was to give when final expected word came that Governor Hutchinson had declined to send the hated ships away. Adams spoke it in the meetinghouse.

"This meeting can do nothing more to save the country."

The crowd roared. The word ran quickly, cry to cry, up Marlborough, Cornhill, and Queen streets to the print shop. The shout on the porch of Old South was answered up the streets by war whoops from the *Gazette* office. Edes flung open the doors. The Mohawks moved by the site of the Boston Massacre, down Pearl Street (then Hutchinson Street), toward Griffin's Wharf. Thousands in the throng at the meetinghouse followed. Some, undisguised, joined the Indians on the tea ships. For three hours they worked steadily with hatchets. Carefully safeguarding all other property, they broke open all 342 tea chests on the three ships, valued at about £18,000. The next morning the tea was heaped up in windrows on Dorchester Beach where the wind and the tide had carried it.

Even the loyalist papers, perhaps intimidated by the mood of the town, emphasized the general good behavior of the Mohawks. No published report appeared of Edes' part in the affair. But the *Gazette*, remembering earlier proposals to seize its printers and carry them abroad for questioning and trial, published a warning with its report. In an article signed "Detector," it told any officials planning such action that they could expect to fall "into the pit they are digging for others."

Nobody touched Edes or Gill, though the stacked guns of the

Bloody Backs, soon commanded by General Thomas Gage, the
new Governor, thickened on the Common. A large loyal element,
particularly among the upper classes, gave him hearty welcome
when he arrived in May 1774. Many of them soon felt, however,
that though he punished the town by closing its port, he was too
hesitant in exterminating insurrection.

In September the impatient Tories flung a letter from the dark
into the camp of the British soldiers on the Common. The letter
writer listed those whom he called the authors of revolution.
They constituted practically a roster of the *Gazette*'s distinguished contributors. The message urged that at their first move
they be put to the sword, their houses destroyed, and their effects
plundered. It added a final bitter injunction:

*P.S. Don't forget those trumpeters of sedition, the printers,
Edes & Gill, and Thomas.*

An uneasy winter passed. Soldiers in an early spring night
marched past the shop of Thomas playing "The Rogue's
March." They had just tarred and feathered a countryman for
some unknown crime. They halted. An officer shouted:

"The printer of the *Spy* shall be the next to receive such
punishment!"

Young Thomas' troubles were piling up at his door, and behind it too. The month before the soldiers came blaring threatening music, he had made another discovery which could not have
been a surprise. As he reported to a divorce court later, he found
his petulant, promiscuous Mary in such familiarities with one
Major Thompson as to "give the strongest reasons to suspect
that she was guilty of Adultery." Thomas not only suspected:
he was convinced. He was convinced that Mary had got into the
adulterous bed not only in Boston but also in Charlestown,
Grantland, Newbury, and Lynn.

Legend has it that Major Thompson was a British officer.
In the spring of 1775 there was no time for much investigation
or identification to prove whether Mary was redcoat leavings or
not. Thomas, as he wrote in *The History of Printing in America*,
was too busy being a hero to spare concern for his position as
cuckold. On the night of April 16, he got his press and type across

the ferry to Charlestown, then by cart to Worcester. On April
18, he rode with Paul Revere and others to warn Sam Adams and
John Hancock that Gage was on his way to Lexington and Concord. He helped warn the countryside. Then, in a combination of
circumstances hardly duplicated by any newspaperman before
or since, he fought as a minuteman when the shots were fired
which were heard round the world. The next day he reached
Worcester. He was quickly printer again and too busy after that
for fighting. When he was drafted later he hired a substitute.

The departure of Ben Edes was pedestrian by comparison. At
forty-two he could not have been expected to cover as much
ground as quickly as Thomas said he did at twenty-six. Nevertheless he managed to get an antiquated press and type upriver
to Watertown and to continue his trumpeting from there. John
Gill, terminating their partnership, decided to stay in Boston.
And evidently the British regarded Gill as the less seditious of
the partners. They arrested him in August but freed him to
"walk the town" in October.

Some other printers who had less to fear merely let their
papers expire. The *Post-Boy* suspended on April 17, before Gage
marched. The *Evening-Post,* teetering uncertainly, gave no more
report of the battles of Lexington and Concord than to speak of
them as "the unhappy transactions of last week." That report
of April 24, 1775, was its last. Only the *News-Letter,* the loudly
scorned "Court Gazette," remained operative in the city to
which Gage came back to stand siege.

The *News-Letter*'s timid printer, Richard Draper, had died a
year before in June 1774. Now his widow and cousin, Margaret
Green Draper, showed a vigor which Draper as a man of
"Equanimity of Temper" lacked. Her anger rose as she was
included by the papers in exile among the "pensioned prostitutes" and described as an "old Lady" with a "malignant
heart." She could hardly have been over fifty—she had thirty
more bitter years to live. If, as her onetime neighbors in printing
said, her paper was published "by permission of ministerial
butchers," she did not hold back her blows at those she regarded
as seditious scoundrels. She even printed a letter, doctored by
the British, which suggested illicit relations by George Washing-

ton with a washerwoman's daughter. Margaret Draper only complained to her readers that "almost all communication with the Continent is shut off."

The news at hand was all too clear. Her slurs at Washington had not prevented that Virginian from occupying Dorchester Heights. Under his guns Margaret Draper's *News-Letter* printed its last issue on February 22, 1776, but scarcely as an intended birthday present to the General. The Widow Draper sailed away with the redcoat army on March 17. She never saw Boston again, or the substantial brick house in which life for a printer's lady had been so serene until the gracious elm on the street in front became the Liberty Tree.

Isaiah Thomas remained in Worcester. His *Massachusetts Spy* flourished there. He turned to books and became the leading publisher of his time. He founded the American Antiquarian Society. After divorce in 1777 from his erring Mary Dill, he married twice again, but only his children by the fertile, feverish Mary survived when Isaiah was honored as a tall, courtly, distinguished, and generous old man.

Other "trumpeters of sedition" fared less well. Ben Edes brought the *Gazette* back. It could, of course, not claim the contributors who once helped it flame. Though he was to become governor of Massachusetts, Sam Adams' great career was over. James Otis, after surviving untouched an insane foray into the thickest of the fighting at Bunker Hill, was killed by a bolt of lightning while watching a summer storm. "Only fire from heaven," Samuel Eliot Morison put it, "could release his fiery soul." No roaring welcome waited the *Gazette*'s return to Boston. Its mission had been performed. The patriot mobs had dispersed. Edes importuned rich former friends in vain. He and his sons nevertheless carried the paper on until September 1798. Edes lived five more years in ill-health, poverty, and obscurity. John Gill had little better luck. Two months after the British left Boston he established the *Continental Journal and Weekly Advertiser*. It was colorless compared to the old *Gazette* when Edes had been at his side.

Now both cause and triumph seemed lost. Not merely printers

felt frustrated. Like the angry men who had listened to Adams and Otis in the Green Dragon Tavern, discontented men now talked in the Bunch of Grapes Tavern in Boston of the ingratitude of the new government to poor men who had served independence. New lines were being drawn. Gradually John Gill moved to support the commercial interests which were shaping the conservative side in the new Federalist and Republican alignments which at last would make even John Adams ready to jail men for "sedition." That growing division put Gill in the company of many who were charged with having been lukewarm in Revolutionary days, even pro-British.

Still it was Gill of the Gill and Edes firm who made his exit from newspaper operation in a way which ironically recalled the entrance of the two young printers into it. In 1785, the new free Commonwealth of Massachusetts levied a stamp tax of two thirds of a penny on each newspaper. Protests arose from citizens and printers that here was the odious old British Stamp Act in new guise. Apparently nobody mentioned the provincial stamp act of 1755 which had prompted Sam Kneeland to let Gill and Edes have the *Gazette* in the first place. Gill disposed of his *Journal* now with the kind of rhetoric which had once made the *Gazette* resound. He preferred to retire, he wrote, rather than "submit to a measure which Britain artfully adopted as the foundation of her intended tyranny of America." Four months later, August 25, 1785, he died insolvent.

Massachusetts was still capable of protest. Indeed, at this time impoverished farmers were mobilizing behind Daniel Shays, a Revolutionary veteran, for a new revolt against what they considered oppression of the poor by the rich. The following year Shays' rebels closed the courts at Worcester, where Isaiah Thomas was printing. They threatened to march on Boston. Governor James Bowdoin, whom Gill had supported, quickly formed an army financed by Boston merchants and smashed the revolt. In the tumult of such discontent, the new stamp act which aroused Gill's roar was inconsequential—and was repealed before it went into effect. Another tax was placed on newspaper advertising—sixpence for twelve lines and a shilling for every twenty lines in longer displays.

In Worcester on his way to wealth, Isaiah Thomas escaped the tax. He changed the *Spy*'s format to that of a magazine. He could not he said "continue the publication of a News-Paper ignominiously FETTERED with a SHACKLE" he had been "taught to abhor!" He had also been taught as he grew older that it was possible to be shrewd and not merely shrill.

4

That Damn Duane

On July 4, 1796, William Duane, with his young wife and three children, came home to his native land, arriving in New York on the ship *Chatham*. Duane was an angry, radical newspaperman. America was a country of escape for a man who needed a second chance but did not mean to change his mind.

In the young United States the name Duane did not suggest republicanism and the rights of man, sympathy for revolutionary France, and faith in a democratic America. Years before, when John Adams cheered on the free press of Boston printers which was inciting the Massachusetts mobs, rich James Duane of

New York was going about among the people trying to quell the
Stamp Act riots. He stayed on the conservative side so long that
during the Revolution some doubted his patriotism. Afterward
he ardently supported the Constitution that created a truly national government.

Many people separated in the old colonies, now states, feared
the Constitution was a device to help the rich get richer while
the liberties of ordinary men were curtailed. The Bill of Rights
which they insisted be added to the Constitution two years after
it came into effect might not be adequate protection. Some men
looked suspiciously at the pomp with which the young Republic
was governed, first in New York and after 1790 in Philadelphia.
The possibility of return to monarchy did not seem slight to
those who had recently escaped from it.

When William Duane landed in New York memories lingered
of his cousin James, who had personified such dramatic fears. He
was recalled as the first Federalist mayor of the city, driving in
his gilded and monogrammed coach through the muddy streets,
scattering dogs and pigs and spattering pedestrians. A good
many of the pedestrians who looked resentfully after him were
those described by high-riding Federalists as ''restless mechanics
who wish to engross all to themselves.'' William Duane took his
American place on the side of the restless—not in any lordly,
lunging coach.

Not all the Duanes who had come early to America were so
rich or so lucky as old James. His cousin John Duane, farmer,
surveyor (and undoubtedly land speculator), had been killed by
Indians near Lake Champlain in the year James was trying to
stop the Stamp Act riots in New York. The now-returning William, who was to become the combative editor of the Philadelphia
Aurora, was five years old then. It was good luck for William, in
view of the furies later around the Alien and Sedition Acts, that
he had been born in America on May 17, 1760—which was his last
luck for a long time.

William's mother, born Anastasia Sarsfield, carried the fourteen-year-old boy back to her secure place and properties in
Tipperary and its county town of Clonmel. In Ireland William

wrote poetry inspired, he said, by Thomas Jefferson's Declaration of Independence. That was all right with his mother, who shared Tipperary's bitterness for the red-coated British. But William's notions of liberty carried him beyond his mother's indulgence. An ardent Catholic, she had hoped that her son might be a priest. Instead, when he was scarcely nineteen, he married Catharine Corcoran, a Protestant. Perhaps the girl was, as some said, "as worthy of a duke as a Duane." Regardless, the outraged Anastasia cut her boy off from all his inheritance except her stubbornness.

Disinherited in Clonmel, William turned to printing for a living. He moved to London, where other young men (and older men, too) were confronting inherited patterns with the ferment that had begun in America and exploded in France. From the pedestal of a column in Covent Garden he witnessed an election riot. Angry Irishmen used the poles of sedan chairs in the cause of a liberal candidate. The old order was defended by British sailors with short swords. Duane watched. This was the last time he stood above the battle.

He had a chance to become rich—and did. Through the influence of his father's brother, Matthew Duane, then curator of the British Museum, the chance came for him to start a newspaper, the *Indian World,* in Calcutta. Beyond bitter British memories of the Black Hole, Warren Hastings had established what was hoped to be a stable civilian government. The paper was to be a part of it. It flourished. But Duane published what the authorities described as "an inflammatory address to the army" in which he set forth the grievances of Indian soldiers against the East India Company.

The Governor-General invited him to breakfast; when he arrived he was not served but seized. He was clapped into the prison which had been the Black Hole. Then, without formality and without any of his property, he was deported on the first available ship. In England, his demands for redress got nowhere. While he worked as parliamentary reporter on a paper later merged with *The Times,* he came quickly into the company of radical reformers. Some of them were arrested and carried to the

Tower on charges of high treason. Duane was being watched.
Two years later, in 1796, with some prudence but no repentance,
he sailed with his family for America.

Duane did not linger in New York. He hurried on to Philadelphia, to which the national capital had moved. There he saw
gilded coaches like his old cousin James' move to impressive
mansions. Smaller substantial brick houses, many with shops on
their first floors, stood on shaded streets. However, on the out-
skirts of the town were slattern sections by stagnant frog ponds
and the stinking waterfront. Party divisions were as sharply
drawn between Federalists and Democrats (then Republicans).
Angrily they described each other as the "monarchists" and
"the mob." A miasma of distrust hung over both gardens and
frog ponds, disdainful aristocrats and sometimes impudent common people. Between walled gardens and rotten edges, politics in
Philadelphia was incessant and pestilence was recurrent.

Lines had been drawn in both city and surrounding countryside before Duane arrived. They divided those most concerned
about the rights of the people and those who wanted in the
Constitution chiefly a mechanism for strict social order and
profitable economic stability. Freedom of the press had been a
point of difference, which symbolized the rights Jefferson insisted be added to the basic document. It seemed less important
to Hamilton, who doubted that freedom of the press could be
precisely defined. Old Benjamin Franklin—who understood both
the need for press liberty and the sting of its lash—put forward a proposal. He suggested that liberty of the press be un-
disturbed "to be exercised to its full extent force and vigor;
but to permit the *liberty of the cudgel* to go with it...." When
Duane came to town the old philosopher's grandson, Benjamin
Franklin Bache, had exercised the one and felt the other. Duane
came striding onto the scene to share both.

Benny Bache, as he was called by those who undertook to
minimize him before they tried to cudgel him, had set up his
Aurora in October 1790. Bache was then twenty-one, social, amiable, impetuous. His grandfather had asked him to start the
paper, he said, before he willed him the shop. So he became
Lightning Rod Junior. He attracted the lightning but he

lacked his grandfather's tact. To his solid house on Market
Street beside his shop Bache brought the vital Margaret Hart-
man Markoe as his bride. Daughter of Danish parents who had
settled in the West Indies, she was "a little bit of a woman"
who only later needed to show the "commanding presence and
impressive manner" contemporaries remembered. Ben had met
her after his education (under his grandfather's supervision) in
France. The *Aurora* could have been only a part of their pleasant life and social prestige in Philadelphia. Then, almost by
accident, Bache—devoted to republicanism and seeing the reflection of American Revolution in tumultuous France—suddenly
inherited the journalistic leadership of the Democratic cause.

Up from the waterfront and the frog ponds came the yellow
fever in 1793, bringing corpses by the cartful. And it drove
before it all who could get away. Among its victims was a newspaper, the *National Gazette*. Its editor, Philip Freneau, "the
poet of the Revolution," had established the sheet under the
patronage of Jefferson. He lashed at the Federalists and their
organ, *Gazette of the United States,* run by solemn, obsequious
John Fenno, a former schoolteacher.

Later it was easy to confuse Freneau and Fenno and their
almost-identically named *Gazette*s. Their differences were clear
at the time. Fenno seemed to Democrats to serve aristocrats and
the possibility of monarchy. Freneau fought both. Jefferson declared that Freneau's *National Gazette* had "saved our Constitution which was galloping fast into monarchy." But Jefferson
was a greater advocate of the theory of a free press than a
willing participant in its rough requirements. Freneau lacked
money. And, with the fever, he lacked both printers and readers.
He shut up shop. To Bache and the *Aurora* fell the job of saving
(in Jeffersonian terms) the country and the Constitution.

Lightning came quickly to Ben Bache's rod. He got a scoop
and shocked the authorities, including President Washington,
when he printed in advance of its secret consideration the un-
popular Jay Treaty with England. Bache cried the Democratic
view that the treaty amounted to the abandonment of American
rights and a truckling to the old red-coated enemy. While Federalists, as he charged, were fawning on Britain and British mo-

narchical ways, he opened his columns to the sometimes impertinent representatives of revolutionary France. Behind his reti-
cence, the eminent Washington was often virtually apoplectic at
Bache's words. And Bache almost asked for the "right of the
cudgel" when he termed the retiring Washington "the source
of all the misfortunes of our country."

When Fenno attacked him on the street, Bache beat him off
with his cane. But carpenters building frigates for possible war,
which he opposed, battered him badly in a shipyard. A new and
better cudgel-worded journalist was put in the field against him.
William Cobbett, sometimes radical, sometimes reactionary, always vituperative controversialist, is better remembered for his
later furious role in British politics. He was only in his middle
twenties when, after some troubles in the British army, he arrived in Philadelphia. In the first issue of his *Porcupine's
Gazette,* he let go with savage sarcasm at Bache. Cobbett shot his
needles at "the white-livered, black-hearted thing Bache" and at
the *Aurora* as "the vehicle of lies and sedition." Cobbett indicated the extremes to which press violence had gone when he
matched Bache's blast at Washington by heaping dirt on the
memory of Franklin. Cobbett wrote of Bache's "crafty and lech-
erous old hypocrite of a grandfather, whose very statue seems to
gloat on the wenches in the State House yard."

In the rising drumbeat of division Bache needed Duane. The
publication of the *X. Y. Z. Papers* in the spring of 1798 turned
Federalist partisanship into roaring patriotism. Those dispatches, indicating that corrupt French officials, identified
cryptically by the letters, would only negotiate a peace if given a
big American bribe, seemed satisfactory grounds for silencing
criticism of the administration's policy. Cobbett's *Porcupine's
Gazette* fed fury with reports of French invasion in the South.
Stories of French incitement of slave insurrection were spread.
Sex and slaves and Jacobins were mixed with atrocity stories.
And with its eyes on the *Aurora* the Federalist Congress began
shaping the Alien and Sedition Laws.

Jefferson noted in a letter to James Madison that the "*Aurora*
was particularly named" in the preparation of the Sedition bill.
Duane was thought to be a prime target of the Alien bill which

gave the President power to deport any foreigner he deemed dangerous. The Sedition Act provided imprisonment and fines for anyone who wrote or spoke against the President or Congress with "intent to defame" or to "bring them into contempt or disrepute." Both acts threw press, speech, and other freedoms into the discard heap.

Plans for political proscription bothered neither Bache nor Duane. They refused to be intimidated. Bache was arrested under common law before the Sedition Act was passed. At the same time pestilence struck the *Aurora*. Duane was stricken with cholera. He was desperately ill. The sickness spread in his household. His son was at one time thought to be dead. Then the disease moved on to Duane's Catharine, for whom he had first put himself in revolt against authority. On Friday, the thirteenth of July 1798, the day before Congress passed the Sedition Bill, Catharine Corcoran Duane was dead, a long way from Tipperary.

August 1798 was hot and angry. The heat came up from the stinking wharves. At night the croaking from the frog ponds was audible and ominous. Facing trial in the sickly summer, Bache avoided a duel with an angry reader. But as September came on no one could avoid the contagion which slipped up from the waterfront and the frog ponds. The yellow fever which had killed the *National Gazette* was back again. Before the mysterious malady the great mansions closed; soon, half the houses were abandoned. Death carts rolled in the streets. The town seemed abandoned to the Negroes and the rats, brave baffled doctors, and the printers. Bache and Duane had no idea of shutting down the *Aurora* as Freneau had discontinued his paper in the epidemic of 1793. Their opponents Cobbett and Fenno went on printing, too.

The plague at least was neutral. On September 10, Bache died of it. In Boston a Federalist editor wrote as obituary: "The Jacobins are all whining at the exit of the vile Benjamin Franklin Bache; so they would do if one of their gang was hung for stealing. The memory of this scoundrel cannot be too highly execrated." But John Fenno of the *Gazette of the United States*

followed Bache to the grave on September 14. He departed, the
Federalist press said, "with all his blooming virtues thick upon
him."

Ironically and unjustly, the same epidemic was fatal also to
Porcupine's Gazette. While the disease raged Cobbett violently
attacked the staunchly Democratic Dr. Benjamin Rush not for
his politics but for his treatment of his patients with violent
purges and copious bleedings. Medical science has since justified
Cobbett's charges in this matter, but when Rush sued he got a
$5000 libel verdict. Unable to pay, the curmudgeon editor left
Philadelphia for temporarily safer scenes and a long controver-
sial life.

Margaret Bache, in her twenties, and William Duane at thirty-
eight were left with two families, the *Aurora,* and plenty of
trouble. Bache had lost $14,700 in his eight years as publisher.
Neither the new owner nor the new editor, however, had any
notion of moderating the paper's policies. The only change was
in the *Aurora's* title design of the radiating rays of the morning
sun. There the words appeared, "Published (Daily) by William
Duane, Successor of Benjamin Franklin Bache, in Franklin
Court, Market Street." The new editor, said a not too friendly
biographer, brought to the paper "venom, vehemence, violence,
virulence, vilification, vituperation, severity, scandal, spite, sarcasm and stab." Certainly he brought to it unrelenting republicanism. Facing not only the Sedition Act but the suspicion that
he was an Irish alien subject to the Alien Act, he struck out
against both.

Duane was not fighting alone. The Democratic forces were
more and more militantly mobilizing behind Jefferson. The Virginian wrote Madison:

"Let us cultivate Pennsylvania & we need not fear the uni-
verse."

As chief Democratic editor, Duane's part in that cultivation
was not to be easy or comfortable. The year of Bache's death had
scarcely ended before his successor was under arrest. On a Sunday in February Duane, one of his printers, and two Irish immigrants entered the churchyard of St. Mary's Catholic Church
during services and put up placards urging Irishmen in the

congregation to remain and sign petitions for the repeal of the
Alien Law. Some did, but other communicants of Federalist persuasion pulled the posters down, crying sacrilege. They attacked
Duane and his companions and knocked one of them down. He
rose to his feet with a pistol in his hand. Officers arrived. No
one had been hurt, but Duane and his companions were charged
with creating a seditious riot. Fortunately for Duane, most of
the Irish—who recognized that the law was aimed more at them
than at the French—stood together. Members of the congregation said they had wanted to sign the petition. The priest testi-
fied that it was the custom in Ireland to post such notices in
churchyards. He saw no sacrilege. There were cheers when the
men were acquitted in the state courts.

Duane found restless Germans, too. In 1798 he had been effective in the election to Congress of Michael Leib, a German physician and radical Democrat. Leib was to collaborate with Duane
as political dictator of Philadelphia. Soon after the Irish riot in
the churchyard, the Germans in Bucks and Northampton counties were in tumultuous action. Under the leadership of an almost comic rebel, John Fries, a Revolutionary veteran and itiner-
ant auctioneer, they loudly denounced the direct taxes on houses
and land levied in eager Federalistic anticipation of a war with
France.

The stubborn Pennsylvania Dutch spent more on revolt than
the taxes would have cost them. They erected liberty poles and
wore red, white, and blue cockades. A fifer and a drummer were
hired to lead their march to run off the tax collectors. They
painted signs—DÄMN DE PRESIDENT, DÄMN DE CONGRESS, DÄMN DE
ARISCHDOKRATZ! Irate housewives used hot water to defend their
homes from the measuring sticks of assessors. President Adams
sent a force under a general to put down Fries' Rebellion. Fries
was captured when his little dog, Whiskey, who followed him
everywhere, betrayed his hiding place. He was twice condemned
to death. Some Federalists were angry when Adams pardoned
him.

Duane had not only opposed the taxes but had also charged
that the undisciplined soldiers had brutally mistreated the German farmers. Some fifteen to thirty (depending upon the

telling) petty officers and privates pushed into his print shop. At
pistol-point they herded his compositors and pressmen into a
corner, then they battered the editor with the butts of their
pistols. He was dragged downstairs into Franklin Court. Duane
asked for the chance to fight any one of them man-to-man. Instead he was knocked down and kicked. He was beaten until he
"could neither see nor hear nor stand." He would have been
killed if his son had not thrown himself across his father's body
and a number of his friends and neighbors arrived to make a
battle of it. The soldiers retreated. Armed Democrats remained
to meet a threat that the assailants might return to destroy the
plant. Also on guard was Bache's widow, soon to be Duane's
wife. One report said "Duane's little Margaret had the butcher
knife hid under her apron."

The *Gazette of the United States,* now edited by the dead
Fenno's son, treated the attack upon Duane as a joke. It declared that "the punishment of this catiff is of no more consequence than that of any other vagabond." It said that everyone
knew "the infernal *Aurora* and the United Irishman who con-
ducts it" were "expressly chargeable with the Northampton
Insurrection."

Undoubtedly Duane was an activator of resentment against
such strutting Federalist forces. At the barricade level he was
making the war against the Alien and Sedition Laws which
Jefferson and Madison were conducting in the protests they
wrote in the Kentucky and the Virginia Resolutions. The *Aurora*
recounted the judicial excesses in the enforcement of the Sedition Law. The paper made it steadily clear that only Democrats
were prosecuted. It gave much space to outrageous invasions of
the liberty of press and speech. Also it reported the case of the
man fined $100 because he said of a salute fired in honor of the
President that he wished the shot had hit him in the seat of his
pants.

So insistently did it damn the acts that a report circulated
attributing to Alexander Hamilton a scheme to buy and silence
the *Aurora.* When the Democratic New York *Argus* printed this
rumor Hamilton demanded prosecution. The *Argus'* editor,
Thomas Greenleaf, like Bache and Fenno had died of yellow

fever. His widow and one of her printers were arrested. The case against Mrs. Greenleaf was dropped but her eight-dollar-a-week printer was fined $100 and sent to jail for four months.

It was ridiculous, of course, to suggest that the *Aurora* could be silenced. It hammered out its indignations. With relentless ridicule, Duane also mocked the army being raised for the mythical war with France. "With all the influence of Hamilton, reenforced by the magical name of Washington," he said, the army was unable to fill its ranks. When the law creating the armed force was passed, he wrote, "there were 15,000 applications for commissions—since the passing of the law there have been only 3000 soldiers." And as a vilified Irishman, he noted that "three fifths of the men enlisted were Irish immigrants."

Also he pressed for peace in opposition to those Federalists, led by Hamilton, who, he believed, were eager for war and were using war fears as a means of suppressing political opposition. He published the convincing letters of George Logan, Quaker farmer and physician who had gone to France at his own expense and received assurances that French officials wanted no war. Logan's efforts doubtless served the peace which was to follow. Publication of his report by the *Aurora* increased popular suspicion of the warmakers. It was difficult to make a Jacobin out of Logan, who always wore homespun to encourage home manufacture. But the Federalist Congress rebuked Logan by passage of the Logan Law forbidding any negotiations with a foreign country by a private individual. Still the *Aurora* had made its point for peace.

There was nothing pacifistic about the *Aurora*'s editor, however. In July 1799, Secretary of State Timothy Pickering, a furious Federalist who was obsessed by fears of French influence which might bring mob rule, wrote President Adams.

Duane, he said, "has lately set himself up to be the captain of a company of volunteers, whose distinguishing badges are a plume of *cock*-neck feathers and a *small* black cockade with a *large* eagle. He is doubtless a United Irishman, and the company is probably formed to oppose the authority of the government; and in case of war and invasion by the French, to join them."

Within the week after Adams received Pickering's letter he replied:

"The matchless effrontery of this Duane merits the execution of the alien law. I am very willing to try its strength upon him."

It was tried, but Duane was able to prove in federal court that he had been born in America. Perhaps that failure made Pickering and other federal officials hesitate about trying him under the Sedition Law. Then in October at Norristown, Pennsylvania, he was haled into federal court. George Washington's slow-witted, one-eyed nephew, Bushrod Washington, appointed to the Supreme Court by Adams, was the chief judge. History seems to have remembered Bushrod chiefly for the amount of snuff he smeared on his face and his sloppy clothes. An indictment for sedition was, of course, brought against the editor. The case was continued until June 1800, and Duane went on about his business of lambasting the Federalists.

In a bitter campaign his candidate, Thomas McKean, was elected governor over Federalist U.S. Senator James Ross, a strong supporter of Hamilton's ideas and policies. This was revolution. With Duane behind him, McKean began the swift removal from office of Federalists. To give an enemy an office, the Governor wrote in words which sound like Duane's, would be "to put a dagger in the hands of an assassin." The defeated Ross, however, was still a member of the Senate. He moved to make no political revolution possible in the administration of the United States. As one of Ross' Federalist associates said, it was bad enough to see brought forward to office in Pennsylvania "every scoundrel who can read and write." Among them the Irish were "the most God-provoking Democrats this side of hell . . . the Germans are both stupid, ignorant and ugly, and are to the Irish what the Negroes of the South are to their drivers." Duane could afford to be amused by such angry screams.

He was not amused, however, when early in February three members of Congress brought him a resolution Ross had introduced in a closed session on January 3, 1800. With the Federalists still in control of both Houses of Congress, what Ross pro-

posed was a plan to keep them in control of the country. A
"Grand Committee" would be set up, composed of six Senators
and six Representatives, elected by ballot, and the Chief Justice
of the United States. They would take charge of the electoral
votes in the approaching Presidential election, throw out such
ones as they felt were tainted or improper, and determine which
votes should be counted. From its decree there was to be no
appeal.

Duane printed the bill in full in the *Aurora*. He baldly
charged an attempt to steal the Presidential election. This
Federalist-rigged committee, he wrote, would be like "the secret
Council of Ten at Venice of old." Stubbornly the Senate passed
the bill by a strict party vote of 16 to 12. But Duane's clamor in
the *Aurora* was rousing protests in the country. Some Federalists were troubled. Modifying amendments were offered in the
House. The Senate refused to agree. The bill died between the
two Houses.

Duane exulted: The "odious bill" had died as a result of
press exposure. He wrote in triumph that some in the Senate
"sought to overwhelm by terror and oppression the men who
dared to publish the bill, which even after numerous amendments was found too abominable to be countenanced by the
House of Representatives." A free press had preserved a free
country. But a greater question of press freedom was raised in
the debate.

On March 14, 1800, the baffled upper House by resolution ordered Duane to appear before it for his publications which
tended "to defame the Senate of the United States, and bring
them into disrepute." The editor first said he would appear and
with some sarcasm expressed his pleasure at the justice of the
Senate in giving him opportunity for defense. Then, on advice of
counsel, he declined to appear. In his absence the Senate found
him guilty of contempt. The sergeant-at-arms was ordered to
take him into custody.

Duane was not to be found. His friends were on hand. Clearly
public sentiment was on his side. A remonstrance sent to the
Senate declared "We had thought that the plain and acknowl-

edged principles of natural justice would have prevented the
accusers from being also the judges, the jury and the pun-
ishers.''

There was no arrest though the *Aurora* continued to resound.
March was a busy month for its editor. Not only was he continuing the denunciation of the Alien and Sedition Laws and describing the judicial tyranny which sent other editors and citizens to jail. He also printed in full gleeful detail articles about
the division among the Federalists. Hamilton had published a
pamphlet designed to prevent Adams' re-election on the Federalist ticket. Adams became aware—with Duane's bedeviling assistance—of Federalists who were Hamilton's spies in his Cabinet. Adams was finally putting an end to the fears of war with
France which Hamilton had nourished. All was grist to Duane's
bone-grinding mill.

If the editor could not be found, his laughter could be heard
and his lash felt. His friends were on hand in mounting number.
In May an action for libel was substituted for the contempt
charge. The beset and belabored Adams instructed his Attorney
General and the District Attorney of Pennsylvania to commence
the action, which was evidently lost in the maze of libel suits
which then and later constantly attended Duane. The sedition
charge brought against him the preceding fall was postponed
again.

Almost as a present to Duane, Adams dismissed Hamilton's
man Timothy Pickering as Secretary of State on May 10. Pickering had served as a sort of persecutor-in-chief under the Alien
and Sedition Acts. And when Adams left Philadelphia without a
Federalist demonstration in his honor, the *Aurora* gloated:
''Did the Blues parade? No? What no parade to salute him
'whom the people delight to honor'—'the rock on which the
storm beats'—the 'chief who now commands'? Did the officers
of the standing army or the marines parade? The new officers of
the army are not fond of the President, he has dismissed Timothy.''

Duane's ridicule followed Adams. His diatribes raked the
whole Federalist field. There was no gagging him. He had become too hot for handling under Alien and Sedition laws or any

other repressive procedures. His place in the advancing political campaign, which seemed a revolutionary movement to the Federalists, was best described by their own angriest organ, the *Columbian Centinel* of Boston.

AMERICANS, WHY SLEEP YE? that paper demanded, as if only the un-Americans were awake. Conservatives then as later liked to think they were the only true Americans. The Irish and the Germans, the Jacobins and the roughnecks were about to carry the Democrats to power. The mob was marching. The rabble was aroused. But this time it was Duane and not the young John Adams of 1765 who cheered on defiance of authority.

In Adams' Massachusetts, where the roar to revolution had been led by the *Gazette* of Ben Edes and John Gill, the Boston *Centinel* warned of the rising Democratic tide. Though Federalist newspapers in this campaign outnumbered Democratic journals two to one, the *Centinel* reported that many new radical organs were appearing everywhere. Such papers, the Boston journal declared, "serve as a sounding board to the notes that issue through that great speaking trumpet of the Devil, the Philadelphia *Aurora.*"

William Duane would not have denied such eminence for himself and his paper. In Pennsylvania, he expected to be consulted and heeded by Democratic politicians from the Governor down. When peace was finally concluded with France in September, he regarded himself as justified in his long insistence that the X.Y.Z. episode was just "one of the best and most successful political *tricks* that was ever *played off.*" When the Democrats triumphed at the polls, Duane undoubtedly felt that much of the victory was his own.

The summer of that great campaign was not only a season of clamor but one of happiness for Duane as well. In June, when the sedition case against him was postponed again, he and Margaret Bache were married. Ben had been dead nearly two years. His widow had stood beside Duane when the going was rough. In the big, crowded house near the office, they added five children to those from their first marriages. The youngest of the children remembered being much in the library with her father as he wrote, of the many guests who came and went, noted Americans and foreigners, and of the sometimes almost too generous hospitality of the house.

Such a scene might serve as happy ending for the Duane story. Sadly, it does not. His expectations were high when Jefferson swiftly pardoned all Sedition Act offenders. The removal of the capital to Washington deprived his paper of its political advantage. With the encouragement of Jefferson, he opened a book-and-stationery store in Washington in expectation of government contracts. There too he might have moved his paper as the government's organ. Thomas Jefferson had other ideas, however. The great advocate of freedom of the press and the great beneficiary of its democratic freedom remained aloof from the press' rough-and-tumble practices and its chief democratic practitioner. Instead of Duane, Jefferson chose as the editor of his Washington organ a mild young man who made it so namby-pamby a paper that even Jefferson's enemies called it *The National Smoothing Plane.*

Historian of the period and its press Claude G. Bowers believed that Duane did more than any other man to discredit the projected war with France over the X.Y.Z. incident, to make the Alien and Sedition Laws abhorrent, to arouse and munition the masses, and to make the triumph of Jefferson in 1800 inevitable. Jefferson himself did not minimize the editor's contribution. Duane's *Aurora,* he said, "unquestionably rendered incalculable services to republicanism through all its struggles with the federalists." It had been "the rallying point for the orthodoxy of the whole Union." And "it was our comfort in the gloomiest days." Duane he knew "to be a very honest man and sincere republican." But "his passions are stronger than his prudence, and his personal as well as general antipathies render him very intolerant."

Duane did have strong feelings after Jefferson's election, as before it. He was eager to remove from office "tenacious" Federalists who had recently been eager to relegate him to outer darkness. In a pamphlet signed "Citizen W. Duane," he compiled a list of hangers-on with his own descriptive epithets beside their names: Execrable Aristocrat, Picaroon, Nothingarian, Nincompoop, Throat-Cutter. He thought other Democrats should

remember as he did similar descriptions of them by Federalists.
He was only one member of the ''Jeffersonian Mobocracy'' described by the Federalist poet, Thomas Green Fessenden. A
couple of Fessenden's verses went:

> Step forward, demagogue Duane,
> Than whom a greater rogue in grain,
> Ne'er fortified by mob alliance,
> Dare bid the powers that be, defiance.
>
> Few good and great men can be nam'd,
> Your scoundrelship has not defam'd;
> And scarce a rogue who ought to hang
> Who is not number'd with your gang.

Such rough exchanges pained Mr. Jefferson. He did not forget
Duane. He gave him a commission in the army and when Duane
was hard up he solicited contributions to relieve his financial
embarrassment. But perhaps Duane was more suited to the battle
than the victory. He went on fighting in Pennsylvania politics,
battling old friends and making new enemies. He served as adju-
tant general in the War of 1812. In Philadelphia he supported
the tailors and shoemakers when they struck for better wages.
Libel suits continued to be directed toward him. Before he retired from the editorship of the *Aurora* in 1822 its delinquent
subscribers owed it $80,000. Still he had influence enough to
become clerk of the Supreme Court of Pennsylvania for the eastern district, a position he held until his death on November 24,
1835. Few then remembered the hot times when Federalists
warned that a godless rabble would be brought to Washington if
Jefferson were elected by people who listened to that damn
Duane.

5

Manhunt of the *Western World*

Humphrey Marshall, publicist and politician, insisted to the end
of his days that he never provoked the personal contentions and
partisan conflicts in which he was continually engaged. Yet he
was always ready to shoot with pistol or pen. He was confident
of his own roaring rectitude even when he arrived in Kentucky
as a twenty-two-year-old Revolutionary veteran in 1782 to pick
up a 4000-acre land grant for his war service.

Though he was of the Piedmont Virginia gentry, his parents
were poor. Tradition says he was educated as a member of the
multiplying family of his uncle, Thomas Marshall (who came to

Kentucky, too), the father of John Marshall, great Federalist and Chief Justice of the United States. Thomas was also the father of Mary (christened Anna Maria) whom Humphrey married in 1784. In Kentucky the Marshalls were known as plain-speaking people. They carried candor even to cemeteries. Perhaps Humphrey's Mary was like the description on her mother's tombstone: *She was good, not brilliant, useful not ornamental, and the mother of fifteen children.* Mary's husband freely admitted his shining superiority and, in the elegant clothes he wore in courts, legislative halls, and even in the newspaper office, Humphrey was ornamental as well.

He had few gifts for popularity. The Marshalls did not let any desire for public-petting interfere with their pursuits. Old Thomas had come west for lands—and also with the job of federal inspector of revenue. On March 12, 1792, he put an advertisement in the *Kentucky Gazette* at Lexington telling people plainly that he was going to collect the taxes of the United States government on the liquor they distilled. That was two years before President George Washington felt it necessary to send a general with 13,000 men to put down the Whiskey Rebellion of small farm distillers against the levy in Western Pennsylvania.

Kentuckians didn't like the tax either. Corn grew to surplus where the wilderness had been. To ship it overland to the seaboard was impossible. Trade down the rivers where the Spanish jealously guarded the lower reaches of the Mississippi was a problem. The federal government, grabbing for its taxes on little stills, seemed less concerned about the welfare of the Westerners and their movement to markets on that stream. But a bushel of corn, worth about fifty cents, yielded three to five gallons of corn whiskey, worth one to two dollars a gallon. It could be moved. It could be kept and drunk at home. Sometimes it became as indispensable as ink on editorial desks. The tax on the liquor was a symbol both of the Marshalls' support of central government in Federalist hands and of the restlessness of many individuals around them.

Young Humphrey Marshall gave early warning of his attitude. He had been sent back across the mountains as delegate when Virginia, which then included Kentucky, ratified the federal Constitution. He had voted for the strong union though he knew his constituents feared it would endanger local rights and might cramp their personal liberties. Having provoked them by his vote, he returned to offend them in person. Very little tact attended his caustic candor. He made no secret of his contempt for the idea of rule by the masses or his scorn for many of those who added up to the majority. He freely expressed his disbelief in revealed religion, a persuasive addition to his unpopularity.

As a lawyer, Marshall was successful. He acquired more and more land. Possibly his suspicions of others were sharpened when he himself was suspected of a breach of trust in grabbing more acres. While working as attorney for an estate the land claims of which were uncertain, he secured a grant of the same lands for himself. Angry heirs made him split the profits from the property. Part of it was the equivalent of $433 which he got for a piece he sold, in 1786, to General James Wilkinson upon which that officer from Pennsylvania laid out the town of Frankfort.

But Marshall was not merely dealing in Kentucky acreage. He regarded himself somehow as the guardian of the land of the young Republic in the West. And as a Federalist member of the legislature in 1793 and 1794, while the X.Y.Z. affair was stirring the East with fears of a French war, he stirred Kentucky fears and anxieties by charges of plots and conspiracies with Spain. Many good men in the West were impatient with ties to the distant central government. If the choice lay between Spain or stagnation, many Kentuckians were ready for Spain or Western separation. Their irritations had been sharpened earlier when John Jay, then managing foreign affairs for the loose Confederation, indicated a willingness to relinquish free navigation of the Mississippi upon which Western upriver Americans depended.

Humphrey's charges of conspiracy stirred Kentucky and weakened the Jeffersonians there. In the excitement the legislature sent him to the United States Senate, where he let his consistent support of the Federalist administration carry him beyond the peril point at home. He even voted for the Jay treaty with England. Its negotiation by Jay seemed to Jeffersonians a subservient relinquishment of American rights to Britain. Certainly Kentuckians in general felt no such affection for this Jay as that which caused Marshall to give his name to a son.

Quickly his constituents passed resolutions demanding a Constitutional amendment to permit the recall of such a Senator. But formal protests did not satisfy. Mobs met Marshall. He was dragged to the Kentucky River; only a stratagem saved him from a ducking. Disheveled though not dripping, he was stoned out of Frankfort. And at the first opportunity, in 1801, he was replaced in the Senate by an ardent Jeffersonian. In the sweep that year of the anti-Federalist revolution, there was little Humphrey Marshall could do but go back to acquiring more and more Kentucky acres.

He waited for a chance to strike back. Fortunately for him, he was not quite alone in his dislike and distrust of the Jeffersonians. Ties of both politics and family bound him to Joseph Daveiss. That young man's plainer people had come to Kentucky in 1779, before Marshall arrived. Daveiss had no schooling until he was twelve; at eighteen he was fighting Indians in a campaign north of the Ohio River. When he was twenty-five, however, he appeared as a lawyer before the U.S. Supreme Court. Chief Justice Marshall found nothing crude about his argument.

The great judge fostered the young man's Federalist leanings. He got President Adams to appoint him U.S. District Attorney in Kentucky. The Marshalls there liked him, too. He was welcomed into the family as husband of Ann, sister of the Chief Justice and of Mrs. Humphrey Marshall. He was twenty-nine, fearless and such a passionate Federalist that he adopted Hamilton as a middle name, after his idol, Alexander Hamilton. Marshall shared his admiration for the able New Yorker who was the great founder and guardian of their political faith.

A journalistic incident that tragically involved Hamilton set in motion the circumstances which led Daveiss and Marshall to crusade in Kentucky. In 1804, in the river town of Hudson, New York, two newspapers—the Jeffersonian *Bee* and the Federalist *Wasp*—were exchanging stings. This was routine conflict, but the *Wasp* hit an exposed Democratic nerve when it reprinted the charge that Jefferson had paid the notorious scandalmonger

James Thomson Callender to write that George Washington was "a traitor, a robber and a perjurer." Despite recent Democratic clamor against Federalist persecution of critical Democratic editors, the *Wasp*'s editor was pulled into court and convicted of libel.

Hamilton entered the case on appeal. Though he made a famous free-press argument that the truth of an allegation must be admitted as evidence before a jury, he lost the case. More serious still, while in Albany arguing the matter, he expressed (as he often did) his bitter feeling that Aaron Burr was a "dangerous man," not to be trusted in government. The remark was quoted in a communication to the Albany *Argus*. It was brought to Burr's notice.

Unlike Hamilton, whose origins were as obscure as his elegance and erudition were real, the handsome Burr had risen from the oldest and best American lineage. Like Hamilton, he had risen from brilliant young soldier to effective politician and lawyer. The two men soared upward side by side. Hamilton's role had been vastly more distinguished in the development of the nation. But in New York, where Burr and Hamilton contested for place, the former had organized the rank and file (whom men like Humphrey Marshall regarded as the rag, tag, and bobtail) to confound Hamilton's Federalist aristocrats. In 1804, however, Burr was surrounded by slurs. His political fortunes were disintegrating. The New York *American Citizen*, operated by Burr's enemies in his own party, had not only sharply questioned his political fidelity but had also charged that his faithlessness had filled the whorehouses of the metropolis with the victims of his philandering. Burr ignored such charges with contempt. He did not bother to answer them—even in his own organ, the *Morning Chronicle*, edited by Dr. Peter Irving, effeminate brother of Washington Irving. The opposition of the more moderate New York *Evening Post*, to which Hamilton dictated policy, he let pass. But Hamilton's steady, private, scornful reflections upon him had passed the point of the harassed Burr's endurance.

Burr demanded explanation. Hamilton hedged. They met in perfectly correct duel by the standards of the times in the East as well as the West. Burr's bullet ended his rival's career. And, though Daveiss in Kentucky had been recently prepared for a similar encounter with young Henry Clay, no men responded in greater outrage than Daveiss and Marshall to the emotional and political cry of *murder!* which rose in New York and helped send Burr, politically rejected and financially ruined, over the mountains and down the rivers. Their anger rose when great houses opened to Burr. Their disgust mounted as others greeted the Colonel in appreciation of the manner and charm which made him irresistible to women and brought to him either the ardent support or the bitter distrust of men. The two angry Kentuckians took particular note when the confident traveler from New York moved down the Mississippi in a magnificent military barge provided by General Wilkinson, ranking officer in the United States Army and Governor of Louisiana Territory.

Marshall had not merely sold Wilkinson land. After being first much impressed by the General's dazzling personality, the tart Kentuckian's suspicions grew concerning him. Wild as were some of his charges about conspiracies in the West, the suspicions were justified. Wilkinson's title had been badly tarnished before he arrived. In the Revolution he had played a minor but shoddy part in the Conway Cabal against George Washington. There had been grave questions about his accounts as clothier-general. Yet he seemed builder and promoter of the welfare of the West when down the river from Kentucky he floated to Spanish New Orleans.

His shipments of tobacco and other produce through that port seemed splendid to those who had been plagued about markets for their surplus corn and taxed whiskey. Wilkinson seemed leader and actor for the West. No one knew, until Spanish archives were opened long after he died, that the General in New Orleans took a Spanish oath and accepted Spain's gold as its secret Agent No. 13. But Humphrey Marshall's suspicions mounted with the amount of "tobacco money" which came by the muleload to the General in Kentucky. Now, in 1805, as Burr enjoyed Wilkinson's hospitality and his elegant barge, those earlier suspicions were revived by Marshall and shared by Joseph Daveiss. They provided the link which might connect Burr and Democrats with treason in the West.

The two Kentuckians moved warily at first. Daveiss traveled to St. Louis, where Wilkinson lived as governor, to try to find out more from him about him and Burr. It was his job as U.S. District Attorney to be on guard. His passion as a Federalist made him more eager. But as a holdover in a Democratic administration, he moved with care though apparently dutifully. In January 1806, after Burr had returned to the seaboard from his first westward journey, Daveiss began to write President Jefferson excited letters. They told of some kind of plot in which he was sure the errant New Yorker was engaged. Perhaps Jefferson understood, as some historians have concluded, that Daveiss, Marshall, & Co. were aiming at him as well as at Burr.

Certainly they would not have regretted any damage done to the Democratic President by connecting him with seeming acquiescence in Burr's projects. The President apparently did take Daveiss' letters lightly—though, unknown to the Kentuckians, he put a confidential agent on Burr's trail. Marshall and Daveiss were ready for public exposure and explosion. At this point the two journalistic assistants they needed appeared on the scene in Frankfort, which had been made Kentucky's capital.

John Wood and Joseph Montfort Street, two travelers as different as possible from the cantering Burr, ambled over the Alleghenies from Richmond.

Wood was thirty. He was described at the time as an elderly-looking man, of middle size and ordinary dress, with a Godfrey's quadrant stringed to his shoulder and a knapsack on his back. A Scotsman who had lived in Switzerland, he had arrived in New York in 1800. Recommended to Burr as a teacher of languages and mathematics, Wood was made tutor to the beautiful Theodosia Burr, whose education as something more than a mere lady of fashion was her father's devoted concern. When her education ended with her marriage in 1801 to the rich South Carolina planter Joseph Alston, Burr put Wood's facile pen to use in politics—or Wood put Burr to his uses with his pen.

He prepared for publication in 1802 a work called *The History of the Administration of John Adams*. It was, a critic of such writing said soon afterward, a book made largely "with the scissors, & what is worse, a dull pair.'' So loaded was it with bitter invective and personal abuse of Adams and other Federalists and with such fulsome praise of Burr and Jefferson that the Vice-President felt it would do his party more harm than good. He undertook to suppress the thing by buying up the whole edition.

There was bickering over the price. Then suddenly it was evident that some copies had been slipped to James Cheetham, editor of the New York *American Watchman,* who was engaged in tearing down Burr for the benefit of rivals in his own party. Burr was made to seem to be secretly protecting the Federalists. To point the charge, the book was soon published as *The Suppressed History.* What Wood got or gave in the business is unclear. On the basis of it Burr's Democratic enemies blasted him. Also, when Wood went to prison for debt shortly afterward, William Coleman, editor of Hamilton's New York *Evening Post,* paid him out.

Evidently, however, the market for Wood's literary wares was exhausted in New York. In 1805 he wandered down to Richmond. The Virginia capital was just recovering from sad experiences with an editorial vagabond. The infamous Callender, whose reported slanders for Jefferson had gotten the *Wasp* into trouble, had fled there from Philadelphia eight years before. He had come south in an unsuccessful effort to escape the Federalists' Sedition Law, the lash of which he, at least, deserved. Jefferson had befriended him financially, for the sake only of charity, he said later. There was no charity in Callender. He soon turned on Jefferson to print the worst slanders about his private life, including the charge that he kept a black harem on his philosopher's hill at Monticello. Callender's slanderous skill became material for literature. From his scurrilous writings Thomas Moore took the malice for his poem about Jefferson:

> The weary statesman for repose hath fled
> From halls of council to his negro's shed;
> Where, blest, he woos some black Aspasia's grace,
> And dreams of freedom in his slave's embrace.

Moore's poem did not appear until 1807. Callender was already dead when Wood passed through the preceding year.

Drunken and destitute, the turncoat traducer had drowned in three feet of water, finding his grave, a critic unrestrained by charity said, "in congenial mud."

Though Wood found little work in Richmond, there he met twenty-four-year-old Joseph Montfort Street. Street's father was a prosperous planter, a member of the county court, and an Episcopal vestryman. His mother was a sister of a governor of North Carolina. The elderly-looking hack writer and the young Virginian began what Wood described to Henry Clay later as an "ardent friendship" such as "frequently entails misery on those who are the slaves of such a strong passion."

In Kentucky Wood and Street found Daveiss and Marshall waiting for them. They produced the first issue of the *Western World* on July 7, 1806. There was no great demand for the paper. Kentucky had had newspapers since 1787, a year after the founding of the first newspaper beyond the mountains at Pittsburgh. Then an antiquated press, type, ink balls, and ink were lugged overland from Philadephia to Pittsburgh and floated down the Ohio River. So equipped in Lexington, the Bradford brothers, John and Fielding, issued the *Kentucke Journal,* soon changing the *e* to *y* at the end of the territory's name on their masthead. Other papers were established. This new *Western World* did not have or require a press of its own. Published in another print shop, it was called by one historian a "pretended Republican newspaper." The pretense was thin. From the first it was the recognized propaganda sheet of Marshall and Daveiss. It was even rumored that Chief Justice Marshall was back of this journalistic enterprise.

In the *Western World* stories of old intrigues with Spain were wonderfully revived and freshened. Without too much regard for proof, it began making sweeping charges about conspirators —including, of course, Burr and Wilkinson, but also about Kentuckians on hand and ready to answer with words or with pistols if necessary. Humphrey Marshall and Daveiss were clearly the responsible writers, but Wood and Street stood visible in the line of fire from those whose partisanship or fear was aroused. There was plenty of both.

Wood, as one historian put it, had no hankering for assassination. As the attack of the *Western World* turned more precisely on Burr, Wood did recall in conscience that Burr had once been his benefactor. The Scottish journalist insisted that only the first of the attacks on the supposed plotters was published with his approval. When he failed to prevent the publication of others, he said, he withdrew from the paper. There was another more personal problem involved. The bolder, younger Street grew more intimate politically and socially with Daveiss and Marshall. In the "misery" of broken friendship Wood accused Street of swindling him out of the money he had invested in the paper. The chains of the "strong passion" were severed. Wood, looking less than ardent, retired soon to Virginia and to hack writing, schoolteaching, and mapmaking. There, too, he acquired the good opinion of Jefferson.

Street stayed. Though Daveiss, an old Indian fighter, and Humphrey, who was ready to face mobs and duelists, needed no protector, Street became the pugnacious operator of the *Western World*. He was the steady object of abuse and revenge. Once he was seriously wounded by a would-be assassin. He fought one duel and was challenged to others. Having established clearly his personal courage and pistol skill, however, he announced, in November 1806, that he had "concluded to file the challenges regularly as they are received, and from time to time give a list of them in the *Western World*."

The paper was roaring in its attacks as Burr approached on his second visit in the fall of 1806. On his way toward Kentucky, the debonair New Yorker stopped at the idyllic island retreat of Harman Blennerhassett in the Ohio River near Marietta. That eccentric Irishman, a graduate in law from Trinity College, Dublin, had become an ardent republican in France. He had a flair for music and science and had, indeed, a contemporary said, "all sorts of sense except common sense." He had fled from the distractions of the world to his island in the Ohio, where he built a costly house of "original ugliness." Burr captivated the eccentric Irishman and his pretty wife.

They were ready to invest in his schemes whatever they might be. Blennerhassett, in communications he signed "Querist" in the *Ohio Gazette* at Marietta, seemed clearly to indicate that Burr planned separation of the Western states from the Union.

Also there seems to have been talk, playful or perfidious, about a
Mexican court in which the innocent Blennerhassetts would be
prince and princess or at least peers of empire.

The "Querist" articles stirred excitement not only around
Marietta. The Blennerhassett house was later raided and looted
by militiamen acting like a mob. The articles also became the
basis of an excited appeal to the people printed in the *Western
World* on October 15. Kentucky declined to be alarmed. It was
no longer a frontier full of fears. By 1800, with 180,000 whites
and 40,000 Negroes, it was the largest community west of the
mountains. Furthermore, Burr's distinguished friends in the
Western state had heard and read the frantic partisanship of
Daveiss and Marshall before and often. The Colonel assured his
friends, as he did the frightened Mrs. Blennerhassett, that the
wild stories that he had any plan to split the Union or strike
Spain were untrue.

That was Burr's story. He stuck to it to the end. Nevertheless
in Frankfort, while Burr was enjoying the hospitality of friends
in the state, the *Western World* intensified its charges. On November 5, 1806, Daveiss rose in the federal court and made complaint against the former Vice-President for violating the laws
of the United States by preparing a military expedition against
Mexico. He added that Burr's plans involved a revolution of all
the Western states and territories. On the bench was Judge
Harry Innes. He had gone to school with James Madison, worked
in the defense and development of Kentucky, and been appointed judge by Washington in 1789. He had many friends in
Frankfort, where he had been active in locating the capital. But
he was one of those at whom the *Western World* had pointed the
finger of suspicion. Three days after Daveiss made his motion,
Innes denied it. Then Burr built his popularity by riding from
Lexington with friends on sleek Kentucky horses and demanding
vindication.

On November 12, while the *Western World* continued its verbal cannonade, Burr appeared in court surrounded by indignant
supporters. At his side as his counsel was the young, stooped,
drawling Henry Clay who had once come close to a duel with
Daveiss. Shrewd, sardonic Clay was not averse to confronting

the stiff Daveiss at once. The District Attorney asked for a post-ponement on the grounds that his chief witness was absent in Indiana. Instead, in the impatient court, Burr was acquitted and the jury discharged. The elegant New Yorker made a restrained and dignified speech. Then he rode away with his friends. But on November 25, the stubborn Daveiss renewed his motion. Burr, calm as ever, was back in court on December 2. Once more the District Attorney's witnesses had disappeared. So on December 5, the grand jury of twenty-two persons signed a paper declaring that they could discover nothing improper or injurious to the interests of the United States in the conduct of Aaron Burr.

This time the handsome Colonel did not ride away quickly. The society of little, lively Frankfort gave a ball in his honor. And the Frankfort *Palladium*, which scorned its strident con-temporary, the *Western World*, spoke sentiments shared by most Kentuckians. Colonel Burr, it declared, "throughout this busi-ness conducted himself with the calmness, moderation and firm-ness which have characterized him through life. He evinced an earnest desire for a full and speedy investigation ... he excited the strongest sensation of respect and friendship in the breast of every impartial person present."

Actually Daveiss and Marshall, who could not win in court, had already raised the clamor for manhunt through the *Western World*. Copies of the paper had been sent east to Washington. Congressmen were talking. The President had seen copies. But the sheet's most agitated reader was General Wilkinson. He began to write the President, too (though in other letters he assured his Spanish patrons that he was taking care of their interests). He told Jefferson in obsequious dispatches that the *Western World* had bespattered him with obloquy. He had in-structed his lawyers to bring suit, he told the President, though apparently they never did. The excited purport of his communica-tions was that Burr moved in "a deep, dark and wicked conspir-acy." Wilkinson was ready to help hang his friend to save his own hide, and Jefferson took Wilkinson's betrayal of Burr as basis for belated action.

A week before Burr was first released, Jefferson (on November 27) had issued his proclamation to stir the country with a warn-ing to beware of treason by a group plotting an illegal expedition against Spain. Jefferson did not name Burr; it was not necessary. An almost panic pressure attended the President's call upon citizens to catch conspirators. All citizens and authorities were enjoined to be vigilant, to seize all boats and supplies of the "sundry persons" involved, and to apprehend the guilty. Those sundry persons included not only "well-meaning citizens" Burr had seduced but also the "ardent, restless, desperate and dissatisfied."

Galloping horsemen, their hair streaming in the wind, brought the news to Frankfort. Burr, of course, was already gone southward, serenely unaware of the tumult at his heels. His expedition was insignificant. In his boats he had only a few men and boys whom he insisted he was only leading to settlement in Louisiana. He was on his way to arrest at Natchez, to another jury's dismissal of the charges against him, then to flight from fears that Wilkinson or others might kill him, to arrest once more, and to the great treason trial in Richmond. In the excitement the President, now Burr's implacable pursuer, gave the *Western World* proprietors not praise but rebuke and punishment.

"In Kentucky," he told Congress, "a premature attempt to bring Burr to justice, without a sufficient evidence for his conviction, had produced a popular impression in his favor and a general disbelief of his guilt. This gave him an unfortunate opportunity of hastening his equipments."

Jefferson, who had kept Daveiss in office despite his politics for a half-dozen years, promptly removed him. He was trusting Wilkinson who, he told Congress, "with the honor of a soldier and the fidelity of a good citizen" had sent him the dependable information about Burr. It reported the horrendous possibility that, if Burr failed in his purpose to pull the Western states from the Union, he meant to "seize New Orleans, plunder the banks there, possess himself of the military and naval stores, and proceed on his expedition to Mexico." Eager now for the conviction of Burr, whom he termed criminal before he was tried, Jefferson could not have a District Attorney who discredited his principal witness. He was aware, too, that Daveiss and Marshall would, if they could, have damaged him as Democratic President.

Daveiss turned back to his pen, using it rather as he would a pistol. His temper flared in a pamphlet, published in Frankfort in 1807, called "View of the President's Conduct Concerning the Conspiracy of 1806." Into it he put equal abuse of Burr, Wilkinson, and Jefferson. It was generally disregarded as the bitterness of a dismissed officeholder. Perhaps, as reported later, the popularity of the *Western World* declined with its continued bitter attacks on the President. Still, some support remained for those who had openly attacked Wilkinson and Burr.

Humphrey Marshall was elected to the lower house of the legislature in 1807, 1808, and 1809. There he moved against the *Western World*'s Kentucky targets. He renewed the charges he had made (as "Observer") in that paper that State Judge Benjamin Sebastian had been in the pay of Spain; he was prepared to prove them. Sebastian was less lucky than Wilkinson; some of his Spanish vouchers had been found among the papers of a dead intermediary in Natchez. When Marshall obtained a legislative investigation, he promptly resigned.

With the backing of Daveiss and Street, Marshall was not so successful in his moves against Federal Judge Harry Innes. Though Innes insisted on his innocence, Marshall pushed through the legislature a resolution calling on Congress to impeach him. Congress refused. Then Innes, not content with this vindication, brought libel suits against Marshall and Street.

Impatience with Marshall was growing as he paraded his prosecutions in the legislature. His peacock arrogance more and more piqued those Jeffersonians who recognized that he was shooting not only at oldtime conspirators but also at the present Democratic administration in Washington and its supporters in Kentucky. In his criticisms of the embargo Jefferson had imposed in the critical British-American situation, he tangled with swift-striking Henry Clay.

That rising politician, who had already served briefly in the United States Senate, introduced a resolution calling upon Kentucky legislators to wear only American-made clothes. Many already wore such homespuns by necessity. But the elegant Marshall snorted. Clay retaliated with the slow-spoken jibe that Marshall was dressed in "belligerent cloth." And the bristling Federalist called Clay a liar on the floor. Clay, who had almost

dueled with Daveiss a few years before, called his associate to the
shore of the Ohio across from Louisville. They met on a cold
January morning in 1809. Perhaps cold, fumbling fingers saved
both of them there. Afterward it seemed almost a comic meeting
to Clay. He wrote:

> I have this moment returned from the field of battle. We
> had three shots. On the first I grazed him just above the
> navel—as he missed me, on the second my damned pistol
> snapped and he missed me—on the third I received a flesh
> wound in the thigh, and owing to my receiving his first fire,
> etc., I missed him.
>
> My wound is no way serious, as the bone is unhurt, but
> prudence will require me to remain here some days.

Marshall drew the most blood on the Ohio shore. The legislature in Frankfort that year sent Clay to the Senate and on to his
national career as great compromiser and Presidential candidate.
At home, Marshall faced the Innes libel suit. Just as Clay's
pistol had misfired, in this conflict a hung jury resulted. Things,
however, were not going too well with Marshall's companions in
crusade. Though the *Western World*'s nagging seemed out of
tune with increasing Kentucky prosperity, Street seemed temporarily to be doing well. In 1809 he married Eliza Maria, whose
father, Thomas Posey, had been lieutenant governor of Kentucky and was later to serve as governor of the Indiana Territory and U.S. Senator from Louisiana.

In 1811, Street executed for his wife's benefit a deed of trust
to one of her kin conveying 6000 acres of land, six Negroes, two
cows, and household furniture. A year later, when a big verdict
was rendered against him in the Innes libel suit, he pled that the
amount was entirely beyond his means. He had lost what control
he had ever had of the paper, so he moved on from Kentucky to
the widening West. There long service as an Indian agent won
him the accolade from his red-skinned charges that he was "an
Indian agent whom the spoils of office could not buy."

Daveiss moved that year, too—on a militant mission. Burr had
been acquitted at Richmond by a court over which the brother-in-
law of Daveiss and Marshall, Chief Justice John Marshall, pre-

sided. This time it was not Daveiss' fellow Federalists but the
Jeffersonians who were furious, because they felt that this greatest Marshall had saved Burr's neck. The judiciary had prevailed
against the Jeffersonians once more. Jefferson was made to seem
almost too eager for the end of an enemy. Nevertheless, any
efforts of Daveiss and Humphrey Marshall to discredit the Jefferson administration and build up a following in the West failed
completely. In Frankfort the purposes of the *Western World*
petered out. Daveiss moved to Lexington to practice law. It is
doubtful that he joined in the conviviality the established editor
of the *Kentucky Gazette* enjoyed at the poker table and over
tumblers of bourbon with Clay and his friends. But, with other
Kentuckians, he was looking toward new war on the frontier. On
August 24, 1811, Daveiss wrote General William Henry Harrison, Governor of Indiana, offering his services in the expected
attack on the Indians in the contested ground along Tippecanoe
Creek. He told Harrison that he regarded him as the man of first
military talent in the West and would much value an opportunity to serve under him.

Later Daveiss was less sure about Harrison. The General accepted his offer and put him in command of his mounted force of
dragoons. At the scene of battle Daveiss and other officers urged
prompt attack. With scruples about his instructions, Harrison
demurred. When the fighting came at last, Daveiss rushed forward among the trees, followed by only a few men. He fell
mortally wounded. Arguments grew about the battle in which
many Americans died for uncertain triumph. Western Republicans met the criticism with more enthusiasm than the encounter
deserved. Ultimately Tippecanoe carried Harrison to the White
House. In Kentucky, however, Humphrey Marshall published a
sharp review of Harrison's report of the battle, hinting openly
that Daveiss had died as a result of the General's blunders.
Genuine grief may have moved Humphrey this time. His caustic
pen described the General as "a little, selfish, intriguing busy-
body" who had led his men to death for his own gain.

Marshall roared alone. Daveiss was dead. Street was gone. Of
all the founders of the *Western World* only the prematurely
aged Wood saw the results of its great crusade at the trial of

Burr. With Jefferson directing his prosecutors from Washington and his Federalist adversary Chief Justice Marshall sitting on the bench in Richmond, that trial provided the dramatic conflict of the Jefferson years. Great lawyers were engaged. Sharptongued John Randolph of Roanoke headed the grand jury. Andrew Jackson of Tennessee marched the streets snorting his contempt of Wilkinson. Lovely Theodosia Burr came to stand beside her father. Washington Irving was there as a newspaper reporter sympathetic to the man on trial.

In such a company Wood was only a little-noticed spectator. He published in Alexandria, Virginia, *A Full Statement of the Trial and Acquittal of Aaron Burr*. Apparently his report offended no one at a time when partisanship touched little men as well as great ones. Certainly it did not offend Jefferson. After the trial he befriended Wood. All angers were subsiding when, in 1817, Wood turned to the former President at Monticello for a recommendation. The old editor of the *Western World* was at the Petersburg Academy then, teaching mathematics, which brought him fewer troubles than journalism. Jefferson wrote recommending him for the task of providing accurate maps of Virginia and its counties. Wood had acquired a reputation in Virginia as an eccentric, but he went competently about the work. He received $33,000 for it. He had almost completed the task when he died, in 1822, and students since have praised his performance for such "fidelity to facts, as was possible, under the difficult circumstances attending such a large survey at that time."

No such mellowing metes and bounds marked the later career of Humphrey Marshall. True, he turned to gathering materials for his history of Kentucky, but that with him was less an enterprise in objectivity than a literary engagement in vindication and vindictiveness. In 1810, refusing to be silenced, he established the *American Republic* as the only Federalist newspaper in Kentucky. And, lest his enemies have any doubts about his defiance, he flew the image of a rattlesnake from its masthead. He went on raging at the old conspirators, almost all of whom seemed to have escaped.

Burr was still in poverty-stricken exile in Europe, where pursuing Jeffersonians made constant troubles about both his free movement there and his wish to come home. After a succession of trials and investigation Wilkinson had been found not guilty of wrongdoing by courts-martial but his tortuous, swashbuckling, drunken path was already leading to his death (hastened by an overdose of opium) in 1825, in the Mexico on which he had said Burr's ambitious eyes were set.

In Kentucky Judge Sebastian, whom Marshall had driven from the bench, was living in safe obscurity as landowner, miller, and storekeeper. Federal Judge Harry Innes still sat on the bench. Feud still sparked between the judge and the angry editor. Finally, on February 17, 1815, when Marshall was approaching sixty and Innes was older, the two men signed a formal agreement not to mention each other disrespectfully.

Humphrey went on collecting the materials for his history. He changed the name of his newspaper to *Harbinger,* a label that presaged no change in his views. Even after Marshall sold this last paper of his own, he wrote letters to other publications and even, somewhat surprisingly, occasional verse. But apparently he was waiting again. Innes died on September 20, 1816. Then Marshall began the revision and expansion of his *History of Kentucky,* in which he printed in detail the earlier attacks he had made on the dead man.

As he outlived his enemies, time swept past Humphrey Marshall. The democracy of Jefferson, which he had resisted, was history. Rule by the masses of men which he had scorned was now triumphant and tumultuous in the new surge of plain men behind rawboned Andrew Jackson. Marshall's aristocratic world seemed caught in the paralysis which at last pulled him down. He died at eighty-one in the house of his son in Lexington. The fury of the *Western World* was something only old men remembered then and even historians have little noted since. Yet it had provided the first baying in the great pursuit of Burr. Jefferson had tried to belittle the great exposure of the paper, but its crusade had failed no more than Jefferson's prosecution. That was that, in Marshall's memory and in history, too. That was something an old man could hold in a palsied hand. Maybe it was more important than the fact that Marshall, for all his devotion to clamor and controversy, grew so rich that Kentucky tradition still recalls that he counted his money by the peck.

He was not rich alone. The bluegrass pastures spread wider between white fences. From the little home stills, where Marshall's father-in-law had sought the central government's tax from reluctant men, greater distilleries had grown. Golden-red bourbon poured where once men had been content with the trickle of clear, fiery liquid from their surplus corn. The new liquor was aged and smooth. But the fire in the bourbon was still the product of a country in which a man could be both proud and quarrelsome and certain that his own politics should constitute the patriotism of his land. That was heady stuff. Perhaps Humphrey Marshall was intoxicated by it—such intoxication is often the first requirement of crusade.

6

King Mob's Men

Frank Blair named his Jackson organ the *Washington Globe*. Like the earth, he said, it was made out of nothing. With the help of Amos Kendall, he had created it in seven days. Its wrath was directed at those whom Jacksonians regarded as wrongdoers, but sometimes its storm fell on the unjust and the just as well.

Other papers served the still gap-toothed National City on the marshy shores of the Potomac. Some reflected "the era of good feelings" which had kept the capital comfortable even while the country was building up economic and social pressures. That supposedly happy period had been labeled by a newspaperman,

Benjamin Russell, editor of the *Columbian Centinel* of Boston.

A vehement Federalist, Russell had led the vituperation against Jeffersonian democracy in 1800. He had published the obituary of his party—assassinated, he wrote, by "the Secret Arts and Open Violence of Foreign and Domestic Demagogues." Now with the arrival of Jackson any amiable era in press and politics was terminated—and, as new men like Russell believed, by demagogues all too American. The hallooing pack —the rabble—the mob—of the new wild democracy had been led not only by sentimental and stalwart Old Hickory but also by writing men like Blair and Kendall.

If the era of good feelings existed at all for Blair and Kendall it was of brief duration. Indeed, two years after Russell made his mellowed declaration, the depression of 1819 swept like a fiscal fire across Kentucky. Reversing its inflationary policies, the Bank of the United States began a sharp contraction. Gold and silver were pulled out of the West and bankruptcies and debtors unable to meet their obligations were left behind.

An era of anger, not soon ended, was begun. Jackson was pushed forward as hero by poor men's resentments and demands in the West and on the restless seaboard. He wanted an editor in Washington upon whom he could depend. Kendall and others recommended Blair. Jackson had never seen Blair before he arrived ready for the job. The Kentucky writer's mild, skinny, ugly appearance startled some of the President's intimates. Jackson met his man and, like the perceptive gambler he was, took his chance.

Francis Preston Blair had always seemed a doubtful risk. Born a sickly child in Virginia in 1791, a tendency to consumption marked him as he grew up in Kentucky where his father, James Blair, became Attorney General. Nevertheless he graduated with honor at Transylvania University. Later he studied law, but a speech difficulty prevented his practice. In 1812, he went off to war with his uncle, George Madison, later Governor of Kentucky. But before he saw bloodshed Blair coughed up his own blood in a hemorrhage at Vincennes. He was an invalid at home while others fought.

He farmed, hoping to regain the health which his friends and neighbors thought was lost forever. But Francis Blair was as ardent as he was frail. He fell in love. The girl, Eliza Violet Gist, was reported to be a woman noted for "her extraordinary mental force and her sagacity." Certainly she knew her heart and her head.

"You'll be a widow in six months," her father warned her when she spoke of marriage to Blair.

"I would rather be Frank's widow," she said, "than any other man's wife."

Soon nobody was doubting Frank's vigor as he pitched into the so-called Relief War in Kentucky. That political struggle put debtor against creditor, poor against rich. It built an image of the Bank of the United States, operating with government authority but for the profit of private stockholders, as the oppressor contracting credit from Philadelphia and creating bankrupts in Kentucky. Blair campaigned for moratoriums for debtors and for state banks with the power to print their own money. When the top Kentucky court declared the laws unconstitutional, he assisted the effort to set up a new court. The ruinous inflation that resulted did not change Blair's view about monopolistic money powers. He became the new court's clerk and president of one of the proliferated banks. He also sank deeper into debt. More significantly, he began to write with startling power and skill for the *Argus of Western America* at Frankfort, edited by Amos Kendall.

Only two years older than Blair, Kendall—a sallow, asthmatic Yankee—came from Massachusetts to Kentucky in the flood of westward migration in 1814. A Dartmouth graduate, he served as tutor in the Lexington household of the already famous and fascinating Henry Clay. There Mrs. Clay taught the newcomer some graces and nursed him when he was sick. Afterward, when he took the Jackson side against Clay, he was charged with ingratitude. Soon he was working as a lawyer, small-town postmaster, and editor of two unsuccessful newspapers. He moved to Frankfort and bought an interest, entirely on credit, in the already established and influential *Argus*. As its combative editor who sometimes had to go armed, he found the fragile Blair his most effective contributor. There was nothing frail about the words of either man.

Kendall and Blair supported the more conservative Clay for President in 1824. From Washington the great Harry of the West wrote Frank amusing letters about his popularity when the election had to be decided in the House of Representatives. Clay, as the candidate with the fewest votes in the electoral college, was suddenly popular with everybody. Out of the running himself, he still had the votes which in the House could swing the election to another candidate in the contest. The Kentucky legislature told him to throw theirs to Jackson, who had led in the electoral voting. Instead Clay brought them to John Quincy Adams, and after the election Adams made Clay Secretary of State. In Kentucky and Tennessee the situation looked like bargain and sellout.

Angers were up and the chips were down. Jackson men, whose more radical policies Kendall and Blair shared, prepared for the election of 1828. They insisted that the *Argus* now take its place squarely behind Old Andy. Otherwise they threatened to set up a rival sheet. Not much persuasion was required. With Jackson's victory, Kendall was welcome in Washington—or hoped to be. He went as a stooped, near-sighted, badly dressed man with prematurely white hair. Blair was left in Kentucky. Not everybody was enthusiastic about Kendall and other editors in the capital. At the inauguration Kendall was one of a multitude creating the image of King Mob which, as the Old Order whined, overwhelmed the Presidential Palace, stood in muddy boots on satin chairs the better to see its hero, broke cut glass, and clamored from the trampled lawns for more and more refreshments.

" 'A great multitude,' too many to be fed without a miracle, are already in the city," Daniel Webster wrote on the eve of the inaugural ceremony. And he added, "Especially, I learn that the typographical corps is assembled in great force." If such were to be Jackson's counselors, the craggy-browed orator concluded, "it is a council which only 'makes that darker, which was dark enough already.' "

Webster went to work to save the country from the "typographical corps.'' The Senate rejected the nomination of Isaac Hill, editor of the *New-Hampshire Patriot,* to a $3000-a-year job in the Treasury Department. The vote against the confirmation of Major Mordecai M. Noah of the New York *Enquirer* was 25 to 23. The situation, which seemed dark already to Kendall, seemed darker still. He considered, he said later, that if he were not confirmed, he would start a newspaper in Washington as the readiest way to provide ''the means of comfort for a destitute family and vindicate the principles of equal rights, violated in the proscription of printers as a class.''

The Senate's vote on Kendall's nomination was a tie. Vice-President Calhoun cast the crucial vote in his favor. Kendall was rescued from penury as fourth auditor in the Treasury Department. He became a leader among Jackson's informal advisors, called the Kitchen Cabinet, and later Postmaster General.

Early in the administration other ardent Jacksonians felt the need for such a newspaper as Kendall considered. Presumably they already had such a paper. Duff Green—lawyer, promoter, journalist of St. Louis—had been sent ahead in 1826 to make the war for Jackson in Washington with the *United States Telegraph.* But to Jackson, Green seemed weak in his support of the confirmations of the editors the President named to office. He also seemed suspiciously unenthusiastic when Jackson, before his inauguration, sent him for publication the list of the Cabinet he proposed to name. The appointment of the President's friend and close associate John H. Eaton as Secretary of War, Green said, would cause ''a great deal of trouble.''

That was prophecy. It was warning that Eaton's new wife, pretty, tempestuous Peggy O'Neale Eaton, innkeeper's daughter and gossips' shining target, would not be accepted by the official society over which the widowed President presided. The rich and aristocratic Floride Bouneau Calhoun Calhoun, wife of the Vice-President, took the leadership against Peggy's acceptance. Calhoun stood solemnly behind his lady. Green, whose daughter married Calhoun's son, was behind Calhoun.

The ''Eaton Malaria,'' which spread like plague, did not of itself create the Jackson–Calhoun conflict or the need for a new newspaper. Jackson's preference for his dexterous Secretary of

State, Martin Van Buren, was not based merely upon that widowed New Yorker's politeness to Peggy. The President's opposition to Calhoun's nullification doctrine was built upon a
national faith, not a social feud, although the right of South
Carolina to reject the law of the land was not made more palata-
ble to Old Hickory by the rejection of a lady he gallantly defended.

"She's as chaste as a virgin!" cried Jackson, remembering
the slanders of his own beloved Rachel in the campaigns behind
him.

But Henry Clay's drawled joke went around: "Time cannot
wither, nor custom stale, her infinite virginity."

Duff Green's unprinted prejudices were growing fast. Soon he
reached the point at which he was sneering at Jackson. In a
letter to a South Carolina nullificationist he spoke of the administration of his old patron as "the empire of the whore of Washington."

A new editor was needed. Jackson advisors, particularly members of his Kitchen Cabinet, canvassed the possibilities. An assistant to the elegant Thomas Ritchie of the Richmond *Enquirer*
was considered. People were already noticing the powerful Jacksonian editorials written by William Leggett as aide to poet
William Cullen Bryant on the New York *Evening Post*. James
Gordon Bennett, who had covered the Jackson inauguration with
rapturous enthusiasm while disdainful diarists sneered, later
sought a job on the *Globe*. Blair was little known in the East.
Undoubtedly, as Blair said later, Jackson brought him to Washington. It is equally certain that Kendall pointed to him.

Blair's recommendations built great expectations. Advance
reports created the picture of a towering Kentuckian whose personality and pen would carry the suggestion of pistols and
Bowie knives, both always ready. Those close to Jackson, who
knew Blair only by relayed reputation, gloated in confidence:

"Just wait till Blair comes."

He would put the wavering Green in his place and into the
discard. "Just wait!"

Blair's arrival at the White House shocked them. The man
was only five feet ten and looked smaller; he weighed little more

than a hundred pounds. On his far-from-handsome face was a
swab of court plaster bandaging a gash he had received when his
coach overturned during the journey. The voice which had been
expected to boom was mild, almost apologetic. Worse still, the
cadaverous figure was wrapped in a dusty frock coat which gave
the appearance of being the only coat he owned.

President Jackson was not dismayed. His own cadaverousness
in a cloak had once saved him in a duel. He did not measure men
by the pound. And this "pint-sized man," as one observer described him, met Old Hickory's eyes directly with clear eyes of
his own. Jackson did not waste time in guardedly gauging this
editor he had never seen before. At once he talked of the divisions in his Cabinet. He detailed the maneuvers of the South
Carolina nullifiers, who were maintaining that the state could
disregard a national tariff law. Jackson told Blair of the activities of the President-makers, including Duff Green, who were
telling themselves and others that Old Andy would not seek re-
election. To sympathetic ears he described the sins of the Bank
of the United States, headed by Nicholas Biddle, who was
spreading largess where it would do the most good while he
lobbied for a new charter. The angry old General damned Henry
Clay. He spoke bitterly of the ostracism of Peggy Eaton. Then
he abruptly asked Blair to stay for dinner.

Dinner turned out to be no family affair. Dusty, rumpled
Blair found himself in the company of smartly dressed ambassa-
dors and other notables. In his flopping coattails, the Kentuckian
seemed to seek a corner in which to hide, but the President
presented Blair as his honored guest and seated him at his right
hand. He was to remain there.

The *Globe*, wrote Historian Parton, "like Jonah's gourd," appeared to spring into existence in a night—without capital, without a press, without type, without subscribers. Actually, Kendall
had been hard at work. He had made a printing contract. He had
mobilized all Jackson's dependables as subscription solicitors.
Officeholders were expected to subscribe. Word was quickly
spread that the tough old man in the White House desired a
shift of departmental printing to the new paper. To eliminate all
doubt about that desire, an order was issued requiring each

member of the Cabinet to report monthly to the President on sums spent for printing and to whom paid.

The money poured in quickly. When one eager gentleman with a private ax to grind sent Blair a contribution of $100, the so-recently penniless editor promptly sent it back. Visitors at the *Globe* office still were amazed to see that this new Blair was the little man sitting in a corner, writing on his knee and hurrying his copy to the printers page by page.

As the forerunner from Kentucky, Kendall had been a little glum about life in the national capital. He was shocked by tight-laced ladies in décolleté. He disapproved the conviviality of gentlemen around sideboards laden with wines and spirits. Blair was delighted with the parties and receptions, at which he was more welcome than Peggy Eaton. Often he counted his hang-overs as feelings which he sadly said "make a man fashionable and miserable." Fortunately he was soon joined by Eliza Violet and their children. She watched his health, though apparently not his drinks. She made him ride horseback every day. Also she insisted that he drink a tumbler of rye whiskey (treason for a bourbon-country Kentuckian) after every meal. Perhaps that enlivened his scribbling.

Blair began mildly enough. The *Globe*'s first issue appeared on December 7, 1830. The paper's purpose and position were clearly asserted, however, on January 21, 1831, when, dashing the hopes of Calhoun and Green, Clay and Biddle, and others, he announced that Old Andy would seek a second term. This was notice, too, that Duff Green's *Telegraph* was out as administration organ and the *Globe* of Blair—"Bla'r," as Jackson ever after called him in confidence and affection—was in.

There could be no doubt as the battle mounted. The *Globe* spoke for Jackson as the feuding Cabinet was dispersed over the Eaton feud, as Calhoun and Green and all nullifiers were rebuked with the famous toast that the Union must be preserved, and as Clay, seeing an issue for himself, prodded Biddle into seeking an early Congressional renewal of the charter of his bank. Blair shaped words which damned nullification. He made the bank The Monster and its president Czar Nicholas. Within the Democratic Party, as he put it, he was always ready "to shoot the deserters." He spilled ink and drew blood.

And he prospered. A new press was bought, a better office found. Then Kendall helped him again by bringing to him a man who had been one of Green's assets. John Rives, a really big Kentuckian, had worked on the *Telegraph*. He had been recommended to Kendall by Green as a devoted Jackson man. One of Kendall's "clerks" in the Treasury, he remained devoted when Green drew disloyally away. Rives had a genius for business as well as an editorial ability to slap small faces while Blair was breaking big heads. He went to work for the *Globe* on April 11, 1832.

Blair needed help. The campaign to run the "Tyrant" Jackson out of the White House and bring Clay in to recharter Biddle's bank began to build up steam. Calhoun had been dropped as Jackson's running mate and Van Buren substituted, despite Green's efforts. Jackson's veto of the recharter, on July 10, 1832, created a spontaneous coalition to defeat him. His declaration that the recharter was a plan to make the rich richer and the potent more powerful at the expense of the humbler members of society received mighty support from Blair. Biddle professed to Clay that he was delighted with the veto message.

"It has," he wrote his candidate, "all the fury of a chained panther biting the bars of his cage. It is really a manifesto of anarchy—such as Marat or Robespierre might have issued to the mob of Faubourg St. Antoine: and my hope is that it will contribute to relieve the country from the domination of these miserable people."

The panthers were loosed, nowhere so fiercely as in the press. Blair derided Green and other opposition papers which investigation disclosed had borrowed money from Biddle. He spoke his scorn when Green, after a visit to the bank, Blair believed, solemnly proclaimed in the *Telegraph*, that he felt "our duty requires us to demonstrate that General Jackson ought not to be re-elected." The *Globe* roared of "briberies," of "profligate apostacies," and of the "low buffoonery" of anti-Jackson spokesmen. He and other of the President's supporters were distressed and angry when suddenly in the midst of the campaign the New York *Courier and Enquirer,* the leading Jackson journal in the East, suddenly switched from anti-bank to pro-bank and from Jackson to Clay.

The shift was made with a sorrowful sneer at Jackson and a sharp slap at Blair. James Watson Webb, the New York paper's swashbuckling editor, began the statement of his apostasy with a sanctimonious statement of his continuing respect for Jackson. He regretted that the President "no longer possesses his former energy of character or independence of mind." But, he declared, the record of his administration and "the tone of the official paper at Washington" all too clearly prove that "a few mercenary and unprincipled officers of the government, possessing the confidence of the executive . . . are bringing disgrace and distress upon the country. . . ."

The editor of "the official paper" could answer sharply. He noted that the editors of the old *National Intelligencer* in Washington, recipients of Biddle's financial favors, had joyously welcomed Webb to the anti-Jackson side. It was natural, said Blair, that the *Intelligencer*'s editors should be charmed with Webb's "honesty and independence in complying with his bargain with the Bank—and the bold, frank and honorable way in which he unsays all that he has said of the President for the price paid him by Mr. Biddle."

For real satisfaction, however, Blair in Washington depended upon William Leggett in New York. Though a poet like his employer William Cullen Bryant, Leggett was scarcely a gentle literary man. Social and convivial, he was combative both as a high-tempered man and eloquent writer. He had been court-martialed from the Navy as a midshipman in 1825 for offenses which included insulting his commanding officer. Strong language was not strange on ships. Leggett's case was lifted mast-high by the fact that the insults he directed at his captain were quotations from abusive verses by Lord Byron and passages from Shakespeare "of highly inflamatory, rancorous and threatening import."

Contemptuous of poets as editors, Webb had scoffed at Bryant and Leggett as "the chanting cherubs of the *Post*." He himself

had left the Army as a result of several duels and brought his
belligerence into journalism. He had undertaken to cane Green
of the *Telegraph*. Later he beat up James Gordon Bennett, who
had worked for him before Bennett started his own New York
Herald. Webb regarded other editors as "over-rating entirely
the sufferings of the poor." Starched and haughty, he spoke of
his "social obligation to act and dress according to our station in
life," which he felt was pretty high. Leggett was neither impressed by his pretensions nor intimidated by his record. Outraged by the apostasy of the *Courier and Enquirer,* one day the
literate ex-midshipman met the pistol-ready ex-soldier on Wall
Street. This time Leggett did not turn to literature for invective.
He put his indignation in simple, direct language.

"Colonel Webb," he said, "you are a coward and a scoundrel, and I spit upon you."

He did just that. Blair rejoiced in any humiliation of Webb
as a deserter. Blair himself was strangely enough not involved in
such encounters. He spat and shot with his pen, and as the
campaign of 1832 proceeded, the *Globe* became the shooting center of the Jackson forces. While Biddle, in the interest of Clay's
Presidential ambitions and the bank's recharter, was subsidizing
the circulation of speeches by Senators and the newspapers
which printed them, the *Globe* aimed its less-long-winded appeal
directly and simply at the large number of new voters, pre-
viously disenfranchised by property qualifications. The Jacksonian revolution was marked by the fact that the number of
votes cast for President rose from 356,000 in 1824 to 2,400,000
in 1840.

Blair and Rives, with Kendall helping, made the newspaper
Jackson's arsenal. Its articles were reprinted in smaller newspapers and the *Globe* collected reprints from them. Sometimes it
placed prepared pieces in the smaller papers which it could
"collect" for republication. It was not a pretty campaign. Old
calumnies about Jackson were repeated. His democracy was described as a tyranny. And on his side, Isaac Hill, the vituperative lame editor of the *New-Hampshire Patriot,* who had been
rejected by the Senate when Kendall was confirmed but had
become a member of the Senate himself, poured out more venom.

He presented his "Twenty-One Reasons Why Henry Clay Should Not Be Elected." Reason No. 20 was: "Because ... he spends his days at the gaming table and his nights in a brothel."

Political fevers raged as high as those from the Asiatic cholera which first swept the American seaboard that summer. Charges were flung back and forth. Clay people claimed that the *Globe* was given away and distributed at government expense. John Rives, now Blair's partner, replied with an affidavit as to the legitimacy of its circulation. Its profits grew; its hopes were high. Jackson men were laying their money on the line in election bets.

Blair was undoubtedly in on the betting. In the campaign of 1844, when his passion was less enlisted in the result, he and Rives bet $22,000 on James K. Polk, a sum almost exactly equal to the debts Blair had to settle when he left Kentucky. Whatever they bet this time they won. Jackson received 219 electoral votes, Clay 49, and William Wirt 7. Old Hickory's popular vote was 124,392 more than the total received by his opponents.

Now just two years old, the *Globe* had run far ahead of its competitors. Blair's prestige soared. The paper was growing rich under the financial management of Rives—everything he touched, it was said, made profits except a farm which he bought in Bladensburg, Maryland, near the favorite dueling ground of the Washington hotspurs. Now Blair and Rives began another profitable enterprise in the *Congressional Globe*, partially subsidized by government, which provided a full stenographic report of debates. It soon supplanted the *Register of Debates* published by the proprietors of the older *National Intelligencer*. With Blair, Rives was rising in the world, but in the city which had sneered at the marriage of a Cabinet minister to an innkeeper's daughter, he married one of the bindery girls in the printing shop.

Blair could be expansive. He still had the almost wraithlike figure he had brought to Washington. But now he could afford many coats as well as a four-story stucco mansion on Pennsylvania Avenue diagonally across from the White House. He also acquired a splendid farm at Silver Spring, Maryland, from which he brought pails of milk to his friend, the ailing and aging

President. He began to be a gentleman farmer. For pleasure as
well as his health, he set out trees.

Nor was Kendall forgotten. In 1835, Jackson promoted him
from the informal place in his Kitchen Cabinet to Postmaster
General in his Constitutional one. That meant the problem of
confirmation by the Senate again and brought the crusaders for
Jacksonian democracy in Washington into cruel conflict with
Crusader Leggett, who had fought for Jackson.

Leggett had grown in stature as an eloquent fighter for social
reform. His strong convictions across the whole range of human
concerns, however, brought him into vigorous opposition on some
questions with men with whom he agreed on others. Early he per-
ceived the relationship—inescapable to him—between Negro
slavery and other forms of class exploitation. He had already antagonized conservatives among both Democrats and Whigs. Some
radicals were amazed by his strong laissez-faire views. He had
sharp things to say of Van Buren. His seemingly erratic course
was already isolating him when in righteous indignation he
struck out at Amos Kendall.

The problem of Kendall, backed by Blair, was a practical one.
Just as the question of his confirmation loomed, he was confronted with a letter from the postmaster at Charleston, South
Carolina, who reported that the mailing of abolitionist pamphlets and newspapers, depicting slavery in its worst light, had
created such public excitement that he feared for the safety of
the mails. The Charleston postmaster had been warned by the
Southern press and by public meetings not to deliver such publications, no matter who directed him to do it. This was nullification—indeed, nullification of a free press freely distributed.
While holding up the delivery of papers and pamphlets of anti-
slavery protest, the Charleston postmaster wrote to the newly
appointed Postmaster General for instructions.

Kendall ducked; this time Jackson hedged too. Fears of slave
insurrection were then troubling Tennessee as well as South
Carolina. A free press momentarily seemed less essential than a
safe people. Furthermore, the confirmation of Kendall required
Southern votes in the Senate. Jackson's new master of the mails
stated that he had no legal authority to exclude any publica-

tions, but he was not prepared to instruct the postmaster in the bristling South Carolina city to deliver incendiary sheets.

Straddling safely, Kendall declared, "I cannot sanction and will not condemn the steps you have taken."

William Leggett could and did speak squarely to the issue. He tore into Kendall, whom he had regarded highly before, for this submission to suppression of abolitionist literature in the mails. He had been the most honest, disinterested, and able independent ally of the Jackson administration. But now he spoke his scorn for Kendall, and Blair answered him with the *Globe*'s thunder. So severe was the attack of the official Jackson organ upon Leggett that the New York editor took it almost as excommunication. So did others. In New York Tammany Hall passed a resolution expelling him from Democratic brotherhood.

Leggett was already a physically sick man. Some shrillness had entered the expression of his passionate convictions. He had antagonized many people who believed he could not be appeased on any issue or idea. The advertising and circulation of the *Post* under his direction while Bryant was in Europe declined perilously as a result of his indiscriminate indignations. Leggett had moved on from the defense of the abolitionists' right of free speech to support of their opposition to slavery. The *Post*'s income had fallen to about a quarter of what it had been. Leggett was forced to sell the one-third share he had acquired in the paper to pay his debts. Under the circumstances, Bryant felt that he could not assure him freedom in the future to write as he pleased.

Leggett was sacrificed, but Kendall was confirmed. Kendall was on the *Globe*'s payroll at $800 a year even while he was Postmaster General. He did an excellent job in his official post, improving mail service and putting the postal service on a paying basis. But when he went out of office with Van Buren's defeat in 1840, he was a tired man and a poor man as well. He planned to try to restore his fortune by starting a paper in New York. But a lawsuit growing out of his post-office reforms kept him in Washington and, until the case was reversed by the Supreme Court, loaded him with an adverse verdict of $11,000.

With no other opportunity at hand he established a fort-
nightly called *Kendall's Expositor*. Blair was jealous of his
command of the party press in Washington. Even so, he and
Rives helped his old friend obtain financial backing and even
offered editorial cooperation. But plagued by poverty, trying to
scribble out his paper in an unfinished house, Kendall began to
resent Blair's opulence. He denounced the *Globe*'s editor to Van
Buren. He began to work secretly for a share of the government
printing Blair guarded as his own. In December 1842, mutual
feelings of ingratitude brought the two men into angry correspondence. Blair wrote coldly, even brutally to his old friend.
Kendall's letters in his helplessness bordered on hysteria.
Mutual friends temporarily adjusted the quarrel. Then, in 1845,
William Rufus Elliott, Rives' brother-in-law, killed Kendall's
son William. The Blair–Kendall break was complete.

In spite of everything, the story of the Jacksonian journalistic
crusaders did not end so sadly. Kindness was shown Leggett. His
health was gone. He was sheltered only by the charity of a
friend. Gideon Welles, a Jacksonian editor who was to become
Lincoln's Secretary of the Navy, urged Van Buren to drop Blair
and put Leggett in his place. To Welles, Blair and his *Globe*
seemed faltering while the frail, forgotten New Yorker was "the
ablest editor in the Union."

Van Buren, who had been among Leggett's targets, took no
such advice. Aware, however, of Leggett's poverty and illness,
the President offered him the post of diplomatic agent to Guate-
mala, thinking the sunny tropics might restore his health. But
Leggett died before he could accept, at thirty-eight. Other men
who should have known of his condition, which brought him to
the contemplation of suicide, were shocked. Some were ashamed.
All confronted the amazing immediate image of the editor as
martyr.

Leggett's death brought him an ironic rehabilitation in trib-
utes, resolutions, and orations. They came from those to whom,
while living, he had seemed erratic. Now they understood that
what had seemed erratic had been an irresistible consistency in
his faith for free men—all men.

Every hard blow he had struck seemed forgotten. Only his

eloquence for good was recalled. Old enemies scurried to honor him. Tammany Hall removed from its records the resolution proscribing him for his attack on Kendall's pusillanimity about abolitionist literature in the Southern mails. A bust of Leggett was solemnly placed in the room in Tammany in which he had been condemned. That justified the derision in rhyme by John Greenleaf Whittier, already the laureate of Abolition, of those who had rejected Leggett in life and now quickly praised him dead:

> Well is it now that o'er his grave ye raise
> The stony tribute of your tardy praise,
> For not alone that pile shall tell to Fame
> Of the brave heart beneath, but of the builder's shame.

Bryant, who as Leggett's boss had almost gone broke, wrote a lyric remembrance:

> For when the death-frost came to lie,
>   Upon that warm and mighty heart,
> And quench that bold and friendly eye,
>   His spirit did not all depart.
>
> The words of fire, that from his pen
>   Were flung upon the lucid page,
> Still move, still shake the hearts of men,
>   Amid a cold and coward age.
>
> His love of Truth, too warm, too strong,
>   For hope or fear to chain or chill,
> His hate of tyranny and wrong,
>   Burn in the breasts he kindled still.

There was resurgence for Kendall, too. In 1844, giving up all hopes in journalism, he became a professional lobbyist for government aid for the telegraph invented by Samuel F. B. Morse. Duff Green's *United States Telegraph* had been set up before there was any real telegraph to dispatch the news. Now, with Kendall's help, news sped on wires, and the old editor

made a fortune as Morse's agent. When he retired in 1860, a
mellowed patriarch, his old journalistic restlessness was re-
awakened. He took up his pen to write of Abraham Lincoln's
indecision and vacillation, as he saw it, in the face of rebellion.
If Jackson had been President, he wrote, "the rebellion would
not have occurred, or if it had, the rebels would ere this have
been driven into the Gulf of Mexico." In 1864, Kendall was still
attacking Lincoln's incompetence and advocating the election of
McClellan. He died in 1869.

Frank Blair outlived him. Jackson's *Globe* had become Van
Buren's *Globe,* too. The swinging, striking exuberance of the
Jackson years was past. Neither Blair nor Van Buren could
repeat the 1832 re-election triumph. When Van Buren came up
the second time William Henry Harrison, with his nonexistent
log cabin and hard cider, won, a phony reproduction of the
strong frontier man Jackson had been. Harrison was not Jackson. Tippecanoe was not New Orleans. They sufficed. The years
of the *Globe*'s glory were over.

In 1844, though Blair opposed the annexation of Texas and
hoped to see Van Buren the candidate again, he supported James
K. Polk after his nomination. He and Rives bet $22,000 on
Polk's election and were rich enough at the same time to tell
aged and financially beset Andrew Jackson that he could draw
on them for any sum from a thousand to a hundred thousand
dollars. The devotion of the editor and the old President for each
other never faltered. Jackson was angry during his last days on
earth about Polk's plan to replace Blair as editor of the Democratic administration organ.

Blair had made many enemies; he had cracked heads in the
party as well as outside it. His "shooting the deserters" had not
eliminated all whom he regarded as such. Evidently some had
exacted his head as the price of support for Polk. Certainly the
new Tennessean was determined on change even if that angered
the old Tennessean. He forced Blair to sell the *Globe* to Thomas
Ritchie, editor of the Richmond *Enquirer.* Ritchie was an able
editor and effective politician, though a little on the pompous

side. He was noted in Richmond as dance leader, perennial toast-master, and conspicuous gentleman in the old-fashioned low shoes and silk stockings he wore.

Blair was pleased when Ritchie changed the name *Globe* to *Union*. Perhaps he got some sardonic satisfaction when, after Ritchie's installation, Congress put an end to the political grant of government printing and required that it be let to the lowest bidder. There could never be a *Globe* again—or another Blair. The one and only Blair was rich and honored in his high house on Pennsylvania Avenue and among his trees and cattle at Silver Spring.

In retirement Blair considered himself still a radical. He rejoiced when, in 1848, mobs again moved against despotism in Europe. The *Globe* was gone, but he tried to write in the unlikely alphabet of trees his faith in the surge of the masses. The revolution in France inspired him to try to plant trees so that they would grow and form a tricolor. In what he expected to be his quiet years, Blair lived long enough to see them grow.

Quietness he was denied. Men came to him for counsel. With other old Jacksonians and his own growing brilliant boys, Frank, Jr., and Montgomery, he joined the departure of the Free Soilers from the Democratic Party. In 1856 he still regarded himself as a warrior in the Jacksonian tradition. His voice was still strong. He remembered nullifiers and he knew them now.

"Who are the leaders in the South who make such loud professions of Democracy?" he demanded. "Men who never were Democrats, but abhorred the name when it rallied the country around an administration that was true . . . to the cause of free government."

He followed his Jackson faith, he believed, into the Republican Party. There was an authentic image he could understand in this new tall, raw-boned man Lincoln. Montgomery Blair went into Lincoln's Cabinet, and old Blair became one of Lincoln's most trusted advisors. Certainly in his great dignity no one ever considered him as one of any Lincoln "Kitchen Cabinet," although the new President gave him the sort of task Jackson would have put in the hands only of men he trusted for themselves, not for their offices. And in that task Frank Blair failed.

At Lincoln's request he asked the ablest officer in the American Army to come across the Potomac to see him. Now a man of seventy, he waited in the tall house on Pennsylvania Avenue which still bears his name as the official guest residence for the world's great whom America welcomes to its capital. The old man talked to the handsome colonel. With Lincoln's authority Blair offered him the command of the Armies of the Union. From Blair's house and from Blair's hopes Robert E. Lee rode sadly back across the river to serve his native South in the war against the Union both he and Blair loved so well.

Blair saw that Union preserved as Jackson long before had said it must be. The frail Kentucky controversialist was durable, too. He died at eighty-five, in 1876. If he had come with only one dusty coat, he never turned it in all his years.

7

"Minister of Mischief"

Elijah Lovejoy was preaching no new, distasteful doctrines when he arrived in St. Louis in 1827. Indeed, in his later purposeful antislavery days, he said that no one could have been "more prejudiced, or more hostile to anti-slavery measures or men" than he was then. He was merely one of those young men who moved West long before Horace Greeley had even established the *Tribune* in which he urged the young to head westward. Son of a clergyman in Albion, Maine, Elijah had no inclination to enter the ministry when he graduated from Waterville

(now Colby) College. Instead he became a teacher in Missouri,
then editor of a conservative paper, the *St. Louis Times*.

In the river town serving the slave South and ministering to
the rough requirements of boat crews, fur traders, and travelers,
he did not look like an ascetic Puritan. If he already wore the
broad-brimmed white hat which marked him later, it was not yet
a target for stones. He weighed, he wrote his pious parents, 180
pounds. He was a muscular young man, five feet nine inches tall
and broadly built, with dark complexion and dark eyes. His
friends found him a man of humor. All playfulness was put
aside, however, when in February 1832 he wrote his "dear and
honored parents" that the Lord had laid His hand upon him.
Converted at a revival, he was going East to Princeton to study
for the Presbyterian ministry. He sent word to his brothers, one
of whom, Owen, was to join him later: "Tempt not God, as I
have done," but hurry to profession of faith.

Elijah was in a hurry. After a year at Princeton he was licensed to preach. Then he hastened back to St. Louis to assume
the editorship of the *St. Louis Observer*, established as their
weekly church paper by Presbyterians who put up $1200. His
first blows were struck for temperance, not too popular a cause
in the tolerant river town. But attacks on distilleries, dram-
shops, and drunkenness brought him only limited antagonism.
He invited more when he began to direct sharp blows at "popery" in a city which had a large Catholic population, including
many ardent Irishmen. Possibly he was right in his later statement that "the real origin of the cry, 'Down with the *Observer*,'
is to be looked for in its opposition to Popery." That would not
have been surprising since, among other things, he wrote that
"the nunnery has generally been neither more nor less than a
seraglio for the Friars of the monastery."

Certainly he had trod on other toes before he began to write
critically of slaveholders, but he was surprised when sharp
words were directed at him. He had never been found, he said, in
"gambling-houses, billiard-rooms or tippling shops." Furthermore, he denied that he had ever, by word or deed, directly or
indirectly, attempted or designed to incite slaves to insurrection.

"God forbid. I would as soon be guilty of arson and murder."

His Puritan pronouncements did not repel everybody. Celia Ann French, the daughter of a planter in nearby St. Charles, Missouri, found him a man to love. They were married two years after Elijah entered upon his ministerial editorship, March 4, 1835—four months before the first serious threats against him began to be made by "respectable citizens" of St. Louis.

Lovejoy was thirty-three, Celia Ann twenty-one. Elijah's combative solemnity fell away from him as he wrote his mother about her. The "lady," as he called her, sat beside him as he wrote. She was "tall, well-shaped, of a light, fair complexion, dark flaxen hair, large blue eyes, with features of a perfect Grecian contour.... In short she is very beautiful." She was more than that in Elijah's eyes: "I need not tell you she is pious, for I hope you know I would marry no one who was not."

Though their baby was on the way before the end of the summer, happiness beside such a lady did not suffice then or ever after for Elijah. He seemed to feel a sense of sin in any sort of peace. He considered his mounting editorials against slavery mild. They were still, as his friend Henry Tanner, who later wrote his story, said, too strong for St. Louis.

"The rabble," said the sympathetic Tanner, "called him—with a curse—an amalgamationist, and threatened to destroy his office: slave-holders were ready to tar and feather him as an Abolitionist, and no man ventured to defend him in that city."

Even his friends and fellow Presbyterians urged that Lovejoy "so far change the character of the *Observer,* as to pass over in silence everything connected with the subject of slavery." Others gave Lovejoy sterner counsel. New charges that he had shipped abolitionist literature for distribution were brought. In October 1835, a mass meeting, in resolutions clearly directed at the editor, denied that the Constitution guaranteed any right to discuss freely the question of slavery "either orally, or through the medium of the press." Far otherwise; such discussions, it said, were "in the greatest degree seditious, and calculated to incite insurrection and anarchy, and ultimately a disseverment of our prosperous Union."

Lovejoy answered both humbly and boldly the threat implied in the resolutions. He had never sent a copy of William Lloyd Garrison's *Emancipator* to anybody, he said, "yet I claim the *right* to send ten thousand of them if I choose, to as many of my fellow citizens." He regarded amalgamation "an abhorrent thing even in theory, and a thousand times more so in practice."

"And yet," he added with solemnity which covered a sharp barb, "unless my eyes deceive me, as I walk the streets of our city, there are some among us who venture to put it into practice. . . . I am sure that if a poor Abolitionist were to be stoned in St. Louis for holding this preposterous notion and the same rule were to be applied that our Saviour used . . . there are at least some amongst us who could not cast a pebble at the sinner's head."

Finally he spoke ringing words: "The path of duty lies plain before me, and I must walk therein, even though it lead to the whipping-post, the tar-barrel, or even the stake."

The respectable and the rabble hesitated. The effects of his statement were "tremendous," he wrote his brother. The Irishman who had been the chief instigator of Lovejoy's troubles at this time beat "his female negro slave" almost to death. Her cries and screams brought a multitude (no word of mob this time) around the house. The woman was rescued. Though he knew, he said, that "the wicked, sooner or later, fall into the pit they have digged for others," this was "sudden retribution."

Nevertheless, the original Presbyterian proprietors of the *Observer* thought he had better give up the editorship of the paper. They dodged the direct issue, however, by giving up the paper's press and other equipment to a gentleman who held a note on the property. He insisted that Lovejoy continue as editor, but twenty-five miles up the Mississippi in the Illinois town of Alton, nearly as populous as Chicago, to which steamboats regularly plied from the Missouri shore. Its people, so Lovejoy understood, were "not only prodigiously enterprising expecting to become a metropolis, but were foremost in fathering all moral and religious reforms."

The St. Louis Presbyterian elders took new heart. Though

Alton had expressed its welcome, they insisted he stay in St. Louis. In the comparative calm which had been restored Lovejoy might have remained there if he had not been the irreconcilable reformer and reporter as well. His hand trembled, he said, when he wrote the story of an occurrence in May 1836, but there was no sign of trembling in the terrible "tale of depravity" he told.

Two sailors got into a fight at the steamboat landing. Officers undertook to arrest the men for a simple affray. Then "a mulatto fellow, by the name of Francis J. McIntosh, who had just arrived in the city, as cook, on board the steamboat 'Flora' from Pittsburgh" attacked the officers and permitted the men to escape. On his way to jail the Negro asked the officers how much time he would get. They told him not less than five years. Whereupon he drew a long knife, killed one of the officers, and desperately wounded the other.

The mulatto failed to cut his way to freedom. Citizens helped the surviving officer put the man even Lovejoy called "a bloodthirsty wretch" in jail. He did not stay there long. The mob came. It tied him to a locust tree not far from the jail. Sticks and shavings were piled about him as high as his knees. The man's pleas that he be shot were denied. He burned for twenty minutes before he died. Then, as Lovejoy reported, a rabble of boys came, playing a game, throwing stones to see who could first crack the grisly corpse's skull.

Lovejoy now put his passion and his prejudices together. When Judge Luke Lawless declared the act of the mob beyond the jurisdiction of human law, Elijah was outraged. The editor was not indignant simply at this verdict upholding the rule of the mob. He saw in the lynchers' escape from punishment the popery which seemed to him almost as evil as slavery. Judge Lawless, he declared, was a foreigner. He was an Irishman who had fought for France against the England to whom his allegiance was due. Those were facts of which Lawless, a law partner of Thomas Hart Benton and a man who hated England and loved his countrymen and his church, was proud. Lovejoy made them seem crimes.

"Judge Lawless is a Papist," he proclaimed, "and . . . we see the cloven foot of Jesuitism peeping out from almost every paragraph of his charge."

Violently Lovejoy rejected the intimation of Judge Lawless that his judicial action had protected the editor and *Observer* from attacks by the same mob:

"This assertion of the Judge is a gross libel upon the city, as we verily believe. We have never heard of any threats to pull down our office, which did not originate with his countrymen. Mark that!"

The Irish were rough, in St. Louis and elsewhere. The saying grew along the Mississippi that the way to handle an incorrigible slave was to sell him to an Irishman. Irish pride and anger were also stirred by attacks upon them as poor immigrants, coming from those who were so concerned for the poor slaves. Lyman Beecher, father of the brilliant, antislavery Beecher tribe, preached on the perils of the increasing Irish migration to the Mississippi Valley in Boston on Sunday, August 10, 1834. The next day Protestant louts burned down an Ursuline convent across the river in Charlestown. Prejudice was not any one group's monopoly. Lovejoy's bitter attacks on Catholics did not endear him to the poor Irish in St. Louis, or the powerful Irish either.

Patience with Lovejoy was growing thin among other people, too. Slaveowning planters were more and more determined to end the dangerous talk of both Abolitionists and more moderate critics of the slave system. Many Presbyterians were more than weary of Lovejoy as the editor of their paper. Also, though Celia Ann always urged him to do his duty, she was ill that crowded summer of 1836.

It was a sickly summer even in the river town which expected summer complaints. In August, Elijah wrote his mother piously wondering why, when God had let loose angry and wicked men upon him, "He should also so heavily lay his hand upon me, I cannot see, but He can." He could see clearly, though, that Celia Ann was "a perfect heroine."

Though of delicate health [he wrote], she endures affliction more calmly than I had supposed possible for a woman to do. Never has she, by a single word, attempted to turn me from the scene of warfare and danger; never has she whispered a feeling of discontent at the hardships to which she has been subjected in consequence of her marriage to me, and those have been neither few nor small, and some of them peculiarly calculated to wound the sensibility of a woman. She has seen me shunned, hated, and reviled by those who were once my dearest friends; she has heard the execrations wide and deep upon my head, and she has only clung to me the more closely and more devotedly.

Even Lovejoy realized that his days and Celia Ann's in St. Louis were coming to an inevitable end. In the June 21, 1836 issue of his *Observer,* in which he condemned Judge Lawless, he announced his intention to move the paper to Alton. The mob took that as signal. Before the press, the type, and the editor's furniture could be shipped, angry men entered the shop to pay Lovejoy good-by by smashing furniture and dumping all other equipment, including part of the press, into the Mississippi River. And the last night they spent in St. Louis, Lovejoy wrote, he lay down "weary and sick, with the expectation that I might be aroused by the stealthy step of the assassin."

Celia Ann seemed almost too much of a heroine when he told her of the damage done to the shop.

"No matter what they have destroyed," she said, "since they have not hurt you."

Elijah seemed, in today's terms at least, almost too hidebound a Presbyterian. The remains of his St. Louis printing press arrived at Alton and were unloaded on the river bank before daylight on a Sunday morning in July. His views about Sabbath observance prevented him from doing anything about it then. A "vulgar crowd," which had undoubtedly heard the news of the earlier attack in St. Louis, inspected it all day long. Night came. On Monday morning, Lovejoy found what had been left of his press by the mob in St. Louis had been dumped into the river at Alton.

In Alton, growing with migration from the Northeast, there were sympathetic citizens, even though just a little farther south many of the people had come from the slave states with strong sentiments for slavery. A public meeting was called. The dumping of the remnant of Lovejoy's press was condemned. Money was raised with which to buy another.

The new press arrived on September 8, 1836, and the first number of the *Alton Observer* appeared. The new journal was not the only paper in that prosperous and pushing Illinois town. The leading paper, the Alton *Evening Telegraph*, devoted itself to the promotion of the community and carefully avoided such a dangerous subject as slavery. In the month in which Elijah's second press arrived, it gave much space to an elaborate description of the prehistoric Indian paintings of the Piasa birds on the nearby river cliffs. They were horrendous creatures, goat-headed and goat-horned, tiger-bearded, with red eyes blazing from human faces. The bravest Indians had feared to look at them. Abolition seemed a monster better not seen on newspaper pages.

But there was no need for the pious editor to feel alone and beset in Alton. Much of its population was made up of emigrants from New England and the Eastern states, some of whom shared Lovejoy's strong feelings about black servitude. He was strengthened, too, by the arrival from Maine of his younger brother, Owen. At twenty-five Owen seemed uncertain in his directions as Elijah had once been. He had attended Bowdoin College, but did not graduate. Then he studied law and tried teaching school. But now he had come to prepare for the ministry under his brother and to share his zeal in the antislavery cause.

When he crossed the river from slave Missouri to free Illinois, Elijah was opposed to abolitionism as the doctrine of immediate emancipation. Accused of being an Abolitionist, he denied the charge and opposed the doctrine. His comparatively moderate views about the evils of slavery were sufficiently popular to bring him readers. Within a year after his move, the circulation of the *Observer* doubled, although that did not mean many subscribers. Even the more famous *Liberator*, established in Boston by William Lloyd Garrison in 1831, never attained a circulation of much more than 3000 copies. Its voice was magnified by those who damned it. Quoted by papers and politicians who regarded its utterance criminal, the *Liberator* received an attention its friends alone could not have gained for it.

Garrison had begun his editorship with an arrogant harangue which still resounds like poetry:

"I *will be* as harsh as truth, and as uncompromising as justice. On this subject I do not wish to think, or speak, or write, with moderation.... I am in earnest—I will not equivocate—I will not excuse—I will not retract a single inch—AND I WILL BE HEARD."

Elijah issued no such ultimatum. To the last, his stubborn effort was to be piously persuasive. His words were less militant than Garrison's, although he shared none of the personal pacifism the *Liberator*'s editor oddly added to literary belligerence. He was as ready to hold a gun in his hands as a hymnbook. In Illinois, close to the frontier between slavery and freedom, his views gradually changed and sharpened. So far as it was possible for him, he had a brief happy time in the first months in Alton. Celia Ann survived the fevers. The baby was well. The flaxen-haired lady could play the piano with Elijah, Owen, and friends beside it. But the peacefulness became a "reproach" to Elijah. He was troubled by his "sloth and inactivity." So, on June 29, 1837, in the *Observer* he issued a call to all friends of the slave in Illinois to collect signatures to petitions for the abolition of slavery in the District of Columbia.

Quick resentment stirred among the Southerners who had settled in and below Alton. Their anger was increased when a week later, on July 6, 1837, just after a great temperance and Sunday-School celebration in Alton, Lovejoy urged that an Illinois Anti-Slavery Society be formed without further delay. He wrote, in the tones of a dare, that he had been called a fanatic and an incendiary by his enemies:

"We feel that we must become more and more vile in their eyes."

He set down those words on the Fourth of July. Outside his window as he wrote, he said, crowds were hurrying to listen to the declaration that "all men are born free and equal" and to hear tyranny denounced.

"Alas! what bitter mockery is this!" His press stamped out his indignation with oratory about freedom in a land of three million slaves: "Not all our shouts of self-congratulation can drown their groans—even that very flag of freedom that waves over our heads is formed from materials cultivated by slaves, on a soil moistened by their blood, drawn from them by the whip of a republican task-master!''

The answer to that editorial came promptly in the form of an anonymous handbill posted about the city calling upon those who disapproved the course of the *Observer* to meet at the public market on July 11, 1837. Some leading citizens took part in the meeting. It was charged that Lovejoy had pledged himself not to discuss the subject of slavery and had broken his pledge—and there was some truth in the charge. When citizens had purchased him a new press after the relic he brought from St. Louis was sunk, he had expressed his intention to edit the paper in the interest of the church alone. If that was a promise, it was an impossible one for Lovejoy. The meeting at the market called on him now to ''discontinue *his incendiary publications*.''

In reply the citizens received a long argument against slavery. The piety with which Lovejoy undertook to persuade his opponents only infuriated them further, and their anger was fanned from across the river in St. Louis. Undoubtedly Lovejoy felt that the papists were still after him when the St. Louis *Missouri Republican* joined in the denunciation of him. Despite its name, which it took long before the founding of the Republican Party, the *Republican* was strong in its Democratic and Southern faith. The paper, widely circulated in Alton, had been founded by Joseph Charless, an Irish refugee. Now it offered advice to the people of Alton ''whose hospitalities have been slighted, and whose friendships have been abused by one who was bound by every moral and political obligation to have acted otherwise.''

''The editor of the *Observer*,'' said the *Republican*, ''has merited the full measure of the community's indignation; and if he will not learn from experience, they are very likely to teach him by practice, something of the light in which the honorable and respectable portion of the community view his conduct.''

And it added, ''Something must be done in this matter, and that speedily!''

The instruction of the ''minister of mischief,'' as the *Republican* called him, began speedily. A disguised mob gathered on the night of August 21, 1837. Its reported first plan was to tar and feather Lovejoy and then set him adrift in a canoe down the Mississippi. It met him, Lovejoy afterward related, as he came from his house more than a half-mile from town to get some medicine from the drugstore for the ever-ailing Celia Ann. He was not recognized at first and he walked nearly through the throng. (Perhaps on this occasion he was not at first recognized because he had changed his wide-brimmed white hat for an un-clerical cap.) Then a man, armed with a club, pushed up close and confronted him.

"It's the damned Abolitionist," he shouted, "give him hell."

The road resounded with cries, "Damn him! Rail him! Tar and feather him! Tar and feather him!"

We have only Lovejoy's account of the encounter. As he told it, moral force there repelled the mob.

"Gentlemen," he said he calmly told his assailants, "I have but a single request to make of you. My wife is dangerously ill, and it is necessary she should have this prescription immediately, and which I was on the way to town to procure. Will one of you take it and see that it is delivered at the house, but without intimating what is about to befall me. I am in the hands of God, and am ready to go with you."

There was silence. Then, Lovejoy reported, a doctor in the crowd spoke.

"Boys, I can't lay my hand upon as brave a man as this is."

Slowly, silently, ashamedly, the crowd dispersed. Lovejoy went on to the drugstore. But later in the same night the mob entered the *Observer* office. Lovejoy's No. 2 press was destroyed.

Once again Elijah offered to resign as editor if his friends and supporters regarded that the proper course. He recognized that "iniquity is coming in like a flood." He only asked that his debts be paid and that he be given sufficient funds to enable him to move himself and family to some other field of labor. The friends declined to accept his resignation. Money was raised for another press.

So quickly was the order executed that it arrived at Alton

about sunset on September 21, 1837. Lovejoy was absent at a meeting of the presbytery at the time. But many of his friends gathered around it as it was conveyed to the warehouse of Gerry & Weller. No violence was offered, though there were cries of "There goes the Abolition press. Stop it!" However, the mayor of the town, John M. Krum, promised to protect it. The constable he left on guard departed early in the night. Then "ten or twelve 'respectable' ruffians" appeared with handkerchiefs over their faces. They broke into the warehouse, rolled the press to the river bank and broke it into pieces. The mayor arrived only in time to observe that he had never witnessed a more quiet and gentlemanly mob. Press No. 3 was dumped into the Mississippi.

The "respectables" were still not satisfied. Celia Ann had gone to visit her mother in St. Charles, just across the river in Missouri. Elijah joined her there. A mob was ready for him. He had preached in the Missouri town that day and in the evening was conversing with a preacher friend at his mother-in-law's house. An ominous knock sounded at the door. There was a call for Lovejoy.

"I am here," said Elijah.

Two men rushed across the portico. One was a former Virginian named Littler. The other man he only knew was a Mississippian.

"We want you downstairs, damn you," they said.

But frail Celia Ann had forced her way through the mob on the porch. When she tried to intervene she was roughly pushed back. One of the two Southerners, according to Lovejoy's report, drew a dirk on her.

"Her only reply," Elijah related, "was to strike him in the face with her hand, and then, rushing past him, she flew to where I was, and, throwing her arms around me, boldly faced the mobites, with a fortitude and self-devotion which none but a woman and a wife ever displayed. While they were attempting with oaths and curses to drag me from the room, she was smiting them in the face with her hands, or clinging to me to aid in resisting their efforts, and telling them that they must first take her before they should have her husband. Her energetic measures, seconded by those of her mother and sister, induced the assailants to let me go and leave the room."

Then Celia Ann fainted. But the raid was not over. Men followed when Lovejoy carried her into another room where their sick child was. While she moaned and shrieked and the baby clung to Elijah in terrified silence, the "mob returned to the charge." Fortunately, the visiting minister, though himself a slaveholder, went to battle for the Alton Abolitionist. The alarm had spread. Others came to help.

Still from the yard "the drunken wretches" shouted their oaths and promises to get Lovejoy. Pistols were fired. They were quieted only after Lovejoy slipped out of the house and found his way through the dark for a mile to the house of a friend.

Even in such darkness Lovejoy was not without friends. Indeed, the gathering mobs insured the mobilization of supporters. This central West seemed crowded with Abolitionists. The Reverend Lyman Beecher had brought his famous family to Cincinnati, where he was president of Lane Theological Seminary. His Harriet was then only twenty-one just seeing, across the Kentucky line and in Ohio, the slavery and flight from it which were to provide the materials for *Uncle Tom's Cabin*. There had been bitter conflicts in Cincinnati. Such antislavery leaders as James G. Birney and Gamaliel Bailey were threatened by mobs roaring in anger about the office of their *Cincinnati Philanthropist*. Even Lane Theological Seminary had been so torn about the right to discuss slavery that many students had gone instead to Oberlin College in the northern part of the state. And Lyman Beecher's son, Edward, had given up a prominent church on Boston Common to assume the presidency of one-building Illinois College at Jacksonville, sixty miles from Alton. Behind them all were well-to-do Eastern men like Arthur Tappan, the New York silk merchant, who had helped launch the *Emancipator* of William Lloyd Garrison. There was little problem about providing the funds for Lovejoy's Press No. 4, nor was there any lack of men ready to defend it.

October 1837 was a busy month for Lovejoy. The attack in St. Charles occurred early in the month. He traveled to Springfield, to which young Abraham Lincoln had moved that year as a poor young lawyer carrying all his possessions in two saddlebags. At the annual meeting of the synod Elijah had opportunity "to counsel with his brethren." He came home greatly refreshed and encouraged. And at home, on October 26 , he took a leading part in the convention called to establish a State Anti-Slavery Society, which turned out to be a rowdy occasion. Many of those most violent against any opposition to slavery presented themselves as delegates. They created disorder and confusion.

Even some ministers, including the Reverends John Hogan and Charles Howard, opposed Lovejoy. The Reverend Joel Parker from New Orleans declared that it is "an un-Christian thing to speak on any subject calculated greatly to disturb and agitate the people." In a private house, however, Lovejoy and his friends established the society and discussed the future of his paper. Then on October 30, the Reverend Edward Beecher addressed the friends of free speech at the Presbyterian Church. He vehemently urged that Lovejoy be defended to the last. But while he was speaking a stone was thrown through one of the church windows. Outside another crowd had gathered, this time after Beecher as well as Lovejoy. But now the militant anti-slavery men were ready.

"To arms!" shouted one of them from the gallery. In a few moments the church door was flanked by armed men ready to meet the mob. Behind them Beecher went on with his sermon. After Beecher's speech, the crowd still threatened but, as one who was present later reported, "a collision between the head of a mobite and the breech of a gun" in the hands of one of the defenders was sufficient to disperse the mob. Lovejoy's friends still questioned whether the new press, which was on its way, should be set up in Alton or with its editor be moved to Quincy further upriver. That question was still undecided when the press arrived.

On November 2, a meeting of citizens confronted Lovejoy with their opposition to him and his paper. Even the mayor of the town, who played a Pilate role in the whole story, offered a resolution of regret that "persons and editors abroad should interest themselves in discussions of matters of which Alton had been made the theatre." Lovejoy had few friends present, but he spoke boldly. The question, he insisted, was simply whether or not he should be protected in his rights under God and the Constitution. If he had been guilty of any crime he invited indictment and conviction. Otherwise, he demanded,

"Why am I hunted up and down continually like a partridge upon the mountains? Why am I threatened with the *tar-barrel?* Why am I waylaid every day, and from night to night, and my life in jeopardy every hour?"

He grew emotional in his stubborn logic.

"I plant myself, sir," he told the chairman, "down on my unquestionable rights, and the question to be decided is, whether I shall be protected in the exercise and enjoyment of those rights,—*that is the question,* sir;—whether my property shall be protected; whether I shall be suffered to go home to my family at night without being assailed, and threatened with tar and feathers, and assassination; whether my afflicted wife, whose life has been in jeopardy, from continued alarm and excitement, shall, night after night, be driven from a sick-bed into the garret, to save her life from the brick-bats and violence of the mobs; *that, sir, is the question.*"

Then he suddenly burst into tears. Even some of his enemies were moved, but in its resolutions the meeting held it *"indispensable* that Mr. Lovejoy should not be allowed to conduct a paper, and that he ought to retire from the charge of the *Alton Observer.*" Piously and coldly, however, the meeting expressed its disapproval of all violence. Lovejoy was not shaken: "If the civil authorities refuse to protect me, I must look to God; and if I die, I have determined to make my grave in Alton."

Four days later, in the dead of night, the press arrived from Cincinnati on the steamer *Missouri Fulton.* As a precaution its captain had agreed to land at midnight even if he had to lay his boat over for a while to do so. This time the press was not unguarded. About sixty young men, well armed and drilled, took it in charge. The mayor of the town was "rather unwillingly present." Someone on the shore blew a horn, which seemed to the antislavery guards to be a signal for the mob. None appeared. The crated press was safely stored on the third floor of a warehouse of Godfrey & Gilman. Men were stationed on different floors in sufficient strength to resist any attack, among them the Reverend Edward Beecher. The night passed without incident.

The following evening, the guardians gathered and congratulated each other on the peacefulness. About nine o'clock many decided to go home. At the request of the owner of the warehouse about 19 men volunteered to remain on guard. An hour passed. Then it was evident that a mob was slowly gathering outside in the dark. One of Lovejoy's friends later spoke of "a party of armed men [which] had come from St. Louis." While some such may have come, said another witness friendly to the editor, "it was never proved that any help came to the ruffians of Alton from that source."

"The fast-growing towns of the West had, all of them," this witness wrote, "an abundant influx of the class of roughs; especially were the river towns so afflicted. Alton had vile men enough of her own for such deeds, especially when merchants of Second Street, doctors, and Lawyers, and even such ministers of the gospel (heaven save the mark!) as John Hogan and Charles Howard either egged on the mob, or were, at best, coldly indifferent."

In the moonlight the crowd about the warehouse thickened. Quietness turned to clamor. The windows of the building were demolished by volleys of the stones abundantly available on newly macadamized streets. In the distance the bell of the Presbyterian Church tolled loudly, rung by the wife of the minister, seeking to summon help. None came. Clearly there were more men about the building than the few defenders could long hope to resist. Two men from the crowd were admitted after they asked for a parley. They let the mob know how few were the friends of Lovejoy in the building. Then an ultimatum was given the besieged to give up the press or the building would be burned.

Some of the volunteers inside proposed that they shoot at the mob and make short work of it. But the milder man who had been chosen as their leader commanded them to withhold their fire. The crowd rushed the doors and tried to force an entrance. Then the captain ordered one man to shoot. He killed a member of the mob. It came back, "reinforced by ruffians who had been drinking to inspire them with courage."

"Fire the building!" they shouted. "Shoot every damned Abolitionist as he tries to escape."

The mayor appeared. He wavered as usual. And the mob laughed when he finally urged the crowd to disperse. A ladder was placed against a side of the building upon which there were no windows. A man ascended toward the structure's wooden roof with a torch in his hands. Then the captain of the defenders called for volunteers to make a sortie. Three men promptly stepped forward with guns in their hands—Amos B. Roff, Royal Weller and, of course, Elijah Lovejoy.

As they emerged from the building into brilliantly moonlit night, shots were fired at them from the shelter of a pile of lumber. Roff and Weller were wounded. Five balls hit Lovejoy. He had strength enough to run back into the building and climb a stair.

He came crying, "I am shot! I am shot! I am dead!"

Without speaking again, he fell into the arms of one of his friends. They lay the body on the floor. Elijah's younger brother, Owen, knelt beside it. There he vowed "never to forsake the cause that had been sprinkled with his brother's blood."

But the night's cause was lost. The swarm outside was thickening. The torch was at the roof. Agreement was reached to give up the press if the building, containing other valuable property, was spared and the defenders allowed to depart in safety. But as the remaining guards left the building, the rioters broke their agreement. Shots followed the defeated defenders but, because of the slope of the ground, passed harmlessly over their heads.

The mob poured into the building. It included two doctors and one drayman, each of whom claimed to have fired the fatal shots at Lovejoy. One of the physicians offered to remove the ball from Royal Weller's leg. He angrily declined. It required no doctor to verify the lifelessness of the corpse of Lovejoy. Mobsters made gross remarks about it. The fire was put out. Lovejoy's fourth press was hauled out and destroyed.

Next morning the dead editor's friends came and took his corpse to the home in which he and Celia Ann had been harassed.

She was not there. Prostrated by grief and so sickened by shock
that her life was despaired of, she had been taken to the house of
a friend. Owen Lovejoy received his brother's body. And in a
tense atmosphere, preparations were made for the funeral on the
following day, which broke rainy and depressing. A few friends
walked through mud and water to the grave. The services were
simple for fear the mob might disturb the last rites of the man it
had killed. There had been no inquest. No flowers were placed
upon the coffin.

"If I had a fife," grimly joked one of the doctors who had
been in the crowd which killed him, "I'd play him a Dead
March."

Greater music quickly rose. Word of Lovejoy's death sped to
Cincinnati, from which the last press had come. There Harriet
Beecher feared for the safety of her brother Edward. He had
just missed being present on the last fatal night. Slavery had
seemed evil to her before. Now her brother had been in close
danger of murder in slavery's defense and in rabble defiance of
a free press. The news of Lovejoy's death came to John Brown,
an Ohio wool merchant, to signal a radical change in his attitude
toward slavery. He began to brood over a plan he revealed in
secrecy to his wife and three elder sons two years later: to in-
vade "dark Africa" and free the slaves at gunpoint.

Not all were indignant. No formal punishment followed the
crime, though aspiring Alton was rebuked by emigrants who
passed it by and its property values declined. In Boston a first
request for the use of Faneuil Hall for a meeting in protest
against the "ferocious assault on the liberty of the press at
Alton" was denied by the board of aldermen on the grounds
that such a meeting would not express the public opinion of the
city and could incite a mob there, too. After all, only two years
before in Boston a mob had dragged William Lloyd Garrison as
a "damned Abolitionist" through the streets with a rope fas-
tened around his waist. Now, in 1837, when the aldermen finally
permitted the meeting, James T. Austin, the conservative Attorney General of Massachusetts, spoke not praise but scorn for the
dead Illinois editor. He even compared the men who killed Love-

joy to the patriots who had dumped the tea into Boston harbor, and many in the old hall shared Austin's view.

Lovejoy, he said, "died as a fool dieth."

In the audience aristocratic young Wendell Phillips listened. He was quickly on his feet. Then with passion and eloquence in his rich, persuasive voice, he caught the imagination of the crowd with the first of his great antislavery speeches. His friend Garrison, so recently victim of the mob himself, draped the *Liberator* in mourning at the news of Lovejoy's death. He filled that journal with notices of meetings, resolutions, speeches, and press comment about the tragedy. Yet he welcomed the martyrdom: "Lovejoy died the representative of philanthropy and justice, liberty and Christianity: well, therefore, may his fall agitate Heaven and earth."

The most effective agitator was the one who marched in determination from his brother's grave. Owen Lovejoy was only twenty-six the night his brother died. Soon after Elijah's death he became Congregationalist minister in strongly abolitionist Princeton, Illinois. He never lost an opportunity to speak for the cause for which his brother had died. He would not be silenced by an Illinois law prohibiting abolition meetings. One existed whenever and wherever he spoke. He faced the threat of violence, but his own boldness and his brother's memory saved him from injury. When he found the great instrument he needed, he showed himself a man who could bend and not merely stand and be broken in the cause.

He early recognized Abraham Lincoln as the only man in Illinois who could wield into an effective force "the rag-tag and bobtail" gang of widely diverse elements which gathered to make up the Republican Party. He urged Lincoln to lead the movement. Lincoln declined. The time was not ripe, the tall lawyer said. But Lovejoy forced the radicals to give up their abolition program and accept Lincoln's more conservative leadership. As a member of Congress, Lovejoy was regarded as Lincoln's henchman. He stood for Lincoln against Douglas, but carefully effaced himself when his too-radical support seemed likely to do

more harm than good. He readily accepted Lincoln's repudiation of abolitionism. He brought those who shared his bitter
enmity to slavery to Lincoln's support for the Presidency.
When, in 1862, William Lloyd Garrison attacked the President
as too slow and indecisive, Owen Lovejoy replied fiercely. He
lived to hear the Emancipation Proclamation. His epitaph could
have been Lincoln's statement about him: "To the day of his
death, it would scarcely wrong any other to say he was my most
generous friend." It is certain that to Owen, Lincoln was the
instrument of the fulfillment of the vow he made beside Elijah's
riddled body.

There are conflicting stories about what happened to Celia
Ann. Henry Tanner, one of the defenders present on the night of
Lovejoy's martyrdom, made her fate a footnote in the account
he wrote about it. He said she never entirely recovered from the
trials of 1837.

"Before her death," he said, "she became quite poor, passed
several days at my house, a broken-down, prematurely-old person, possessed of scarce a trace of her early beauty. The prophecy
regarding her, made in 1837, that 'her strong heart would break
down her physical frame,' was, indeed, most sadly verified."

Another version was that of Dr. Samuel Willard, also an eye-
witness of Lovejoy's death. At Tanner's request, he added notes
to Tanner's account. Dr. Willard stated that Celia Ann married
Royal Weller, who made the sortie into the mob with Lovejoy
and was wounded when Lovejoy was killed. That may have made
her story sadder still. Weller, the doctor said, was for a time
insane in his later years.

One certain item in Elijah's and Celia Ann's story is that
long afterward on the third floor of the courthouse at Edwards-
ville, Illinois, seat of the county in which Lovejoy died, the
Madison County Historical Society carefully preserved among
Indian and pioneer relics the square piano which belonged to the
Lovejoys. Its historical guardians presumed it was made by the
firm of Astor and Company, established in this country in 1772
by the brother of John Jacob Astor. Certainly by the time the

young Lovejoys played on it John Jacob Astor, who had come to America with only seven flutes among his merchandise, was becoming the richest man in America with interests spreading from Manhattan real estate to a fur empire which ran from St. Louis to the Pacific. The martyrdom of Lovejoy seemed to many a very little thing in the rich, expanding, exuberant land.

8

James King of William

"Bets are now offered, we have been told," wrote James King of William on November 22, 1855, less than two months after he had launched his San Francisco *Bulletin*, "that the editor of the *Bulletin* will not be in existence twenty days longer...."

The odds were not stated. In the wide-open, jerry-built metropolis by the Golden Gate a man could get covered on almost any wager then. Miners in red-flannel shirts and dandies wearing gleaming tall hats were always ready to hazard gold dust and gold coins. And in a hazard like that involving James King of William, some were ready also to fix the result with pistol or knife in duel or brawl. Thirty-four-year-old, black-bearded, stooping James King of William scoffed.

"Pah!" he wrote in his bristling paper. "We passed unscathed through worse scenes than the present at Sutter Fort in '48. War, then, is the cry, is it? War between the prostitutes and gamblers on one side, and the virtuous and respectable on the other! War to the knife, and the knife to the hilt! Be it so, then! Gamblers of San Francisco, you have made your election, and we are ready on our side for the issue!"

The issue was not quite that clear. Undoubtedly James King of William, in his public indignation as well as his private angers, believed himself on the side of the angels. But the devils he confronted were not merely the whores and gamblers of the swiftly grown town on the foggy hills above the Bay. The polyglot place contained not only Sydney ducks (paroled criminals from the Australian penal colonies) and native American toughs who had earlier formed themselves into a gang called the Hounds. Some of those he opposed were bankers, politicians, lawyers, insistent on their respectability and quick to defend their "honor" which some seemed to carry as ostentatiously about as they did their pistols and knives. Not all fell neatly into the kind of alliance of the respectables and the roughnecks which has been the shame of other cities since.

King of William had no doubts about the villainy he confronted; others also felt surrounded by a sinful city. Only his boldness and verbal vigor surprised those who had known him earlier. His emergence to brief, violent eminence was strange. Born of Scotch-Irish parentage in the sedate Georgetown section of the national capital, he had been a restless boy. At fifteen he had wandered up through Pennsylvania and westward to the wilderness shores of Lake Michigan. But that rough country proved too tough for his constitution. He came home to a life which seemed designed for durable and dull domesticity.

The young man took a job as a postal clerk. Then he received first-rate journalistic training working on Amos Kendall's *Expositor* and the Washington *Globe* of Frank Blair. No promise marked him on those papers. At twenty-one he married Charlotte Libbey, a girl of his own neighborhood. The children came rapidly. He found a job as a bookkeeper in the banking house of Corcoran and Riggs. He began to count figures, as he had sorted letters in the post office.

Clearly, however, he had a strong sense of his individuality. There were other James Kings whose names appeared on the letters he handled and the bank accounts he kept. To James King he ostentatiously added *of William* (his father's name), and James King of William he remained.

Evidently he was torn between routine domesticity and restless quest. He was excited by the letters of an older brother off exploring with John C. Frémont in 1846. In 1848, leaving Charlotte and their four children behind, he set off on a roundabout journey to the Pacific Coast. In Valparaiso, Chile, he heard the news that gold had been discovered in California. No mere prospector with a pick, he hired ten Chileans to go with him in the search for the glittering ore. He got to San Francisco before the full tide of the rush from the East of the Forty-niners.

In the fortune fever which King of William and his band found in San Francisco, seven of the Chileans deserted to go off prospecting on their own. King of William hurried with his remaining loyal three to a place called Old Dry Diggin's east of the village of Sacramento. Two men were reported to have dug $17,000 in dust in a week's time from one small ravine there. Quick wealth brought outlaws there, too. When a band of robbers calling itself the Owls was seized in the manner which was to mark the Vigilantes, tried in the street, and strung up on an oak, the name of the place was changed to Hangtown. In more placid times it became Placerville.

King of William and his men dug. In three weeks they found enough gold to pay the Chileans and their travel expenses from Valparaiso. Some historians say he had a tidy nest egg left over. However, during this short period he concluded that digging was not the way to fortune for him. Briefly he traded in gold dust and claims in Sacramento—which had been laid out on lands of Captain John Sutter who was to be overrun, not enriched, by the Forty-niners now on their way. In that rough town by Sutter's Fort, King of William held his own. However, in this supply center of the miners, he saw the banking possibilities in the new country. He went back East, found capital, and opened a banking house in San Francisco on December 5, 1849.

He found plenty of competition. Others had also realized that digging was not the only way to get gold. Some Eastern banking houses opened offices; so did men of varying competence and character. Young William Tecumseh Sherman, feeling left behind as his friends were promoted, resigned from the Army and opened a bank. In such company James King of William prospered. He began in a small frame building, then a substantial brick structure was required. He survived a swift panic which punctuated flush times in 1850. In 1851, he was one of the substantial citizens who formed the first Vigilantes to use rope and pistol to punish hoodlums, including the Sydney Ducks, whose murders and depredations mocked the regular forces of justice.

In that year of the first Vigilantes, he was prosperous enough to bring Charlotte and their four children West. They came to a fine house. James King of William kept a carriage and horses. In 1853, thirty-one, and five years up from commonplace bookkeeping in Washington, he was reported worth $250,000. But constant good luck was not assured in golden California.

King of William sent a large sum of money to Sonora, in a mining area off toward Yosemite Valley. Sonora had settled down since the rough days of June 1850, when Yankee newcomers had put a head tax on Mexicans and Chileans as foreigners and marched against the Latins with fife and drum under the American flag to drive them out. The richest pocket mine in the Mother Lode, the Big Bonanza on Piety Hill, had been discovered in 1851. Business boomed. King of William instructed his agent to buy gold dust with the funds he sent him. Instead the agent diverted the money to a local hydraulic association organized for the washing out of gold in placer mining.

King of William's capital was tied up. With a financial panic mounting, he realized that in any sudden run he could not pay off those who were still depositing funds in his bank. Friends assured him that his business was as sound as any in town. He waited and worried. Then he moved, regardless of sacrifice, to put himself into a position in which his liabilities would certainly be met.

A Mr. Woods of the banking and express firm of Adams and Company amiably offered to be helpful. His firm agreed to assume King of William's liabilities in exchange for his assets. King of William gave up a business building, vacant lots, valuable stock as well as his fine house, which sheltered Charlotte and the children, his carriage, and his horses. His losses were not eased by Woods' excessive satisfaction with the bargain.

"King is entirely too honest," he told a mutual friend, who told King of William later. "He underrated everything he had.... I am satisfied I shall make from $100,000 to $150,000."

But Woods was too optimistic. He had, perhaps as a sop to his conscience, given King of William a job at a good salary. It was no job at all when, on February 23, 1855, "the Black Friday" of early San Francisco, the local office of Adams and Company closed its doors. It could meet neither King of William's liabilities nor its own. This firm, which in the West had seemed as strong as the Bank of England, had liabilities to pay and less assets to assign.

Alfred Cohen, a rich and prominent San Franciscan, was named receiver. Associated with him as an assignee was Edward Jones, partner in the banking firm of Palmer, Cook and Company. Other debtors did not like the arrangement. They had another receiver named in place of Cohen. Cohen and Jones declined to give up the assets. They were arrested. Then, King of William and others believed, by improper influences in the courts they were released—apparently with the money still in their hands.

Then King of William moved from accounting pad to copy paper. If he had lost his money, he did not mean to lose his good long name. In a card published in the newspapers he made it clear that he was involved in no finagling in the matter. He made it equally clear that his opinion of Cohen's operations and character was not high. The two men met on Montgomery Street; words passed between them. In the blows that followed Cohen got the worst of it. So he formally dispatched a challenge to a duel. King of William declined.

He thereby risked his reputation. *Honor* was a high, hot word in San Francisco. The physical courage to meet an adversary on the dueling ground could be the measure of a man. King of William retracted nothing he had said. He declared that he had "ever been opposed to dueling on moral grounds." But he also made the practical point that Cohen was rich. If Cohen fell, King of William said, he would leave ample means to support his wife and child. King of William's situation was different.

"Recent events have stripped me entirely of what I once possessed. Were I to fall, I should leave a large family without the means of support. My duties and obligations to my family have much more weight with me than any desire to please Mr. Cohen or his friends in the manner proposed."

Public support rallied to his position. Some have said his example helped reduce the too-prevalent dueling practice. Still, if King of William declined to risk his life on the field of honor, he seemed almost eager to risk it in the tough city. He made a brief effort to re-establish himself in the banking business. Then, on October 8, 1855, he published the first issue of his paper, the *Daily Evening Bulletin*. And although he had declined the dueling pistol, as editor he opened with artillery.

San Francisco had no lack of newspapers. Eight years earlier, on January 9, 1847, Samuel Brannan, the Mormon pioneer who was to become a political power, had set up his weekly *California Star*. Four months later, tall Kentucky emigrant Dr. Robert Semple moved his *Californian* from Monterey. Both papers were skeptical about first gold-discovery reports until Brannan himself went to investigate. In April 1848, he came home roaring "Gold! Gold!" and waving a whiskey bottle full of dust to prove it. The discovery put a temporary end to San Francisco journalism. Printers and readers all stampeded for the fortune-filled hills. But by August 1848 the *Californian* was back in business. A month later it bought the *Star* and became the *Alta Californian* of which Bret Harte was later an editor and to which Mark Twain contributed.

The *Alta Californian* by no means monopolized the field. And when King of William entered it, he believed that some of the papers, like too many of the politicians, were part of a corrupt system which controlled the city. He was not long in making his views known. He was in the business to make a living, he said. A few friends had advanced a few hundred dollars for the enterprise. He wasn't looking for a fight, "but if forced into one, we are 'thar.' "

Actually King of William needed no pushing toward combativeness. He already knew the nature of the complex target he confronted. On October 11, he fired his first shot at Palmer, Cook and Company, which he branded the "Uriah Heaps of America." He was more specific in his charge.

"They are unlike other bankers," he wrote, "because forevermore they are at some scheme to elect, not good men to office but their own or such as can be so fashioned, and then, becoming bondsmen for them, get hold of public money with which to bribe and corrupt other public officers, both state and federal."

Mr. Jones of Palmer, Cook promptly called. The only account of the visit comes from King of William's report in the *Bulletin*. The banker was evidently as suave as his friend Cohen had been pistol-ready. He assured the editor of the new paper that he was not offended and his firm would not reply to the *Bulletin*'s description of his bank. He had not come to discuss the merits of the articles "as much as to have defined to him certain personal relations between him and us. . . ."

Carefully Jones defined the relations of the bank to the *Bulletin* and its editor as battle or blackmail.

"Mr. Jones gratuitously informed us," wrote King of William, "that no newspaper, that had ever attacked the firm of Palmer, Cook & Co., had made anything by so doing, but that his firm had always succeeded in silencing such journals. Mr. Jones did not intimate by what means his firm became so successful in these contests, but in a subsequent part of our interview in which the altered fortune of the editor of this paper was alluded to, Mr. Jones expressed much sympathy, and remarked that had he known it he would have aided us with pleasure, which aid we told him we would have felt bound to decline."

The editor added: "A very remarkable man, that Mr. Jones!"

King of William was a remarkable man, too. He seemed to court enemies. He declined to take the advertisements of quack doctors and described them as obscene. Rather than take them, he said, "we will shut up our office and head for the mines."

But he was not content with such general cleansing measures in his paper. The antagonism of Cohen and Jones was not sufficient for him. He deliberately collected more and more dangerous antagonists. He hit heads high and low in a swinging description of the pervasive corruption he saw around him:

"A man, unworthy to serve the humblest citizen in the land, has filled the highest office in the gift of the people. Judges have sat on the bench, whose more appropriate station would have been the prison house. Men, without one particle of claim to the position, have filled the posts of Mayor and Councilmen in this city, for the sole purpose of filling their pockets with the ill-gotten gains of their nefarious schemes, their pilfering and dishonesty. City and County Treasurers, and Recorders, have sought to obtain offices of trust and honor, who, had they met their deserts, would in other countries have formed part of the chain-gang years ago. And all the while the *press*, THE PRESS, either silent through base fear of personal injury, or yet more shameful, is basely bought to uphold this iniquity."

Then he swung at the epitome of political power:

"Of all the names that grace the rolls of political wire-working in this city, the most conspicuous of all ... as high over all his compeers as was Satan among the fallen angels, and as unblushing and determined as the dark fiend, stands the name of David C. Broderick."

Certainly "David Cataline Broderick," as King of William called him, was power in California. Thirty-five years old when the *Bulletin* attacked him, he had been born in Washington, D.C., where his father was a stonemason on the national Capitol. Orphaned at seventeen, he had pushed his way forward in New York as powerful brawler and effective politician. As a saloon-keeper he was an unsuccessful Tammany Hall candidate for Congress in 1846. In 1849 he closed his saloon, emptying his casks of liquor in the street and swearing that he would never again "sell or drink liquor, smoke a cigar or play a card." In California he kept his vow as to personal behavior, but applied his Tammany training to both politics and business. Within two years, he was described as "the Democratic Party in Cal-

ifornia." When King of William attacked him he was fighting
his way toward the United States Senate.

Undoubtedly King of William's words sometimes fell like rain
on the innocent as well as the guilty. Josiah Royce, the philosopher, who was born in California in the year King of William
launched his crusade, concluded in his history of the state that
King of William was not altogether "free from selfishness in the
conduct of his mission." The editor, Royce wrote, "not infre-
quently felt a good deal of personal spite against the sinners he
assailed." In any event he showed rash courage and attracted
swift attention for his paper. Within a month it had a circulation of 2500 and within two months 3500, more than that of any
other paper in the city.

Under any circumstances King of William's boldness would
have attracted readers. But in November 1855, the month after
the *Bulletin* appeared, a murder in a city of too many unpun-
ished murderers dramatized his crusade. In the tolerant inter-
mingling of all sorts of characters, the wife of U.S. Marshal William H. Richardson quarreled at a theater with a prostitute who,
in token of her intimacy with gambler Charles Cora called herself Belle Cora. The marshal and the gambler were drawn into
the feminine dispute.

Sharp words ensued. Accounts of what followed differ. The
spat seemed settled; the two men were seen together. Then, on
the evening of November 17, the marshal and the gambler were
seen walking arm in arm from the Blue Wing Saloon on Montgomery Street. Around the corner on Clay Street, Cora drew his
gun, grabbed Richardson by his coat collar, and shot him down.
Others said that when Richardson entered the saloon Cora,
standing at the bar, whipped out a derringer as the marshal
approached and shot him in the chest.

Excitement spread through the town. Crowds gathered shouting for the rope for Cora. Men who had been participants when
the first Vigilance Committee hanged hoodlums in 1851 called
for a revival of its methods. Samuel Brannan, founder of the
California Star, shouted so loudly for Cora's summary execution that he was arrested for inciting a riot. Tempers toughened.

But when Brannan was released and Cora was held for trial the crowd calmed.

James King of William made his paper almost a one-man posse in a city that lacked confidence in its courts. Gamblers and politicians were rallying to Cora's defense; Belle Cora provided gold from her brothel. Willing witnesses were found to say that Richardson had tried to slash Cora with a knife. The gambler was well defended—and not merely by knaves. One of his lawyers was Colonel Edward D. Baker, an Englishman who became American soldier, politician, and intimate of Abraham Lincoln.

Baker took the case, it was stated, out of a sense of legal duty. The legend remains, however, that he undertook the defense because Belle Cora promised him $30,000 in gold and paid him $15,000 on the spot. He could not withdraw from the case later when public opinion condemned him because he had lost the $15,000 the same night in a faro game and thus could not return the retainer. Certainly his celebrated oratorical powers, as well as witnesses said to be "gamblers and agents for cock-pits," helped win a jury disagreement. Awaiting a second trial, Cora remained comfortably in a jail presided over by one Billy Mulligan, whom King of William had pilloried in print.

King of William was not alone in condemning the verdict. The *Alta Californian* declared on January 17, 1856, that "it has been understood for some time past that criminals, having money or friends, could not be punished in this community.... Men were placed upon that jury who should never have been there. They went upon it in order to defeat the ends of justice—in other words to 'tie' the jury."

King of William was less restrained.

"Hung be the heavens with black!" the *Bulletin* proclaimed. "The money of the gambler and the prostitute has succeeded, and Cora has another respite.... Rejoice, ye gamblers and harlots! rejoice with exceeding gladness.... Your triumph is great—oh, how you have triumphed! Triumphed over everything that is holy and virtuous and good; and triumphed legally—yes, legally!"

Gamblers were not the only ones to mutter at the sweeping charges against them as members of a perfectly legal profession.

Gaudy girls cried resentment in the whorehouses. There was angry talk in mirrored saloons. Fears grew among officeholders and in the offices of the political bankers, Palmer, Cook and Company, as King of William went on attacking the firm's members as the "greatest enemies to the public weal." Already he was driving that firm to the ruin which later overtook it. But he multiplied the company of his enemies as he roared at corrupt judges, dishonest officials, bought jurymen, and political hirelings.

Furthermore, while openly opposing lynch law, he made a sort of left-handed suggestion that a revival of Vigilance justice might be required.

"We want no Vigilance Committee, if it can be avoided," he said; "but we do want to see the murderer punished for his crimes. . . . The people of this city are not in favor of taking the law into their own hands if justice can be done in the courts; and no class of men can be found in this community more in favor of law and order than the members of the old Vigilance Committee. But if the courts were to relapse into the former farcical apologies we had, it would require but a few hours to again call into action the same body of men."

King of William knew some men were eager for his elimination. A gambler named Selover had tried to bring him to the dueling ground and threatened his life when he refused. King of William made a news item of it:

"Mr. Selover, it is said, carries a knife. We carry a pistol. We hope neither will be required, but if this rencontre cannot be avoided, why will Mr. Selover persist in perilling the lives of others? We pass every afternoon about half past four or five o'clock, along Market Street from Fourth to Fifth Street. The road is wide and not so much frequented as those streets farther in town. If we are to be shot or cut to pieces, for heaven's sake let it be done there."

He was not so unconcerned, however, as his words suggested. His family had grown even if his fine house was lost. Two more children had been born since Charlotte arrived. Now in the yard behind their dwelling she and the children watched him practice with his pistol. One of his sons, then a schoolboy, remembered

seeing him "many a time hit the mark he was aiming at repeatedly in succession."

He went on with his verbal shooting, too. He aimed at Colonel
Baker as the leader of those seeking some pretext to attack him.
In view of Baker's earlier and subsequent career, it somehow
seems doubtful that he was the instigator of murder. Still, undoubtedly, many hoped that some man would stop forever the
pen of the storming editor. By chance or choice the lot came to
James P. Casey.

Casey was hardly an obscure killer. He had recently been
elected a city supervisor by vote-rigging in a district where he
did not live and where his name was not even on the ballot. He
had also started a paper, the *Sunday Times.* Bitterness later may
have prompted the statement that he was incapable of writing a
word for publication. His paper had printed articles which
aroused a much more famous man than James King of William.
William Tecumseh Sherman, who as a banker had survived the
slump which had brought James to failure, let Casey see his red-
headed anger. When Casey's *Times* printed articles which Sherman and other bankers regarded as a blackmailing effort,
Sherman strode up the stairs of his banking building to the third
floor where Casey had his shop.

"If you repeat this," said the man destined soon to become a
great Union general, "I'll throw you and your presses out of the
window."

Casey moved to more friendly quarters but, according to Sherman's biographer, he continued to harass "the better element."
Certainly he became the instrument of the worse element. Full of
bluster, on May 14 he walked into King of William's office at the
Bulletin. King of William had not only charged him with ballot-
box stuffing; he had also casually mentioned the already often-
published fact that Casey had once been an inmate of Sing Sing
Prison in New York. Men in the adjoining room heard the angry
conversation about it.

"What do you mean by that article?" Casey demanded.

"What article?"

"That which says I was a former inmate of Sing Sing
Prison."

"Is that not true?"

"That is not the question. I don't wish my past raked up. On that point I am sensitive."

King of William's anger flared.

"Are you done?" he demanded. "There's the door—go! And never show your face again."

Casey retreated but paused. "I'll say in my paper what I please."

"You have a perfect right to do as you please," King of William told him with contempt. "I'll never notice your paper."

Then Casey warned, "If necessary, I'll defend myself."

"Go," King of William commanded again. Casey went.

More resentful because he had been repulsed, he walked to the Bank Exchange bar, a favorite gathering place, not far away. The news of his visit had already spread. Friends asked him about it. Casey began to brag: He was not a man to be trifled with. He gave the impression that King of William had apologized. Evidently nobody quite believed him. One of those who listened was Judge Edward McGowan, a former Philadelphia policeman who was now a close associate and chief aide of David Broderick, whom King of William had called the presiding devil of corruption. Ned McGowan, said once to have been a fugitive from justice himself, was fat, jolly, hard-drinking, noisy. He was no fool, and he had a gift for troublemaking. Some historians claim that he had furnished the evidence that Casey had once been in Sing Sing. But now he spoke with encouragement and incitement to Casey. He called him aside for quieter talk. The story spread that there he furnished Casey with a Navy revolver.

King of William left the *Bulletin* at his usual time. Absorbed in his thoughts, he walked northward in front of the Montgomery Block, then crossed diagonally toward the Pacific Express office. Apparently he did not notice that a crowd had gathered in some sort of expectation. He was wearing, in the fashion of the time, a short cloak or *talma*, which was buttoned together in front and covered his arms. Then, as King of William himself told the story, he suddenly heard a cry, "Come on!" Others maintained that the assailant shouted "Arm your-

self!'' Whatever happened, no time was given for defense. Only
a few paces from him Casey put his bullet into King of William's breast. The *Bulletin*'s editor staggered into the Express
office. Medical aid was quickly secured. It seemed possible that
the wound might not be fatal.

But the shot had loosed pandemonium on the streets. Crowds
gathered quickly. Demands grew that Casey be strung up on a
lamppost, but friends surrounded him. He was hurried to the
station house. The clamoring mob grew about the building. For
his greater safety Casey was moved in a carriage containing
Sheriff Dave Scannell, whom King of William had damned, to
the county jail, presided over by Billy Mulligan, the killer
Cora's friend. There Gambler Cora was comfortably ensconced,
confident of release after another trial.

Armed gamblers seemed ready to protect the jail, but the
crowd about it grew in number and noise. Efforts to quiet it by
the mayor only brought cries of the remembrance of Cora's escape from the noose. Soldiers were called to protect the building.
The crowd still roared for vengeance. But more than noise and
cries from the street filled the night. Implacable planning went
forward, as was revealed in a notice in the morning papers:

THE VIGILANCE COMMITTEE

The members of the Vigilance Committee, in good standing, will please meet at No. 105½ Sacramento Street, this
day, Thursday, 15th instant, at nine o'clock A.M.
By order of the
Committee of Thirteen.

This call from the old Vigilance leaders of 1851 brought thousands to Sacramento Street. Some historians describing the Vigilantes at this point have made them appear simply well-
disciplined angels gathered against unruly devils. But not all of
those opposed to so-called popular tribunals were evil men. One
story is that the owners of the *Alta Californian* tossed a half-
dollar to decide whether or not to support the new Vigilance
Committee. The committee won. But the *Herald*, which King of
William had charged was a paid paper of Palmer, Cook and
Company, dismissed the shooting of King of William as ''an

affray.'' It was promptly punished by the withdrawal of advertisements by businessmen who had lined up with Vigilantes under another merchant, William T. Coleman.

Those who stood for "law and order," which the Vigilantes called "law and murder," still included even Sherman—who had himself threatened to throw Casey out of the window. Only the reluctance of federal commanders to furnish him arms prevented his leading, at the request of the Governor, a military body to suppress the extralegal forces of popular indignation. That could have meant civil war. The drilled and armed Vigilantes meant serious, sudden business.

They did not wait for the determination of the result of King of William's wound. Hope rose that he might live. He carefully dictated his story of the assault. But he weakened as Charlotte sat beside his bed. Some said that the improper ministrations of many doctors reduced his chances of survival. On Tuesday, June 20, six days after the shooting, King of William's ten-year-old son, Joseph, who had scarcely seen his mother since his father had been shot, was in school. At half past one, a bell tolled. Soon numerous bells were mournfully ringing throughout the city. The teacher called the boy. She told him that his father was very low, but he knew from the continued ringing of the bells that he and his brothers and sisters were fatherless.

The funeral was held two days later. Crowds followed King of William's bier to his grave in the fog-swept, barren neighborhood of Lone Mountain. Just as that procession moved, Casey and Cora, already taken from the jail and swiftly tried by the Vigilantes, were brought to platforms before the two-story granite headquarters at 105½ Sacramento Street. A short time before, in the jail, Cora had been married to Belle the prostitute. He marched to the noose like a gambler whose nerve was not shaken by his last, losing hand. But Casey cried almost incoherently to God, and to his mother who, he whimpered, would not believe him a murderer. The two men were swung simultaneously to their deaths.

The story of James King of William was done. So great was the sympathy for his family that people contributed nearly $32,000 as a gift to them. But retribution for his death was incomplete. The Vigilantes sought those believed to have encouraged Casey to his killing, including Judge Edward McGowan. McGowan fled in disguise to the hills and hid for months in distant thickets and lonely canyons. Finally, he got himself tried and acquitted in a more friendly jurisdiction. He lived to write a book about the times when he was "persecuted" by the Vigilantes.

Two other murderers were hanged. Twenty-five men were shipped out of San Francisco. Others were notified to leave, and some left without waiting for warning. Billy Mulligan left with a pious declaration of sin and repentance. He went on to New York, however, where he hung around hotels to beat up any visitors he recognized as Vigilantes.

Gradually the informal power the Vigilantes had grasped grew more difficult to hold safely. David Smith Terry, associate justice of the state supreme court, tried to organize resistance to the Vigilantes. In an altercation he seriously wounded one of them. He was seized and tried. The wounded man lay precariously between death and recovery, and the Vigilantes faced the alternatives of a show of weakness or the possibility of hanging a judge of the state's highest court. If he were hung, all might hang in an anti-Vigilante movement. Fortunately the wounded man recovered. The judge was released; Vigilante leaders were relieved. And in August, three months after the death of James King of William, the Vigilantes of 1856 marched out of history in a parade which displayed their power. Dispersing, they left behind them various assessments of the benefit or the damage they had done to justice in San Francisco and safety in the West.

Strangely some of those who received the scorn of the *Bulletin* and the resentment of the Vigilantes were men well remembered in history. David Broderick, whom James King of William had described as the great Satan of San Francisco, not only entered the United States Senate in 1857 but became noted there for his hostility to slavery and political corruption. Finally and ironically, he met in a duel the Judge Terry whose custody had embarrassed the Vigilantes. Broderick fell, and the old New York saloonkeeper who brought Tammany methods to San Francisco said on his deathbed: "They killed me because I was opposed to the extension of slavery and a corrupt administration."

Broderick's funeral oration, was a strange summing up of the views of opponents of the Vigilantes. Eloquent and impressive, it was delivered by Colonel Edward D. Baker, who had defended the gambler Cora. Baker had been urged upon President Taylor by Abraham Lincoln for a Cabinet position. Later, as United States Senator, he was a chief advisor to President Lincoln on checkmating secession movements in the Pacific states. He died violently, but as a Senator-soldier in the Union Army at Ball's Bluff.

Terry died violently, too, but not in the Confederate Army in which he served. In 1889, after a violent contention with a judge who had decided a lawsuit against him, he attacked the judge and was shot by a bodyguard assigned to the jurist by the Attorney General of the United States. Violence died slowly in California. Coleman, who had led the Vigilantes, lived long and died quietly in his bed in 1893. But in 1877, in his fifties, he had come forward again as the head of a Committee of Safety to put down rioting workmen who may have considered themselves in some way Vigilantes, too. Resentful of the job competition of Chinese, they lynched nineteen of them. Private "justice" could get out of hand. And crusade can sometimes lead to deadly confusion in the violence it stirs.

9

Barren Ground

Edmund Ruffin seemed always to be hurrying on his mission across the South. He was "on the cars" hastening to Harpers Ferry, the "seat of war," the early morning of November 26, 1859.

Southern indignation over the raid of John Brown a month before was fully shared by Ruffin, but he hoped for more than a hanging. He wished Abolitionists would attempt to rescue Brown and that all engaged in such an enterprise might be "put to death like a wolf." Nevertheless, to him Brown was not only the red-handed emissary of the enemy. He was also a possible instru-

139

ment of Ruffin's own fierce aims. The stern Southerner declared
that he would have welcomed Northern efforts to free battered
old Brown, a move which "successful or not . . . would be the
immediate cause of separation of Southern and Northern
States."

Ruffin was sixty-five the morning he arrived in the little village by the heights and the river, now crowded with troops from
all parts of Virginia. With his long, lank white hair about his
sharp-featured face, he looked every day of his age. In the tense
atmosphere of the time he was saluted by those who recognized
him as a stirring Southern radical, though perhaps too precipi-
tate a prophet to be followed. He was given permission to join
the cadets of the Virginia Military Institute to be sure to witness
the execution of Brown at nearby Charles Town. Some of the
adolescents in arms smiled at the old man wearing their uniform—a scarlet flannel shirt crossed by two white belts and a
long gray military overcoat. Remembering the drills in the War
of 1812, Ruffin swung into the early morning march to the execution field.

By the gallows grim against the morning sky he waited in the
ranks two hours before Brown, sitting on his coffin with his arms
pinioned to his sides, was brought to the scene in an open wagon.
Ruffin watched as "old John Brown," younger than he, ascended the scaffold "with readiness and seeming alacrity." The
condemned man showed no terror. He seemed to Ruffin "a willing assistant instead of the victim." After a full day of long
standing and much marching, Ruffin wrote his impressions of the
dead man in his diary:

"The villain whose life has thus been forfeited possessed . . .
one virtue (if it should be so called) or one quality that is more
highly esteemed by the world than more rare and perfect virtues.
This . . . [was] physical or animal courage, or the most complete
fearlessness of and insensibility to danger and death. In this
quality he seems to me to have had few equals."

Ruffin's reluctant admiration revealed his own qualities. Indeed, across the execution field he almost understood that he and
Brown had come together at the event which made inevitable
what both most wished. Brown had hastened the collision both

desired. He became the martyr of a menacing North. But he
served as well the long-pressed purposes of Ruffin for a South
withdrawn from the Union to save the Southern land. From
Harpers Ferry Brown quickly became the abolitionist symbol—
or, as Ralph Waldo Emerson put it, the "new saint who will
make the gallows glorious as the cross." And Edmund Ruffin,
an old man in the fighting clothes of youth, moved at accelerated
pace to become the lonely victim of a cause to which he gave his
life and would gladly have given his blood.

Farmer and editor, Ruffin had quite literally assumed the task
of saving the Southern land as a young man. Its chief fruits
were his inheritance; so were its dismaying difficulties. He was
the fifth of his line to bear his name in America. Ruffins had
settled in Virginia in 1666. On the new rich soil their acres
broadened and the number of their slaves increased. Gracious-
ness, pride, and responsibility marked them as Tidewater gentry.
When Edmund was born the broad lawns before his father's fine
house spoke concern for spaciousness and beauty in an ordered
society.

His father, George Ruffin, and other typical Virginia planters
contemplated the problem of an increasing slave population
while need for its labors decreased on worn lands which had been
too long exploited. As his eldest son, Edmund was an heir to this
puzzle. Nothing about the frail, restless boy suggested he could
solve it.

His mother died soon after his birth in 1794. A stepmother
came. He was educated at home among half-brothers and -sisters
until he was sixteen, when his troubled father died prematurely.
That home teaching was about all the formal education he ever
had. He crossed the James River to William and Mary College in
Williamsburg. But he was soon suspended for neglect of his
classroom work. One of his extracurricular preoccupations was
evidently a pretty, aristocratic girl named Susan Travis. After
brief and battle-free service in the War of 1812, Edmund and
Susan were married in 1813. The nineteen-year-old bridegroom
brought Susan home to the house on the James at Coggin's
Point which he had inherited.

The house stood high. It was ranked in quality only below

such neighboring mansions as Shirley, Westover, and the Brandons. But now Edmund confronted the problem which had begun to plague his father and other Virginians, gentry and yeoman alike. To some it seemed that "an angel of desolation" had cursed the land. Two centuries of tobacco farming had left it worn out, washed out. Much of it was left to the briars and the brush, the wild turkeys and the deer.

It was no simple problem for a nineteen-year-old. John Taylor of Caroline, Thomas Jefferson's friend, had suggested better farming practices. After Edmund brought Susan to Coggin's Point, Jefferson, who considered himself the agrarian philosopher, was trying in vain in his debt-plagued old age to find a purchaser for his lands who would pay enough to meet his liabilities. Nobody wanted Virginia farmland. From its barren ground "an emigrating contagion resembling an epidemic disease" spread among the people. Virginia's population growth faltered. And those planters and yeomen who did not move to new lands in the Southwest were beginning in reluctance, sometimes in shame, to sell their "people"—their slave surpluses—to the new Deep South. Young Ruffin faced a gloomy prospect.

"There was scarcely a proprietor in my neighborhood," he wrote later, "who did not desire to sell his land, and who was prevented only by the impossibility of finding a purchaser, unless at half of the then very low estimated value. All wished to sell, none to buy."

Ruffin's own acres were poor. The yield was more disappointing each year. He began to experiment. He tried new methods and practices; he began to read and study as he had never done before. He failed, while his neighbors laughed. He himself was about ready to seek "the rich western wilderness" where his "whole income and more" would not be necessary to the barest support of his "small but fast growing family." He thought of the future of both his children and his slaves.

Then by chance Ruffin found a copy of the *Elements of Agricultural Chemistry* which Sir Humphry Davy had published in 1813, the year Ruffin came back to the farm. In it he came upon the statement that sterile soils containing "the salt of iron, or acid matter ... may be ameliorated by the application of quicklime." The young Virginia farmer applied this to his observation that only sorrel and pine abounded on poor lands, lands lacking calceous earths or an adequate calcium content. He concluded—or guessed—that this trouble could be corrected by the application of marl (common fossil shells) which were abundant in the neighborhood.

In February 1818, he put his puzzled Negroes to the task of digging the marl from pits in his lower lands. Two hundred bushels of marl were spread on a few acres of newly cleared but poor ridge land. He planted corn. He waited. The crop he grew was fully 40 per cent better than he could have otherwise expected. More carts went to the marl pits. Fields flourished. And Ruffin, now twenty-four, opened an era in the agricultural history of Virginia. Marl could save the Old South and the order upon which its landed security had rested.

With the zeal of a discoverer, Ruffin turned from plants to pen. The report of his results, made first to the Prince George County Agricultural Society, was published in the *American Farmer*, a new agricultural journal started in Baltimore by John Skinner, later to serve Horace Greeley in the agricultural interests of the New York *Tribune*. That connection of Ruffin through Skinner to slavery-hating Greeley pointed a common concern, North and South, of lovers of the land.

In that agrarian preoccupation Ruffin needed his own farm publication. Though agricultural leaders acclaimed his work, some of his planter neighbors still scoffed at his ideas. They referred to the marl pit from which he took the first shells as "Ruffin's Folly." The good news had to be spread. So in June 1833 Ruffin published the first issue of the *Farmer's Register* at his plantation. Though he set the high subscription price of five dollars a year on it, it swept from the field an earlier agricultural periodical, the *Virginia Farmer*. The earlier paper drooped, it was said, "like the harebell before the sun." At the end of the first year, Ruffin moved his editorial activities from his plantation to an office in Petersburg. He had subscribers from 85 counties and towns in Virginia and 197 more from 15 other states and the District of Columbia.

Few papers with a cause were ever more successful. Its teach-ings spread. Where marl was introduced talk of migration to the West subsided. Fields flourished. The land values of Tidewater Virginia rose by over $17 million between 1838 and 1850. It was even estimated that the total increase from the application of marl, after 1820, amounted to over $30 million. By 1843 the scoffing neighbors in Prince George County were giving thanks to a native son who "single and alone . . . [had] buffeted popular prejudice" and enabled them to grow two ears of corn where only one grew before.

But what Ruffin wanted to see grow and flourish again was not merely grass and corn but the faltering aristocratic agrarian order. The eroded lands around the philosopher at Monticello disturbed him no more than Jefferson's "corrupting and poisonous" political theories "of democratic perfection." He believed that Jefferson had devised "false and foolish" words as an instrument for Abolitionists in his "free and equal" Declaration. Now it was not merely abolitionist sentiment that grew in the North. The evil power of numbers grew there, too, to the disadvantage of the once-dominant South.

Even in Virginia Ruffin saw aggressive moves against the agricultural interests of the planter class. Throughout he regarded protective tariffs as taxing Southern agriculture to support Northern industry. He was not only hauling marl, he also had loads of protest to move against forces he believed were exploiting and eroding the landed South which depended not only upon a good earth but also upon beneficent Negro slavery for prosperous plantations.

Gradually the *Farmer's Register* moved from marl to men, from agriculture to politics. Ruffin began moderately in his attack on banks and banking practices. The banking problem following the panic of 1837 was national, but under the system of state charters his adversaries were at hand in Virginia. Opposition from the targets of his criticism sharpened his language. Bankers and their political friends, some of them planters, resented his attacks. Subscriptions were canceled by some who had welcomed his agricultural articles. Ruffin resolved to use no "holiday words." The words he did use—"pillage . . . lying, fraud and swindling"—brought him more abuse.

He met it. In September 1841, he established a new publication, the *Bank Reformer*. He had no ready remedy for what he regarded as erosion of economic morals. He had scorned the methods of politicians when he had served briefly in the Virginia state senate. He had shown arrogance there and become "tired and disgusted with being a servant of the people." But he was no match for those who disliked his diatribes against the entrenched financiers. The *Bank Reformer* survived only five months, and the *Farmer's Register* followed it in failure. Furthermore, though in 1841 Ruffin was named a member of the first Virginia State Board of Agriculture, enmities he had made resulted in what he regarded as "niggardly support & contemptuous treatment." He was ready to withdraw from all public affairs.

When he felt that the public of Virginia was "wearied" of him and his writing, the call came from South Carolina. Governor James Henry Hammond, a planter and politician who had also been an editor, invited Ruffin to become agricultural surveyor of the Palmetto State. Ruffin gladly accepted. His sense of neglect at home made the invitation even more welcome. Hammond was his kind of gentleman, attacking banks and tariffs, upholding slavery as the greatest of great blessings, and moving toward the radical view that the time for secession was near. Ruffin fell in love with Charleston. It could be likened, he wrote, "to a gentleman born and bred, simply but perfectly well dressed, compared to a mustachioed dandy and exquisite."

His work was not in Charleston, however, but in laborious quests in swamps and river bottoms for the marl beds which the worn South Carolina land required. He received warm appreciation, honors, and friendship, but the work was too much for his frail constitution. Regretfully he went home, but he arrived to find that he was not forgotten or unappreciated. Not only did good harvests come to him from carefully restored soils at a new and well-loved home, Marlbourne, which he had acquired on the Pamunkey River, northwest of Richmond. People and papers praised him. Ex-President John Tyler hung his picture beside Daniel Webster's above his mantel. Ruffin, never happy away from the press, agreed to take on at his "discretion or caprice...

something like the sub-editorial duties for an agricultural column or two in each No. of the Richmond *Enquirer.*"

The plow did not keep him from the pen; it was never to do so.
Though his own editorship ended when he sadly shut his shop in
Petersburg, his writings for the papers increased. His subject
matter became less and less exclusively agricultural. His mood
had mellowed toward Virginians. He accepted the presidency of
the Virginia State Agricultural Society which he had rather
brusquely declined before. But agriculture had now ceased to be
his chief concern. His mission was a separate and independent
Southern nation.

As early as 1836 he had written bitterly of the Abolitionists.
Five years before that, in southeastern Virginia, the slave Nat
Turner had staged his insurrection which began with the murder
of the whole family of Joseph Travis. Ruffin's wife, Susan, bore
that surname. Still Ruffin declared, "From our slaves of themselves, and from any political effects of the institution of slavery,
as it exists in the South, we have *nothing* to fear . . . —but the
South, *and the Union,* have everything to fear, (and danger far
greater than from servile insurrections) from the restless,
mad, and *sustained* action of Northern abolitionists."

Ruffin's faith in his own slaves was demonstrated by his elimination of white overseers. To his "faithful and intelligent"
slave foreman, Jem Sykes, he even gave "charge of the keys." If
that resulted in an unusual amount of pilfering, he said, he
would still prefer no white overseer. Under slave direction the
lands continued to grow in fertility at Coggin's Neck and at
Marlbourne, which became his residence.

From Marlbourne came the increasing flow of his writings for
Southern newspapers, not only for the *Enquirer* in Richmond
but also for the *Mercury* in Charleston and other Southern
papers. The *Mercury* was already the organ of Robert Barnwell
Rhett, then moving along the course which was to make him "the
father of secession." Other papers welcomed Ruffin's steady
stream of editorial contributions. He wrote for the *Virginia
Index, The South,* the Charleston *Courier, DeBow's Review,* and
the *Southern Literary Messenger.*

He published books, one of which, *Anticipations of the Fu-*

ture, was serialized in part in the *Mercury.* In imaginative prophecy it pictured a South pushed into such ruin that secession was accepted. Then followed a short devastating war in which the South suffered from a blockade but Northern merchants were bankrupt and their cities overwhelmed by mobs of "undigested foreigners." Finally the West broke with the North and joined the South. The end, of course, was a South rising from ruin to prosperity, adding industries to its agriculture and trading directly and profitably with Europe.

No one was more misled by his own imaginings than Ruffin. In 1855, when he was sixty-one, he entirely gave up the management of Marlbourne to devote himself to his mission. Despite his growing associations with angry editors and politicians, he was lonely. Susan had died in 1846. And a few years before that he had been shaken when a lifelong friend, Thomas Cocke, a relative of his stepmother, unwilling to impose his invalidism on others, committed suicide. Ruffin wrote that he would not judge this "greatest offense" of his friend's life.

"When death calls me from this world," he wrote, "may my dread account of sins over-balancing virtues, be not greater than that of my self-slaughtered friend."

Confident in his loneliness of the virtues of his own views, he became a more intense propagandist. Articles signed "A Virginian" appeared in the Richmond and Charleston papers. They ran to the relentless radical conclusion that for a South beset by Northern fanaticism there was but one "defense or means of safety left"—"separation from, and independence of, the present Union." Delay meant only loss of Southern "wealth and strength." The alternative, under increasing abolitionist pressure for Negro freedom, he believed would be a South sinking to the "condition of Jamaica, and later [to] the bloody horrors of St. Domingo, and then the extinction of the white race, and the brutal barbarism of the black."

That dread prospect appeared closer and closer to him but the South seemed slow to see it, even after a majority of all Northern votes were cast for John C. Frémont as the Free Soil candidate for the Presidency in 1856. Ruffin quickened his campaign. He traveled about the South. He again found more congenial associ-

ates in Charleston, where he spent much time in the offices of the
Mercury arguing for the early secession of the Lower South as a
unit. He and Barnwell Rhett mourned together over the fact
that too many Southern politicians were bribed by their own
national ambitions and other men seemed lost in "sullen despair."

Ruffin's locks were whiter now, his features more pinched. He
was an undisguised agitator when he went to Washington, where
his old friend Governor Hammond had entered the U.S. Senate.
Even Hammond was doubting the wisdom of Southern secession.
But his passion rose as Ruffin's did when William H. Seward,
voice of the "irrepressible conflict," boasted that the North
henceforth would rule the South as a conquered province.

"You dare not make war on cotton," Hammond cried, as he
made a phrase which became a great delusion; "No power on
earth dares make war upon it. Cotton is king."

Ruffin almost feared the truth of that statement. The North
would not fight and the South would not secede. And he had
already arrived at his absolute determination upon the necessity
for separation as a basis for Southern survival. Moving about the
capital, lean, his face intent under his long white hair, he already had the aspect of a prophet of destiny or doom. He carried
a cane which looked like a staff. To some he seemed a Southern
Peter the Hermit preaching a great crusade.

The problem now was not resisting the Abolitionists but arous-
ing the South. As he had labored with South Carolina's ardent
Rhett, Ruffin worked with a congenial associate in incendiarism,
the eloquent Alabama firebrand William Lowndes Yancey. At
Rhett's suggestion Yancey, who had begun his career as a
Unionist editor in South Carolina, published in the Montgomery
Advertiser and Gazette a plan designed by Ruffin that proposed
the organization of stanch states-rights men in a League of
United Southerners.

They were organizing, but in the face of stubborn conservative
Southern resistance. Ruffin pushed the plan in Charleston and in
North Carolina and Virginia. As the summer of 1859 drew to a
close, Ruffin wearily regarded the task of bringing the Southern
people to the realities as he saw them. In Virginia he found that

"talk of secession would ruin any man with political aims."
Ruffin had none, but he wanted to keep safe from change the
Southern order which he had labored in his fields to make secure.
But even at his beloved Marlbourne all that enriched his life
seemed unraveling.

In the autumn his daughter Mildred told him of her plans for
marriage which would take her far off, over the mountains to
Kentucky. A sense of loss settled thick about him. He hid his
unhappiness, only celebrating it secretly on a last evening before
her wedding when old songs rose around the harmonicon—songs
which had warmed his hearth and home more than any fires. On
October 18 she was gone and he wrote, "I have lived long
enough—and a little more."

He did not know then that on the morning of the day before
John Brown—"Old Brown of Osawatomie"—had seized the
U.S. armory at Harpers Ferry in his manic move to free the
slaves. But he learned quickly. Vague word of the almost incredible invasion reached him on October 19. Word came, too, of
Northern approval of everything about Brown's blow except its
"rashness and impudence." The old planter at Marlbourne
roused as a propagandist again, his weariness forgotten. Brown
had shown, Ruffin believed, what he had preached for nearly a
decade: "the great mass of the people of the North" as "enemies
of the South" would "sympathize even with treason, murder
and every accompaniment of insurrection ... to overthrow
slavery." And because, as Wendell Phillips said in Boston,
Brown might have carried "letters of marque from God," Edmund Ruffin roused from his sense of loneliness to march as
anointed protector of his faith.

At sixty-five, he armed himself first with his pen and then
with John Brown's own pikes. He dispatched resolutions to ardent Southern-rights organizations urging that "the only safe-
guard from the insane hostility of the North" was secession.
Then he took the train to Harpers Ferry. He used the occasion to
press his purposes. He printed his resolutions and petitions in
the local papers. There as elsewhere he knew his way into newspaper offices. An agricultural paper, the *Farmer's Repository*,
had been printed there before Ruffin entered the editorial field.

At Harpers Ferry was the *Virginia Free Press* and at Charles Town the *Spirit of Jefferson.*

As he stood in VMI cadet uniform watching the execution, his respect for Brown's courage did not make him see Brown as a sort of perverse mirror of himself: both men of old American stock, both stepchildren not only in their families but in their times as well, both ready to step far ahead in causes so dissimilar as to seem much the same. It is unfortunate to conclude that Edmund Ruffin could not have heard one of the calm last statements of John Brown as the wagon brought him into the square of troops.

"This is a beautiful land," old Brown said as his eyes swept the Southern hills.

Old Ruffin, who meant to make it so, could condemn but not despise old Brown. He came homeward from the hanging by way of Washington, carrying with him everywhere one of the pikes with which Brown had armed his men. The knife-tipped weapons were, he wrote the Richmond *Enquirer,* "devised and directed by Northern Conspirators, made in Northern factories, paid for by Northern funds, and designed to slaughter sleeping Southern men and their awakened wives and children. . . ."

Ruffin apparently cornered the market on Brown's knife-pointed shafts. His proposal that the legislature of Virginia send one to each of the slaveholding states to be displayed in their capitols was not accepted. But Ruffin himself sent the deadly mementoes to the states. The South seemed ready to rise in resentment. Ruffin was encouraged. But passions cooled. As 1859 turned into 1860, there was Southern talk of the dangers of Southern folly. Ruffin went on traveling, preaching, working for secession. Now he seemed an even more dramatic prophet in a suit of cheap homespun, "manufactured in Virginia," which he began to wear with his wide, flat, flopping black hat.

He rejoiced at the split among the Democrats. He was only afraid that in naming Lincoln the Republicans had not nominated their ablest man, whose election would assure Southern reaction. And he was disgusted at home where too many people seemed willing "to swallow black republicanism, nigger, tariff and all." As the election of 1860 approached, he found politi-

cians from many of the Southern states enjoying the society and
the waters at White Sulpher Springs.

Among them he was the only "avowed secessionist per se."
That seemed so everywhere. He was saddened on a visit to his
daughter in Kentucky to find her husband "a submissionist."
He wrote Yancey in Alabama urging him to become the Patrick
Henry of Southern liberties. He sent more of his incessant contributions to the *Mercury* in Charleston, stressing the necessity
of swift action if Lincoln was elected: "One state will be enough
to begin the movement. South Carolina will not fail."

Lincoln's election was not the signal for the Southern determination to withdraw, however. The old agricultural reformer
spoke of the "sterile Virginia soil." North Carolina also seemed
barren for the sowing of any crop of dragon's teeth. But in
Columbia, South Carolina, where the secession convention first
met in December 1860, he was welcomed with applause and the
music of bands. He was asked to speak, though his powers were
not in oratory but in the pen. When the convention moved to
Charleston he wore the blue cockade of Southern "minute men"
on his wide hat. He wrote his sons that this was the happiest
time of his life. In Charleston the editor of the *Courier* called to
announce a serenade in his honor. He was cheered by the cadets
of the Citadel. A prominent place was provided for him when
the ordinance of secession was ceremoniously signed.

Charleston was the seat of his spirit. A brief visit home only
disgusted him more with Virginia's reluctance to follow South
Carolina. He hastened back to the Carolina city he loved as
tension grew there before the Union flag defiantly flying from
Fort Sumter. He borrowed a rifle from cadets at the Citadel.
Various South Carolina units invited him to join them. He chose
the Palmetto Guards. And on the evening of April 11, the captain of the guards sought him out and reported that the company had chosen him to fire the first shot on the fort in the
harbor. He lay down without undressing. At four o'clock he was
up at the beat of drums. At four-thirty the old planter-
propagandist fired the first cannon shot. The war he had wanted
had begun.

Virginia's secession ended what he called his "voluntary

exile.'' He was as honored now in the Old Dominion as he had
felt neglected before. Still he felt inactive. He tried to re-assume
plantation management when his son Edmund went off as soldier.
He went into Richmond when his own Palmetto Guards passed
through. The plow could not hold him. In July he was in the city
again, purchasing supplies and completing plans to join his
young South Carolina comrades at the front.

He found his company on the eve of the Battle of First
Manassas (Bull Run), and a dreadful experience followed. New
shoes hurt his feet before there was any threat of battle. The
food for the troops was too hard for his poor teeth. He was cold
in the camp. He could not run with the younger men as they
maneuvered forward. Finally he was persuaded to retire, but
when he heard the thunder of cannon he hurried back to his
company. Kind young men let him ride on the caisson of a cannon. And when a halt was made to shell the federal retreat
down the road toward Centerville, once more the men insisted
that Ruffin fire the first shot at the blue troops. His shell fell
squarely among the Union soldiers retiring across the suspension
bridge over a creek called Cub Run. This retreat was turned into
confusion. Eagerly and proudly the old man counted his dead.

He was nearly dead, too, when he got back to his son's home
on the James. There his expectations that the Bull Run victory
would swiftly end the war slowly faded. He wrote a little. His
hearing had been injured by staying too close to the cannon he
had fired. He took consolation in the picture of himself which
Leslie's Weekly had printed in the North. He was, that Yankee
weekly said, a secessionist who must have ''imbibed with his
mother's milk the desire to break up the compact that binds this
great Confederacy together.'' It described him as ''laden with
years, and having the air of a patriarch,'' but ''not yet by any
means'' at ''the doddering state.''

But now all the earth trembled about him. His elation faded.
Union gunboats appeared in the river before his house. Still he
clung to the faith that the Southern patriot, ''clothed in the
armor of a just cause,'' would be superior to Yankee ''banditti
and pirates.'' When Robert E. Lee struck at McClellan's
threatened move on Richmond, Ruffin again rode up to the

Chickahominy to the battleground. And again soldiers cheered him. But there, too, he learned that his grandson, Julian Beckwith, had been killed in battle.

He shouldered this first sacrifice with pride. But when he returned home, Yankee soldiers were in the fields below Coggin's Point. Only when they were withdrawn could he go back to find his stripped fields and looted mansion. His books and papers were scattered. So was his collection of shells and fossils. The old harmonicon at which Mildred had sung was shattered. And Jem Sykes, the trusted slave, had slipped away to freedom with new Yankee friends. Obscene phrases were smeared with filth upon the walls.

"This house," said a mild one, "belonged to a Ruffinly son-of-a-bitch."

He wanted not peace but vengeance, retaliation by raids into the North. But, at the place where he had first tried to save the worn Southern land, dangers grew. Not only did Yankees and wandering Negroes threaten. So also did poorer Southern whites resentful of the war Ruffin had helped bring upon them. Once he had to hide in his fields when Union riders swept into his yard. A move to Marlbourne only brought him to the country through which Grant hammered toward Richmond. He had bought a small farm in Amelia County—unaware, of course, that it would be on the way of Lee's troops' retreat from Petersburg to Appomattox. The harried old man moved about. In the fall of 1863, he visited beleaguered Charleston again. There he enlisted —this time among the city's old-man defenders. His spirits rose. Charleston would not know surrender. But back in Virginia, in January 1864, he recognized his own feebleness at seventy. Then word came that his beloved Mildred was dead in Kentucky. In May the news came that his son Julian had been killed at Drewry's Bluff. He was, he thought now, incapable of grief.

Moving implacably forward, Union toops occupied Marlbourne. The New York *Herald* proudly told its readers of headquarters set up in the home of "the old rebel who fired the first gun in the present war." And its correspondent commented on its well-tended fields and fine library of agricultural books. That was a report before swift devastation. All that was not carried away from Marlbourne was left in ruin. In March 1865, Ruffin sent to the Confederate government all the cash in his possession, Confederate bonds, family plate, even at last his gold watch.

On the night after Richmond was evacuated on April 3, at his Amelia County farm he wrote in his diary that he was left "without any resources of either property or escape.... Even the dependence on one or the other of my two sons and their wives must fail now, because they will be stripped of everything.... I cannot consent to live a pauper on the charity of strangers abroad, or of impoverished children and friends near our present home."

Not far away from that home Lee surrendered. Soldiers passing through Amelia County remembered afterward the shade of the great oak trees, and fences over which roses and honeysuckle tumbled. The April opulence was deceptive. In May and June men began coming back in ragged clothes and on tottering horses to the lands which Ruffin so long before had tried to save from misuse, erosion, and infertility. Most of the old slaves were gone. Such stock as survived was scrawny. The implements were broken.

On June 18, little more than two months after Appomattox, the old agitator withdrew to his diary. The pen was still steady in his veined white hands. In a bold scrawl he wrote, and at the bottom of the last page of his crowded record, he set the phrase *The End*. But above it, in loneliness and bitterness, he inscribed not repentance but a curse.

"I here declare my unmitigated hatred to Yankee rule—to all political, social and business connections with the Yankees and to the Yankee race.... May such sentiments be held universally in the outraged and down-trodden South, though in silence and stillness, until the now far-distant day shall arrive for just retribution for Yankee usurpation, oppression and atrocious outrages, and for deliverance and vengeance for the now ruined, subjugated and enslaved Southern States!..."

At midday he put down his pen. Calmly he braced himself in his chair. Then he carefully arranged the silver-mounted gun his son had loaded for use against horse thieves in the disordered land. With the gun resting on a trunk before him, he pulled the trigger with a forked stick. The first cap exploded without setting off its charge. He adjusted the stick again. This time there was no misfire. On the porch below, the young women of the family heard the blast. His son came running from the barn. They found the old man's body still upright in his chair. In the cause in which he still believed he had saved the last shot for his own life.

10

Scarecrow of Courage

Sidney Gay brought Horace Greeley the news that the mob was advancing on *The Tribune* hollering for Horace's head. Gay, former active agent of the Underground Railroad, was a natural managing editor of *The Tribune*. Everybody, of course, knew of Greeley's concern, among a multitude of other causes, for the freedom of the slaves. Gay was excited at the approach of the rough crowd carrying crude banners—NO DRAFT, KILL THE NIGGERS—and shouting "To *The Tribune!* We'll hang Old Greeley to a Sour Apple Tree."

"This is not a riot," Gay told his carelessly dressed chief at his cluttered desk. "It's a revolution."

"It looks like it," said the editor with the face of a cherub framed by gray chin whiskers.

It was time to arm for defense, Gay said.

Greeley, who was often described almost as a scarecrow as he moved about New York and America in his familiar wide-brimmed floppy hat and his rumpled white coat, calmly surveyed the crowd.

"It is just what I expected," he said, "and I have no doubt they will hang me. But I want no arms brought into the building."

Greeley's pacifism was not out of character. There had never been a more peaceful man whose whole life was devoted to verbal violence. Since 1841 when, a queer-looking printer from Vermont, he had set up his *New York Tribune,* he had missed no fight, fad, or fancy in his writing. He had damned Democrats, divorce, and drink. He had fought as a Whig for internal improvements and protection of industry, but he also sought a better chance for labor. He had flirted with socialism and promoted the arts. He had mixed much in politics, often with a hunger for public office for himself. As the Civil War began, his daily, weekly, and semiweekly *Tribune*s reached more than a quarter of a million Americans.

"Greeley," said Ralph Waldo Emerson, "does the thinking for the whole West at $2 per year for his paper."

His lack of surprise as he watched the mob crying for his blood could have expressed only his knowledge that the rioting had been going on for hours. Apparently organized crowds, starting with the destruction of the Enrollment Office at Third Avenue and 46th Street, had roared across the city, burning, killing, looting. But Greeley knew too that the anti-draft mob had exploded from spreading slums. White-poverty servitude had grown even as the war to end black servitude went on. As a crusader Greeley often seemed eccentric and inconsistent; so was the life he confronted. Now the war for freedom and union created bitterness and the danger of lasting divisions, not only

between sections but also at home. Crusading could be confusing
to less eccentric-seeming men than Horace Greeley.

Below his windows the menacing mob thickened in Printing
House Square.

"Down with *The Tribune!*" rose the cry.

And then the clamor for its editor: "Down with the old white
coat that thinks a nigger is as good as an Irishman."

Greeley seemed more sad than afraid. Excited friends and
aides tried to persuade him to slip out the back door and leave
town. He shook his head. But finally, more testy than terrified,
he agreed to go to dinner.

"If I can't eat my dinner when I'm hungry," he said in his
squeaky voice, "my life isn't worth anything to me."

So he clapped on his floppy hat and walked straight out into
the crowd. With his specs hanging on his nose, he stalked arm in
arm with a friend through those who had been shouting for his
blood. He looked benign, not fearful. Not a hand was raised to
touch him. Obviously this was no simple mob. It contained hoodlums, but it had grievances. In the city of 813,000 people, half of
them foreign-born, including 203,740 Irish, thousands were
packed in warrens of poor housing and poor men. Wooden shan-
ties and rows of grim tenements stank from their own primitive
toilet facilities and from the offal of stockyards and breweries.
Homeless children ranged the streets. Women, Greeley found in
the midst of the war boom, were receiving an average of $1.54 a
week from Army clothing contractors. Such wages had to be
supplemented by prostitution. Many men received little more,
and the anger of men trying to support families as laborers on
$3 to $5 a week was misdirected at gangs of freed Negroes imported by employers to break strikes and depress wages. Now the
draft, which exempted all able to pay $300 for a substitute, as
owners of twenty slaves were exempt in the South, readied the
cry in the North—as in the South—that it was a rich man's war
and a poor man's fight.

There were those in politics and journalism ready to take
disloyal advantage of discontent. Newspapers like *The Herald,
The Sun, The Times,* and Greeley's *Tribune* are better remem-

bered in the war's story. All of them, certainly including *The Tribune,* were often critical of the Union effort. But at the outbreak of the war New York had seventeen daily newspapers, of which nine defended slavery and five were definitely Southern in sympathy. Most significant among them was the New York *Daily News,* operated by Benjamin Wood, brother of the Democratic Mayor Fernando Wood. Fernando, as war approached, had declared that the Union would soon be dissolved and that New York should "disrupt the bands" which bound it to upstate government and become a free city.

The *Daily News* was so fervent in its opposition to the "war against brethren" that in August its postal privilege was revoked. A month later it suspended publication. But in the spring of 1863, when Union fortunes seemed at low ebb, it reappeared with all its poisonous Copperhead colors intact. Even Greeley was writing about a possible negotiated peace. But the *Daily News,* when by draft the Union sought the only apparently possible reinforcement of its armies, set flame to the tinder of discontent.

"The people are notified," it said, "that one out of about two and a half of our citizens are to be brought off into Messrs. Lincoln & Company's charnelhouse. God forbid!"

Greeley and his *Tribune* were devoted to the welfare of the poor, but the *Daily News* made itself the poor's paper, circulating chiefly among the half-literate swarm in the tenements. Men and women, it was said, who had scarcely enough to eat found a penny for the paper. It not only gave them the most sensational news, it also carried the reports of lottery and policy drawings. Both Fernando and Benjamin were licensed gamblers. The listings of the lucky numbers were followed by the poor who knew that only the longest shot would ever pay them out of poverty. The *Daily News* did not have to prod them to hatred of this new draft lottery. Yet Carl Sandburg, in his study of Lincoln's life, concluded that "somebody had done some thinking, somebody had chosen a time when all the state guards the governor could scrape together had gone to Gettysburg."

At first the riots began with evidence of incitement and organization. Then the mob, captained only by chaos, armed with clubs and sticks, torches, and stolen rifles, frenzied with looted liquor, moved like a torrent through the streets. And down the avenues of the island it advanced in the July heat toward *The Tribune* building. Greeley, who had watched from his office window and moved through the angry crowd, looked still benign as he ate his dinner within hearing of its hooting in nearby Windust's Restaurant.

Dusk came and stones were flung at *The Tribune*'s windows. A sort of phalanx formed by brawlers from the Bowery and toughs from such slums as Hell's Kitchen and Cow Bay battered at the paper's doors. Gangs like the Dead Rabbits and the Roaches Guards of New York were now supplemented by the Plug Uglies and the Blood Tubs of Baltimore and the Schuykill Rangers of Philadelphia. But before the hoodlums had a chance to wreck the presses, help came.

Across the Square at *The Times* Henry J. Raymond had no pacifist scruples against arms, and in this situation he nursed no grudges. Greeley had given Raymond his first job at $8 a week. He had proved a brilliant assistant. But when the younger editor, no longer with *The Tribune,* began to challenge Greeley in press and politics he became to his old boss "a little villain." He felt now that what this mob required was "grape, and plenty of it."

From the Army he had obtained two mitrailleuses, a new-fangled breech-loading machine gun with a number of barrels. A helpful stockholder, Leonard Walter Jerome, grandfather of Sir Winston Churchill, manned one. Raymond was ready at the other; he had also armed his reporters and printers with Minie rifles. Seeing the center of the assault at *The Tribune*'s doors, he sent sixteen rifle-armed *Times* men through back streets to help embattled *Tribune* employees. Two hundred policemen from all parts of the city rushed into the Square with pistols cocked and nightsticks flailing. Three score of the mobsters were left lying in the Square when their companions scurried away.

Next day Greeley came back to the office through streets that were debris laden, acrid with the smoke of many fires, and crossed by barricades behind which rioters had fought the police. He was shocked to discover that his associates had made almost an arsenal of the *Tribune* building. He surveyed a howitzer, some bombs, other weapons ready for use in the editorial offices overlooking the Square.

"Take 'em away! Take 'em away! I don't want to kill anybody, and besides they're a damned sight more likely to go off and kill us!"

Fresh rioters were gathering outside. Reporters came with more stories of street battles between the mobs and soldiers who were being hurried in from the Gettysburg area. Unperturbed, Greeley walked through the crowds again. He listened to an address of Democratic Governor Horatio Seymour, who had recently said things about the federal government's mistreatment of citizens which might have served as incitement to the rioting. Now, urging order, the Governor spoke with sympathy rather than rebuke to the crowd.

Greeley stalked back to the battered *Tribune*. This time he only said he did not want to work in his editorial office with all those guns around him. So he took one of the never-enough battered chairs which the paper provided for reporters in its news rooms. Toward evening he started to go home, as was his custom in ordinary times, by horsecar. Reluctantly he let the excited Gay and others prevail on him to go in a private carriage.

More men of the thirteen regiments ordered from Gettysburg were arriving at the depots. Volunteer Specials, gentlemen who (some felt) got into action too late and tried to take too much credit, helped patrol the streets. "The Irish cattle," one of them said, "have had impressed on them a respect for order." That called for apology which was published in *The Tribune*: "The Irish in the police department have won the respect of good citizens. They nobly shot down their fellow countrymen and women."

Apparently nobody yet knows how many people were "nobly" or otherwise shot down. One of Greeley's biographers put the number at 400, but an historian of the slums from which the mobs emerged suggested that 2000 lives were lost in the tumult. The draft went on. But what the mob could not accomplish in open violence was still served in covert ways by politicians and editors like the Wood brothers with the aid of papers like the *Daily*

News. According to Sandburg, upwards of $5 million was appropriated by the municipality of New York for draft-evasion purposes. Of the 292,441 men whose names were drawn from the revolving drums, only 9880 were inducted.

The Tribune, though looking a little ramshackle, stood against the mob. And in it old Horace, though often doubtful of the capacity of Abe Lincoln in the White House, saw the triumph of his greatest cause. But even as the war advanced toward its glorious termination, the great crusades which Greeley had made in his life and his paper appeared almost an exercise in futility. Certainly the editor expressed some of his own fears when he wrote in December after the riots of the ceremonial hoisting of the Statue of Freedom to the dome of the completed Capitol in Washington. In *The Tribune* Greeley thought the statue might prove either "a mentor, a censor, a scoffer or a satirist," or perhaps "no more than a mocking memorial of fading traditions and of virtues which have grown antique."

Poverty still swarmed in the tenements. Even though William B. Astor was making a million dollars a year, he could not afford to provide toilets and running water for his teeming tenants. Labor unions, which Greeley had long supported, were weakening or broken, thanks to the continuing importation of freedmen to break strikes and depress wages. As the nation moved to victory and Grant held Lee immobilized in Virginia, *The Tribune* sent out reporters to describe the poverty in a New York which was helping build new ostentatious mansions on Fifth Avenue. At the war's end the Negroes were free but the old nation seemed torn almost beyond repair. Some politicians and businessmen were ready to keep it so.

And what of "Go West, Young Man," Greeley's best-known preachment? That had been optimistic advice to young men to go where they could be sure their capacities would be appreciated and their industry and energy rewarded. Now in Union victory, though Greeley favored transcontinental railroads, it was clear that the westward movement had become a part of the Big Barbecue. In it, sauced with corruption, railroads, promoters, and politicians were served a bounty which mocked Greeley's meaning. Crusades and the crusader were not menaced merely by the mob; Greeley had to reckon with rampant righteous indignation.

In advance it could not have seemed possible that this fact would be best demonstrated in Greeley's life in the case of Jefferson Davis, late President of the defeated Confederate States of America. As the war began the editor had proposed a large reward for the apprehension, trial, and execution under martial law of Davis. But among the things which troubled Greeley in the spring of 1867 was the treatment of the Confederate President. He had been captured within a month after the assassination of Lincoln. There was not the slightest evidence that he was implicated in that crime. Not even the most vengeful Yankees were prepared to hang all the Rebels—or even the leading ones. And while there were plenty of sour apple trees available, the government found it difficult to fashion a legal noose for Davis' neck. Nevertheless, without ever having been brought to trial, for nearly two years he had been kept a prisoner in Fortress Monroe, Virginia.

Greeley was sure that if the "shrewd and kind-hearted" Lincoln had lived he would have preferred that Davis be allowed to slip off into exile—a nuisance he didn't want on his hands. Also the editor suggested without too much compunction that when captured Davis "might have been forthwith tried by a drumhead Court-Martial, 'organized to convict,' found guilty, sentenced, and put to death." But, with others, Horace was more and more troubled about the endless imprisonment of Davis "with aggravations of harsh and (it seems) needless indignity" and without ever being brought to trial.

"Meantime," Greeley thought hopefully, "public sentiment had become more rational and discriminating."

So when the United States Circuit Court in Richmond finally agreed to free Davis under $100,000 bond, put up by a group of reliable citizens from all parts of the country, Greeley was in the court to sign. Joining with Greeley was a diverse company of men. One was Gerrit Smith, rich reformer, who as a longtime Abolitionist had backed John Brown in his raid on Harpers Ferry. Another was Cornelius Vanderbilt, whose name alone would have proved the financial responsibility of the bondsmen. Greeley, however, seemed the single target of resentment. The warmth of his greeting to Davis, whom he hardly knew, was exaggerated by angry critics. But there could be no exaggeration of the heat of the indignation against the editor concerned for a gesture of reunion and good will.

"I was quite aware," Greeley wrote later, "that what I did would be so represented as to alienate for a season some valued friends, and set against me the great mass of those who know little and think less; thousands even of those who rejoiced over Davis' release, nevertheless joining, full-voiced in the howl against me."

He could not have foreseen the dimensions of the outcry. Into the dilapidated-looking *Tribune* shop which Greeley himself called the "old rookery" poured furious letters, including thousands of subscription cancellations. Advance orders to the new volume of Greeley's *American Conflict* were withdrawn. Friends ignored him in the street, and in the business office of *The Tribune* stockholders—who owned more of the paper than he now did—were angrier than people outside. The old paper and its editor seemed more besieged than when the draft mobs seethed outside in Printing House Square.

At the height of the furor, he received a note bristling in its brevity. It was a call from thirty-six "stalwart" members of the Union League Club for a special meeting "for the purpose of considering the conduct of Horace Greeley, a member of the club, who has become a bondsman of Jefferson Davis, late chief officer of the Rebel Government."

The Union League could speak with power and authority. It had been organized in the January preceding the draft riots to put behind the cause of the Union "men of substance and standing." It was radical but exclusive. It included some undoubted idealists. Many of its members, leaders in business and society, had always thought Greeley pretty much a crank even when they recognized his effectiveness and his right to belong to any group devoted to the Union. Many of them had profited from the war; some of them were anxious to rake in more profits in the peace under the protection of the Republican Party. Certainly they welcomed no such moderation as might reflect a willingness to forget the bloody battles in the South—and on the streets of New York—both of which to them made the Democratic Party synonymous with the South and with treason.

Greeley received their note when he was most beset. It might have been a final blow. He made it the instrument not of defense but of defiance. He wrote not only for his elegant accusers in the club but also for the public, which included some who liked neither him nor the superior airs of other Union League members.

"Gentlemen:" he began in polite scrawl. He had, he said, received the note from "our ever-courteous President," notifying him of "a requisition" for his appearance at a meeting for the consideration of his conduct.

Then, behind the same smooth word *gentlemen,* he put down his words like blows.

"I shall not attend your meeting. . . . I do not recognize you as capable of judging, or even fully apprehending me. You evidently regard me as a weak sentimentalist, misled by a maudlin philosophy. I arraign you as narrowminded blockheads, who would like to be useful to a great and good cause, but don't know how. Your attempt to base a great, enduring party on the hate and wrath necessarily engendered by a bloody civil war, is as though you should attempt to plant a colony on an iceberg which had somehow drifted into a tropical ocean. I tell you here, out of a life earnestly devoted to the good of human kind, your children will select my going to Richmond and signing that bailbond as the wisest act, and will feel that it did more for freedom and humanity than all of you were competent to do, though you had lived to the age of Methuselah."

Then he flung back his answer as a challenge.

"I ask nothing of you, then, but that you proceed to your end by a direct, frank, manly way. Don't sidle off into a mild resolution of censure, but move the expulsion which you proposed, and which I deserve if I deserve any reproach whatever. All I care is, that you make this a square, stand-up fight, and record your

judgment by yeas and nays. I care not how few vote with me;
for I know that the latter will repent it in dust and ashes before
three years have passed.''

When the draft rioters were charging the doors of *The Tribune,* burning houses and damaging property, the home of the
Union League escaped without so much as a cracked window-
pane. But now its member Greeley had really sent a volley into
it. Greeley was not alone in thinking his letter worth printing.
So did many other papers. Even many of those who condemned
his act as bondsman approved the quality of his prose and the
position he took in it.

The challenged club met in solemn assembly on May 18, 1867.
Its hall was packed. Reporters gathered outside the locked doors.
From the noise they could hear and the facts they gathered from
departing members, the newsmen described the meeting as
''riotous,'' though no cops were called or any troops ordered
from Gettysburg to deal with it.

The Radicals who had initiated the proposed censure offered a
resolution which practically condemned Greeley of treason along
with Jeff Davis. In their mood they would have decorated one
sour apple tree with the remains of both. Then from Moderates
and other Radicals came amendment after amendment. All were
defeated. The unamended condemnation motion was put to the
vote. A shout of ''No'' ended it.

In their turn the Moderates proposed a resolution that ''there
is nothing in the action of Horace Greeley, relative to the bailing
of Jefferson Davis, that deserves censure.'' The fight began all
over again. It was after midnight when this motion, unamended,
was adopted. Greeley had won all he could have asked except the
one thing he had specifically requested. ''Unfortunately,'' said
the club's historians, ''the minutes do not record the number of
'Ayes' and 'Noes,' '' nor the names of the persons who cast such
votes.

Greeley had won another fight. And as victor he still looked as
cherubic and mild as he had when he arrived in New York as so
sloppy a young printer that his crusading predecessor had objected to his working in his shop of respectable journeymen.

Now, thirty-six years later, he was, thought the consciously superior E. L. Godkin, editor of the *Nation*, still a bumpkin with "a hopelessly peaceable face." It was difficult to see how so mild-appearing a scarecrow of a man could be so often the center of storm.

"To see him walking up Broadway," Godkin said, "you would take him for a small farmer of the Quaker persuasion, who had lost all the neatness of the sect, but had appropriated in his disposition a double portion of meekness."

That was a mask for courage he had needed many times and would require again.

11

Mr. Jones and the Tiger

On September 20, 1870, startled citizens read and then reread a long editorial in *The New York Times*. Its punch was packed into one paragraph.

We should like to have a treatise from Mr. Tweed in the art of growing rich in as many years as can be counted on the fingers of one hand.... You might begin with nothing and in five or six years you can boast of your ten millions. How was it done? We wish Mr. Tweed... would tell us. The general public says there is foul play. They are under the impression that monstrous abuses of their funds, corrupt bargains with railroad sharpers, outrageous plots to swindle the general community, account for the vast fortunes heaped up by men who sprang up like mushrooms.

In the bulging city, where some were so suddenly rich and many others liked the spectacle of such possibility, the surprising thing about the passage was not seeing the words, which almost everybody had been saying privately, in print. More amazing was the man behind them, George Jones, publisher of the paper. His was a name so commonplace as to be easily forgotten, and as a figure in American journalism he has been neglected. Elmer Davis, historian of *The New York Times*, found that less had been written about George Jones, during or after his lifetime, than about any other newspaper proprietor of the period. That would have suited George Jones.

When *The Times'* attack on Boss Tweed began, Mr. Jones was a conservative, ponderous-appearing gentleman. An ample beard seemed to mark rather than mask his mildness. He peered at the world around him through the thick lenses of gold-rimmed spectacles. He liked the company of successful and not always too scrupulous men in the better clubs. Certainly, in September 1870, he seemed the last man likely to upset a corrupt and contented metropolis and to take as his target William Marcy Tweed.

Tweed, Sachem of Tammany Hall, was boss of city and county. In Albany the Governor was his political creature. Bankers bowed to him. Poor men praised his charities. Behind an air of benevolence he embodied the Tammany Tiger. That cat was no kitten. Almost anyone could have told George Jones that behind its purring—its parades and picnics—it was a man-eater. As *The Times'* publisher quietly entered his sixtieth year, he set out on his safari in the jungles of power and politics of America's Gilded Age.

Mr. Jones had become editorial director of *The Times* by accident. He was probably the least conspicuous figure at the funeral of his partner, the brilliant, dashing Henry J. Raymond. At the funeral in Green-Wood Cemetery in Brooklyn in June 1869, among the pallbearers was Greeley, whose competitive *Tribune* Raymond had helped protect in the draft riots. Another who attended the coffin was James Watson Webb. He strutted even in the graveyard as the elegant "Brimstone" Webb he had been in his younger, dueling, cowhide-swinging days as editor of *The Courier and Enquirer.*

Others present recalled the first roaring days of newspaper competition for mass circulation. Raymond's death seemed to mark a sort of mellowing pause in current journalism. James Gordon Bennett, of the lively snarling *Herald,* had retired two years before in increasing feebleness. The second Bennett had not yet matured in eccentricity. William Cullen Bryant of the New York *Evening Post,* saddened by his wife's death, was relaxing as editor and seeking to rid himself of depression by translating Homer. Certainly no newspaper explosion was suggested when Raymond's death brought Jones to responsibility for the policies as well as the profits of *The New York Times.*

Raymond had been the dramatic journalist. Even his death, had later gossip been gathered, might have made sensational copy. Found dying at his doorway of a cerebral hemorrhage, it was reported that he had been left there by companions who thought he was drunk. Then there were whispers that the stroke had been brought on by "an emotional crisis" involving a celebrated young actress. No such dangers or whispers threatened Jones.

Jones was nine years older than his departed partner. He had been safely, happily married for thirty years to a sensible woman from Troy, New York. Solemnly he read the plaudits for his partner, whose charm and powers were not forgotten in the grave. Greeley doubted editorially "whether this country has known a journalist superior to Raymond." The erudite Edwin L. Godkin, then editor of the *Nation,* declared that Raymond's *Times* had brought the American press "nearer the newspaper of the good time coming than any other in existence." Even the serpent-tongued *Herald,* while taking credit for the kind of news journalism which Raymond had perfected, said that *"The Times* will go on as before."

That seemed highly doubtful. The dash, the drive, the drama

had departed with Raymond. There was little to suggest that
Jones was more than the dependable business-office drone. He
had had no editorial experience in his life. He had no literary
talents. He had been a grocer's boy when, in Poultney, Vermont,
he had first known Horace Greeley as printer's devil on the East
Poultney *Northern Spectator*. Later Greeley had asked him to
become his partner, in 1841, in the founding of *The Tribune*. But
with less money than even Greeley then had, he took a job in the
business office instead. There he met Raymond, whom Greeley
was reluctantly paying $8 a week.

While Raymond rose as a newspaperman, first with Greeley
and then on Webb's *Courier and Enquirer*, Jones moved to Albany, where he made money as a "free banker" dealing in the
fluctuating and varied currencies of the time. Jones and Raymond met in the New York capital and talked of an idea they
had discussed earlier of starting a newspaper of their own. They
heard rich reports of Greeley's profits. Raymond was becoming
restive under Webb, who never was happy with his subordinates
long, nor they with him. And Jones' profits as a banker were
threatened by a proposed law to "reduce the redemption rate
on country money." The law was enacted.

With the help of another banker, Edward B. Wesley, in whose
office Jones had desk space, $70,000 of the $100,000 capital they
sought was secured, largely on the basis of Raymond's reputation. That was opulence compared to the shoestring on which
Greeley had started *The Tribune* or the "plank across two flour
barrels" upon which Bennett had produced the first issue of the
Herald. Between the sensationalism of the *Herald* and the sanctimonious semisocialism of *The Tribune*, *The Times* announced
in its prospectus that "its main reliance for all improvement,
personal, social and political, will be upon Christianity and Republicanism. . . ." Its determination was to be "the best and
cheapest family newspaper in the United States."

Enough readers believed it was. But the paper's prosperity
reflected Raymond's performance. Jones, as the first big newspaper publisher in editorial command, initially regarded himself as
a sort of trustee for the Raymond family, which owned thirty-
four of the hundred shares of *Times* stock. Jones himself held

only thirty. It soon became evident, however, that young Henry Warren Raymond, who had graduated from Yale the year his father died, was not qualified to take his father's place.

Jones began as caretaker, not crusader. Indeed, if he had wished to strike at the corruption all around him in the year after Raymond died, he could have been both embarrassed and encumbered. One of the directors of *The Times* was James B. Taylor, Boss Tweed's partner in the New York Printing Company, one of the mechanisms by which Tweed drew off his loot. The New York Printing Company did most of the public printing as well as that of railroads, ferries, and insurance companies which wanted to stay in business in New York. At one time it had more than 2000 employees, all busily setting type for the power and glory of Tweed and his favored friends.

Taylor died in September 1870. Perhaps it was only coincidence that *The Times* began its editorial attack that same month. At any rate, the assault was long overdue. An historian of *The Times* reported that every newspaperman in town had long known that the Tweed Ring was "up to its hairy elbows in municipal thievery." So did elegant gentlemen whose carriages took them to the most exclusive clubs. Already Jay Gould and Jim Fisk, Jr., had found Tweed and the Tammany judges he controlled useful in looting the Erie Railroad and other properties. More respectable rich men were sharing behind the scenes.

It was time to tackle the Tiger. A younger Tweed, rising in politics as head of the volunteer fire company Americus No. 6, had taken that beast as his symbol. Its head was painted on the fire engine. In derision and defiance, it was to be the Tammany symbol ever after. Jones went after it. His chief aides in the fight were not native to the American jungle. His editor was a brilliant Englishman, Louis J. Jennings, who had learned his business on papers in London and India, and had come to the United States as Washington correspondent of the London *Times*. Jennings had a gift for the sharp word and the barbed phrase. Working with him as reporter was John Foord, a Perthshire Scot, who could array facts in telling fashion.

Jennings began with his request for a Tweed treatise on how to get rich quick without any visible honest means of accumula-

tion. Tweed's accumulation, however, was visible to every naked
eye. *The Times* undertook to illuminate it even for the blind.
Only a few years earlier Tweed had spent his last dollar fighting
his way to power in Tammany. In power, he quickly began to
recompense himself. He was a lawyer with little legal training,
but he paid almost no attention to the law he knew, and collected
huge fees for legal services. Gould and Fisk got their money's
worth when they paid him more than $100,000 for help in loot-
ing the Erie Railroad. Money rolled in from the New York
Printing Company's business. Kickbacks flowed from public employes and contractors. Mr. Tweed was glad to help the city and
county get the marble for their public buildings. He picked up
$40,000 in stock on the Brooklyn Bridge project. By such thrifty
and industrious methods, by 1867 he had provided for his transition from the lower East Side to a mansion in Murray Hill just
off Fifth Avenue. He had a glittering yacht. He and his family
moved in custom-made carriages behind prancing horses. Police
and plutocrats saluted when they passed.

In the midst of such riches Tweed, as Meyer Berger said in his
The Story of The New York Times 1851–1951, was only "mildly
startled" by *The Times'* attack. True, *The Times* might only
have been flexing its Republican muscles for the upcoming election. But the Grand Sachem's reaction suggests no mildness. A
month after Jennings' impertinent questioning a mass meeting
was held in and around Tammany Hall to demonstrate faith in
Tweed and his associates. Perhaps the thousands in the streets
included the "band of thugs" *The Times* said it was fighting.

On the platform sat Horatio Seymour, former Governor of
New York and recent Democratic candidate for the Presidency
against Ulysses S. Grant. Beside him was current Governor John
T. Hoffman, Tweed's creature who gave the Boss control of state
as well as city. The hit speaker of the evening was Jim Fisk, who
had impudently survived the Black Friday on the Stock Market
which he and Gould had brought on the preceding year. To a
cheering multitude he announced that though he had never voted
the Democratic ticket, now for Tweed he would vote it happily
and often and bring 25,000 men with him to vote it, too. Most
remarkable figure on the platform, however, was the then chair-

man of the Democratic State Committee, the rich railroad lawyer
Samuel J. Tilden, who later was to get—and deserve—much
credit for Tweed's prosecution.

This monster meeting was not Tweed's only quick answer to
The Times' campaign. In October he called in six of New
York's richest respectables: John Jacob Astor, Moses Taylor,
Marshall O. Roberts, George K. Sistare, E. D. Brown, and Edward Schell. They were shown city accounts by Comptroller
Richard ("Slippery Dick") Connolly. And they solemnly
emerged with the announcement that "the account books . . . are
faithfully kept. . . . We have come to the conclusion and certify
that the financial affairs of the city . . . are administered in a
correct and faithful manner."

It was later charged that in return for this courteous cooperation these gentlemen were relieved of taxes. On the other hand, it
was alleged that they were threatened with a sharp increase if
they did not make the report. Certainly they were a significant
company in the situation. It was, historians have concluded,
difficult to believe that any of these men were "unaware of the
gigantic frauds then being committed." Astor, the third of that
opulent name, was noted for his acquisitiveness as an investor in
real estate. He preferred for whole blocks of his houses to burn
down rather than pay insurance on them. Moses Taylor, banker
and railroad investor, was the son of a confidential agent of the
first Astor and himself had become a partner of Cyrus W. Field,
remembered for his part in laying the Atlantic Cable. Cyrus was
also brother of David Dudley Field, later Tweed's chief lawyer.
Edward Schell, banker, was one of four rich brothers, the most
prominent of whom, Augustus, succeeded Tweed as head of
Tammany.

Jones on *The Times* may have taken particularly bitter note of
the fact that among the "whitewashers" was Marshall O. Roberts, one of the owners of *The New York Sun*. Roberts' activities
in chartering and selling steamships to the Union during the
recent Civil War constituted profiteering which set a pattern for
the "greedy" or "shoddy" postwar years.

None of this helped Jones of *The Times*. The respectables had
spoken. Further, prodded by Tweed, big advertisers and smaller

ones pulled out of the paper. Questions were raised about the
title to the land on which *The Times* building stood. Other newspapers, including *The Sun* (part-owned by Marshall Roberts),
scolded *The Times* for slandering the good and the mighty. *The
New York World* demanded, "Why does that journal [*The
Times*] so stultify itself?" Jones accepted the cold shoulders
turned to him by Wall Street men in his clubs. He took his
advertising losses. He told Jennings and Foord to fight. They
did.

It did little good for Jennings to point out that reputable
accountants declared that it would have taken three months for
the respectables really to have examined the books they had approved after a few hours. Perhaps it even hurt for *The Times* to
charge that such gentlemen were guilty of a breach of faith
toward the public. Tammany swept the city in the elections of
1870.

Jones looked at the results through his thick lenses. He ordered his editors to hit again and harder.

Jennings wrote: "No Caliph, Khan or Caesar has risen to
power or opulence more rapidly than Tweed I. Ten years ago
this monarch was pursuing the humble occupation of chairmaker
in an obscure street in this city. He now rules the State as
Napoleon ruled France, or the Medici ruled Florence.... His
immediate personal followers are a more despicable and unclean
herd than has ever surrounded the paltriest Asiatic despot....
And there he sits today, pocketing our money and laughing at
us."

Foord carefully prepared an article about Tweed's payroll
padding. Within six weeks the Boss had put 1300 new names on
the city rolls. With a less objective attitude than *The Times* later
came to cherish among its newsmen, he described them as "row-
dies, vagabonds, sneak thieves, gamblers and shoulder-hitters."
Tweed, he said, bred adherents on a diet of whiskey and black
cigars. More work was made for hoodlums by painting park
lamps on rainy days so that the work would have to be done over
again. Taxpayers, he wrote, were paying the bill to support the
criminal population in idleness and debauchery.

Tammany had more than toughs behind it. *The Sun,* then

under the editorship of Charles A. Dana, sneered at *The Times* and slandered its editor.

"The decline of *The New York Times* in everything that entitles a newspaper to respect and confidence, has been rapid and complete. Its present editor, who was dismissed from the London *Times* for improper conduct and untruthful writing, has sunk into a tedious monotony of slander and disregard of truth, and black-guard vituperation. . . . Let *The Times* change its course, send off Jennings, and get some gentleman and scholar in his place, and become again an able and high-toned paper. Thus it may escape from ruin. Otherwise it is doomed."

The situation did indeed look dark. Jennings was damned not only because he was an Englishman but also because his wife was an actress—the word, of course, being used to suggest an older profession. He had never been fired by the London *Times*. Later his reputation in Britain was to be demonstrated by his election to Parliament. Now, as he wrote with vivid vituperation, he had the steady, courageous support of Jones, who stood to lose most in the doom prophesied by the *Sun*.

The words were written by Jennings but the determination behind them came from Jones when *The Times* said: "Forebearance has no place in a fight like this. We are battling with a band of thugs supported by the freebooters of the press. It would be worse than useless to go into such a fight armed only with rose water."

Nevertheless, *The Times* needed luck as well as acid ink. Death provided it. The Grim Reaper had seemed almost a welcome visitor when, in 1870, he removed a *Times* director who was a Tweed partner. In January 1871, a fatality served the paper again. In a blinding snowstorm a sleigh pulled by a $10,000 horse collided with another at Harlem Lane and 138th Street. In the accident James Watson, the County Auditor, was fatally injured. That made only an insignificant news item for *The Times*. The aftermath provided the paper's biggest news of the year.

Tweed made his fatal mistake in appointing Watson's successor. The job went to a man who at the time was working secretly for a Tammany insurgent, former Sheriff James

O'Brien. Head of the Young Democrats, O'Brien was completing a prosperous term in his fee-paid office. He wanted a bigger
cut of the graft and also, it was said, even Tweed's place as
Grand Sachem of Tammany Hall. O'Brien's grasping hand was
restrained, but through his agent O'Brien had his hand on the
County Auditor's incriminating accounts.

Evidently Tweed was fearful that *The Times* had more to tell.
Early in 1871 Henry Raymond's widow, who held thirty-four
Times shares, asked Jones for a general accounting. He gave it to
her. But soon afterward a *Times* editor passing through City
Hall chanced to hear a snatch of conversation between two of
Tweed's aides.

"I think that deal with Mrs. Raymond will go through."

The remark illuminated rumors that Gould, Tweed's old associate in the Erie Railroad and other matters, and Cyrus Field,
brother of the lawyer who was to be Tweed's own chief attorney,
were eager to help the Boss by the secret purchase of control of
The Times.

In March Jones fully realized the danger. But this time,
standing visible and vigorous before his writers, he wrote on the
editorial page that *"No money"*—he put the words in italics—
could persuade him to sell any of his *Times* stock to Tammany
"or to any man associated with it or indeed to any person or
party whatever until this struggle is fought out." He added that
if he lost control he would "immediately start another journal to
denounce these frauds which are so great a scandal to the City."
In the continuing crusade he would have Jennings and Foord
by his side.

Tension mounted. Quite possibly Tammany heard that Sheriff
O'Brien had offered his incriminating figures to the New York
Sun, which declined to touch them. There were rumors that he
approached other papers. It was still a surprise when on a hot
night in early July the Sheriff came casually into Jennings'
office in *The Times* on Printing House Square. *Times* historians
report the conversation.

O'Brien mopped his sweating forehead. "Hot night," he
said. In an envelope he carried fiscal dynamite. He handled it
uneasily.

"Warm," Jennings agreed.

O'Brien allowed that *The Times* had had a tough fight.

"Still have," the editor admitted.

"I said, '*had*,' " the insurgent Sheriff announced. With what a *Times* chronicler described as "a damp, bediamonded fist," O'Brien thumped Jennings' desk.

"Here's the proof to back up all *The Times* has charged. They're copied right out of the city ledgers."

Still sweating, O'Brien got up and left. Only after he was gone did Jennings eagerly snatch open the envelope.

The Times was ready to move with roaring confidence now. But a frightened Tweed and his friends were moving, too. Mrs. Raymond had inherited the stock, not the paper's tradition. Separated from the former editor, she had lived abroad before she was reconciled with him, more in form than in fact, shortly before his death. Her eldest son lacked the talents to become his father's successor. She had three younger children. Gentlemen like Gould and Field had ready money.

Gossip, conjecture, and intuition warned Jones of the danger. He wired Colonel Edwin B. Morgan, one of the original stockholders in the paper. Morgan, then sixty-five, was a founder of the Wells Fargo Express which brought him wealth as it roared to California with stages and ponies. Now he rushed to the rescue. From retirement in Aurora, New York, he hurried to the city. Jones told him the situation.

"The old Colonel," said an Irishman who was a *Times* office boy then, "was angry right down to his woolen socks."

Next day, armed with his checkbook, Morgan called on Mrs. Raymond. But Jones and his writing assistants did not wait to learn the result of his visit. They began to let loose the O'Brien ammunition on July 8. Another disgruntled Tammany man added to their store of evidence. Jennings began the disclosures.

"We lay before our readers this morning," *The Times* said, "a chapter of municipal rascality which in any other city but New York would bring down upon the heads of its authors such a storm of public indignation as would force them to a speedy accountability before the bar of a criminal court, or compel them to take refuge in flight and perpetual exile."

Pardonably the editor gloated a little.

"We apprehend that no one will complain of a lack of facts and specifications in the articles to which we now call the reader's attention; and that not even *The Tribune* or any other of the eighteen daily and weekly papers that have been gagged by Ring patronage will be able to find an excuse for ignoring the startling record presented here, on the ground that it is not sufficiently definite."

This specific sneer at *The Tribune* of Horace Greeley, who regarded himself as master of reform, and Whitelaw Reid, who had become *Tribune* managing editor, could not have pleased them. Other editors were more surprised than applauding. New York's editors and New York's readers were amazed at the articles by Foord which followed. That hard-hitting Scot listed small saloons and shabby stables for which the city was paying enormous rentals as city armories. The charges for "repairs" and furnishings were even more staggering. Shocking, too, were the prices for arms for the National Guard paid to a Tweed firm.

The Times was in no hurry. Its pace was as ponderous as Jones appeared to be. It waited ten days to release more news about the ramshackle armories. Then it promised to prove that not less than $90 million a year passed through the hands of Tweed's stooges "and that they and their fellow conspirators steal a large part of the money." Two chief aides, handling the warrants on the new County Court House, it bluntly described in its headline as TWO THIEVES.

The Times not only had the facts; Jones had won its security. On the same day the paper spoke of the TWO THIEVES and indicated it was ready to uncover forty thieves or more, it carried an announcement by Publisher Jones:

It has been repeatedly asserted that the Raymond shares were likely to fall into the possession of the New York Ring, and it is in order to assure our friends of the groundlessness of all such statements that we make known the actual facts.

The price paid in ready money for the shares in question was $375,000. Down to the time of Mr. Raymond's death the shares had never sold for more than $6,000 each. Mr. Morgan has now paid upwards of $11,000 each for thirty-four of them, and this transaction is the most conclusive answer which could be furnished to the absurd rumors sometimes circulated to the effect that the course taken by *The New York Times* toward Tammany leaders had depreciated the value of the property.

In terms of its value or danger to desperate Tammany leaders and their friends, *The Times* was soaring. Its stories about the phantom armories went on to show that the fraudulent repair bills amounted to almost a million. The "cost" of carpentry came to $431,164, plastering $197,330.24, plumbing $142,329. Chairs, for which Tweed as a onetime chairmaker seemed to have a special fondness, amounted to $170,729. These sums, *The Times* said, went "to meet the expense of the Ring in the matter of fast horses, conservatories, handsome houses and newspaper editors."

The Times was especially sharp in its comments on the other papers which either defended Tammany or long delayed forthright attack upon it. The paper's contempt for its journalistic contemporaries in this fight seems justified. Indeed, almost the only effective and consistent periodical support Jones and his editors received in their fight was from *Harper's Weekly*—particularly its great political cartoonist, Thomas Nast.

The young artist's war pictures were so effective that near the close of the war Lincoln declared, "Thomas Nast has been our best recruiting sergeant." He showed little of Lincoln's charity in his cartoons of the South in Reconstruction. But he saw clearly that not all was pretty in the Reconstruction period in the North where native civilians and not outside politicians and soldiers were in control.

The Times had prepared the way when Nast turned his pencil on Tammany, but those not moved by figures of looting were stirred by his tough satire of the looters. He made Tammany the tiger—and the man-eater. His caricatures of Tweed were devastating, yet so accurate that the Boss was later identified as a fugitive in Spain from one of them. Nast drew him with a great belly and a moneybag head. He aroused laughter and indignation. In the whole Tweed tale Nast emerges as the best-known figure of the crusade.

Yet behind him, as behind Jennings and Foord, was a new type of fighting publisher. Perhaps there was a closer relationship between *The Times* and *Harper's Weekly* than has generally been noted. Meyer Berger, in his history of *The Times*, wrote that in 1856, under owners Raymond and Jones, Fletcher Harper, Jr., was publisher of the paper. Fletcher Harper, who had established the *Weekly*, was sixty-five at the time of the Tweed fight. A contemporary of Jones, he showed the same sort of stamina. Harper & Brothers, publishers, were vulnerable to political attack. That gave Tammany its target when Nast's cartoons pilloried it.

When politicians retaliated on Harper's textbook contract, the book firm wavered, though not for long.

"Gentlemen," Fletcher Harper is reported to have said in rather strange formality to associates composed principally of his brothers, "you know where I live. When you are ready to continue the fight against these scoundrels, send for me. Meantime, I shall find a way to do it alone."

His brothers stood by him, and all backed Nast. Nor was that stubborn sharp-penciled Bavarian to be shaken though his life was threatened. He was contemptuous when a Tammany emissary came to him to say that he had great talent and some hundreds of thousands of dollars could be made available for his art studies abroad. Such generosity was declined. He was, Nast said, going to be too busy "for some time getting a gang of thieves behind the bars."

The drumbeat of *The Times'* disclosures continued. Astounding item after astounding item appeared. The figures *The Times* had obtained showed that the total for repairs and furniture for the new County Court House in 1869 and 1870 amounted to

$5,663,646.83. One obscure carpenter, C. S. Miller, was supposedly paid $360,751.61 for one month's work. The Tweed government paid $2,870,464.06 in the same years for plastering—of this $394,614.57 was listed as paid to one plasterer, Andrew J. Garvey.

"As C. S. Miller is the luckiest of carpenters," *The Times* said, "so Andrew J. Garvey is clearly the Prince of Plasterers. His good fortune surpasses anything in the Arabian Nights."

Obviously the plasterer and the carpenter were not getting all this money. A detailed supplement of *The Times,* issued in 500,000 copies, was grabbed up by eager readers. Reporters went looking for the workmen supposed to have received vast sums. They had disappeared. And as the election of 1871 approached Tweed men were frantic.

"If I were twenty to thirty years younger," Tweed is supposed to have said about this time, "I would kill George Jones with my own bare hands."

The hairy fist no longer sufficed. Instead Tammany sought in Jones the greed that had bred corruption not only among politicians and plasterers but among some plutocrats—even newspapermen, as *The Times* kept saying. One afternoon while the disclosures were appearing, a lawyer who had offices in the *Times* building asked Jones to come to see him for a few minutes. When Jones went he met not only the lawyer but also City Comptroller "Slippery Dick" Connolly.

"I do not care to see this man," Jones told the attorney.

But Connolly begged, "For God's sake, Mr. Jones, let me say a word or two. Listen for just a moment. Wouldn't it be worth, say, five million dollars, to let up on this thing? Five million dollars, sir."

Jones admitted later that he was appalled at the sum. But he shook his head in distaste and disgust. Connolly persisted.

"With that money, Mr. Jones, you could go to Europe— anywhere— You could live like a prince.... You could——"

The publisher's eyes were cold within the frames of his spectacles.

"True, sir," he broke in. "All true. But I should know while

I lived like a prince, that I was a rascal. I cannot consider your offer—or any offer. *The Times* will continue to publish the facts.''

It did. But afterward Jones looked back on the incident with some humor as well as indignation.

''I don't think the devil will ever make a higher bid for me,'' he said.

But now the respectables who had stayed silent so long were emerging in the armor of righteous civic indignation. On September 4, 1871, a few days short of a year after *The Times* had begun its lonely crusade, a great meeting was held in the Cooper Union. Joseph H. Choate, conservative Republican and lifelong foe of Tammany, served as chairman of the committee on resolutions which called for the creation of a Committee of Seventy to clean up the corruption. The active figure in leading the cleansing job was Samuel J. Tilden, Democratic State Chairman, who less than a year before had sat beside Tweed on the platform at the rally showing confidence in his municipal government. Tilden's later nomination as Democratic candidate for President in 1876 was based in large part on his successful prosecution of the Tweed Ring.

Tammany was badly beaten in the elections of 1871 soon afterward. Strangely, however, in his home district, where there was much affection for him, Boss Tweed was re-elected to the state senate. But at noon on December 16, 1871, one of the Boss' old friends and appointees, Sheriff Matthew T. Brennan, came nervously into Tweed's richly furnished office. The Sheriff twisted his hat. He laughed in embarrassment. Then he touched Tweed on the shoulder.

''You're the man I'm after, I guess,'' he said.

Tweed went with him, though not to jail but to a suite in the Metropolitan Hotel, which he owned. Next morning a friendly judge was found who fixed bail. Tweed's fixing days were dwindling. He still had money for a magnificent array of attorneys headed by David Dudley Field, described by the *Dictionary of American Biography* as a ''law reformer,'' and including young Elihu Root, then in his twenties, who later became U.S. Senator and Secretary of State.

Tweed's lawyers' fees cost him more than half a million, but the attorneys got him off with a $250 fine and twelve months in the Tombs and on Blackwell's Island. Then, while under $10,000 bond in connection with a civil suit, gentle jailors let him visit his Madison Avenue mansion. He slipped out a back door. He hid while waiting for a secretive schooner. In disguise as a common sailor he made his way to Spain. Identified there, he was brought home, a tired, disheveled old man though only fifty-three.

In 1876, he pled only for "the shortest and most efficient manner in which I can yield an unqualified surrender." He submitted freely to all sorts of questioning, but nobody could ever quite figure out how much had been stolen. Estimates varied from $50 million to $200 million. Tweed himself did not know.

He died suddenly in prison. Though he thought, as he lay dying, that he had tried to do good by everyone and that God would receive him, moralistic preachers held his sins high. Edwin L. Godkin, editor of *The Nation,* noted that poor people in New York felt that he was less a villain than "the victim of rich men's malice."

"The odium heaped on him in the pulpits last Sunday does not exist in the lower stratum of New York society...."

And much of the higher stratum had found him odious only after *The Times,* with little support and no applause, uncovered the civic danger which Tweed only symbolized. He was buried in Green-Wood Cemetery, where Raymond's burial had attracted so many of the leaders of the press little more than half a dozen years before.

Lewis Jennings had already left his post as *Times* editor when Tweed died. So he was not editor when the great election contest between Tilden and Rutherford B. Hayes had its inception in *The Times* newsroom. There was a final irony in this story. When other papers were conceding the election of Tilden, who admitted he had killed the Tiger, John Reid, managing editor of *The Times,* persuaded the Republican National Committee to claim victory for Hayes. George Jones seems to have had no part in that incident in newspaper history. It led to what Democrats called the "crime of '76," by which Carpetbag governments

in the South helped national Republican leaders steal the
Presidency of the United States. In comparison perhaps Tweed
was a piker.

George Jones was already almost forgotten. He did not cry for
more credit than he got for bringing Tweed down. Quiet and
retiring, it was hardly noticed in his lifetime and has been little
remembered since that he was the prototype of the modern
business-office newspaper proprietor. Some moderns have not
recognized all the necessary qualities of courage and determination which he put into that pattern. Certainly few later understood George Jones' pride that while he controlled *The Times* no
man was ever asked to subscribe to it or advertise in it.

He went his own way with editors of his own choosing. That
brought him troubles as well as satisfaction. Respectables in the
Union League Club, of which he was very fond, turned their
backs on him again when the Republican *Times* bolted to support
Grover Cleveland in 1884. Again subscriptions and advertising
were canceled. But Jones advanced happily and quietly into
honored old age.

12

Pistols and Palmettos

Mark Twain was not strictly autobiographical when he described the journalism of his youth south of the Ohio—and Potomac— but the humor in his exaggeration about the bloody business of editing in Tennessee was related to hard reality. Writing in the first person, he described the instructions calmly given to a young editorial aspirant as his chief left to meet company at dinner:

> Jones will be here at 3—cowhide him. Gillespie will call earlier, perhaps—throw him out of the window. Ferguson will be along about 4—kill him. That will be

all for today, I believe. If you have any odd time, you
might write a blistering article on the police—give the
chief inspector rats. The cowhides are under the table;
weapons in the drawer—ammunition there in the
corner—lint and bandages up there in the pigeon holes.
In case of accident go to Lancet, the surgeon, downstairs. He advertises—we take it out in trade.

Editorial duties were not generally that violent even in the
South, where the pistol seems to have remained longest as the
essential adjunct of the pen. Yet tradition says five successive
editors of the *Sentinel* in Vicksburg, Mississippi, came to violent
deaths. And in South Carolina in the decades after the Civil
War much turbulence attended editorial efforts to end personal
encounters and riotous violence.

Captain Francis W. Dawson was a strange individual for this
enterprise. Born Austin John Reeks in London of an aristocratic
Catholic family which had come on hard times through the father's speculations, he was well educated by relatives. He made
the Continental tour essential to a gentleman's education. His
baritone voice was trained for a possible singing career. Before
he was twenty he was a promising playwright appearing about
the theaters in an impressive Inverness cape. He was boyish still,
with fair complexion, light blue eyes, and curly hair. Not even a
cigar between his lips made him look like a warrior when, much
against his father's will, he undertook to fight the Yankees in
the Civil War.

"They'll hang you," said his father. "No Reeks has ever
been hung."

So to avoid that danger to the name young Austin became
Frank and as Francis Warrington Dawson got himself aboard a
Rebel ship at Southampton which had run the Federal blockade.
He donned the kind of dress described in Frederick Marryat's
novel *Mr. Midshipman Easy*. He also procured what he supposed
to be standard Southern equipment, a fifteen-inch Bowie knife.
He had his troubles in the forecastle. His big sea chest was looted
by tough sailors. Storm tossed the ship. But by the time he
reached Beaufort, North Carolina, by his evident education and

gentlemanly manners he had so impressed his officers that he was made a master's mate in the Confederate Navy.

The action he saw in the Navy was too tame for him. He shifted to the Army of Northern Virginia. Rising from private to captain of ordnance, he fought in a dozen important battles, was three times wounded, once captured. He made friends, including a young naval officer, James Morris Morgan, important in his later career. By his own accounts, he met and served under great Confederate generals and became acquainted with the fairest and richest of the Virginia gentry. War's end found him a twenty-five-year-old veteran with a postage stamp and the change from a five-dollar bill. Characteristically he spent that on oranges and cigars. Some defeated Southerners were leaving the South. He decided to stay.

Dawson and a friend tried to start a small weekly. Federal soldiers seized the type they hoped to use. He worked as a bookkeeper. But his future was fashioned when he got a job as reporter on the revived Richmond *Examiner* which had grown famous under editors ever ready to defend their words with their bullets. The "smell of battle" was still on Dawson's clothes, it was said, when he joined the paper. And soon he was given the "honor" of serving as second to the paper's new editor, Henry Rives Pollard, in the Virginia editorial tradition of cowhidings and dueling which he maintained. In one duel Dawson stood beside Pollard in the rotunda of the Virginia capitol. No damage was done except that a shot intended for the editor of the rival Richmond *Enquirer* hit a statue of George Washington and took the tassel off his sculptured cane. Hair—and perhaps some hide—was lost when Dawson stood by with a pistol to prevent any interference in a brawl between his editor and E. P. Brooks, a *New York Times* correspondent, in a Richmond hotel. Pollard swung his whip. Brooks grabbed Pollard's beard. The South triumphed when Pollard pushed Brooks' head through a panel that fronted the clerk's desk.

Much of Dawson's record of his Richmond days, however, is more idyllic than explosive. He helped gentle ladies organize the first Confederate memorial association. He was engaged to and "unceremoniously jilted" by pretty, witty Mary Haxall, the daughter of a rich Orange Courthouse planter. In a longer lasting relationship, he met Bartholomew R. Riordan, an older newspaperman who had worked on the fire-eating Charleston *Mercury* during the war. Riordan, soon to return to the South Carolina city, talked of starting a paper there, including Dawson in his plans. And when Dawson, after a futile foray into the express business, was jobless again, Riordan got him a job on the *Mercury* in Charleston. Riordan, already there, was working on the old *Courier.*

Still under military supervision, Charleston journalism was in the doldrums when Dawson arrived in November 1866. At the war's end, not merely grass but bushes grew in the city's streets. Still the young Englishman found much to charm him in the proud port from which, as Yankee reporter Whitelaw Reid said, gentlemen had dashed into war as into a waltz. There were shell-scarred buildings now and many women in black. There were fears of black Reconstruction backed by military force. Yet under the palmetto trees youth was gay and charming even in catastrophe. And some, young and old, were still hot-headed.

The brief winter turned into luxuriant spring. There seemed no question about the young stranger's welcome acceptance in the old city. As soon as he obtained his American citizenship, his application for membership in the Survivors Association was both endorsed and blessed by Generals Longstreet, Fitzhugh Lee, and others. Less than a year after he arrived he married the delicate Virginia Fourgeaud, daughter of an old French family. General Robert E. Lee, when he visited cheering Charleston, Dawson wrote, granted a special interview at which the Captain presented her to his old frail commander.

But all was not tenderness, recognition, and romance. Dawson did not get along too well with Colonel R. B. Rhett, Jr., editor of the *Mercury,* who still breathed a sort of secessionist fire in the ruins of secession. Later Dawson said Rhett required him to assume responsibility under the *code duello* for all the *Mercury* said. Rhett then sneered that Dawson had been little more than a clipper of other papers. Their antagonism grew when Dawson and Riordan, in 1868, bought with borrowed money the faltering Charleston *News.* Dawson set out to rebuild the battered city.

Far from being dead, he argued, Georgia, Alabama, Louisiana, Mississippi, and Texas were only the "back country of Charleston." The port was "the Liverpool of America."

Dawson swiftly claimed climbing circulation. Rhett claimed more. Then Dawson's ridicule of Rhett's veracity brought a cold challenge from the *Mercury*'s editor. In the summer of 1868, Dawson took his position against dueling for the first time. The possibility of endless encounters may have prompted it. His membership in the Catholic Church, he said, forbade it. Rhett made that the basis for his lasting sneer that Dawson's religious scruples were "the shield of a base hypocrite." Their argument was ended temporarily, however when, still sneering, Rhett was forced to suspend the *Mercury* in November 1868 for lack of business.

Dawson had more concerns than Rhett. His wife was dying of tuberculosis. Business occupied him as he built the *News*. In August 1872 the paper moved to a new fine plant at 19 Broad Street. At the same time he and his partner were watching the difficulties of the old Charleston *Courier*. In 1873, they bought that paper, too, with more borrowed money—some of it Yankee money, it was brought out later as if that were a crime. And, while his wife lay dying, Dawson met Sarah Ida Fowler Morgan, whose abhorrence of dueling was greater than his own.

Gunfire brought them together. They met when Dawson hurried up to Columbia to see his old wartime friend James Morris Morgan, who had been seriously wounded in some shooting between gentlemen in a café at the capital. When Dawson met Sarah she was no longer a girl. Thirty-one, tall, violet-eyed, with very long gold hair tinged with red, she had had plenty of beaux. Some of them had died and some had been dismissed. She was a woman with vivid memories, including not only the horror and the humiliations of war but also the death of a brother at the war's beginning in a duel with shotguns following a trivial quarrel.

Sarah Morgan was not merely beautiful. She wrote with perception and grace. Dawson was enthusiastic about her contributions to the *News and Courier*. At first, recognizing the custom which barred women from newspaper work, she insisted that he

copy them in his own handwriting before passing them to editors
and printers. Then, increasingly, she wrote book reviews, articles, even editorials—all signed with the pseudonym of "Mr.
Fowler" or "Feu Follet."

The recently widowed editor began to look at his contributor
with something more than editorial approval. At first Sarah rebuked Dawson's ardor, but on January 27, 1874, Frank and
Sarah were married.

Their life together was to be no retreat to serenity. Dawson
had already sounded a spirited call to South Carolina conservatives to rescue the state from the radical Carpetbaggers and
Scalawags—"a motley crew of vagabonds whose only principle
is greed, and whose only policy is to plunder." Industriously he
exposed the greed and the plunder, the venality and vulgarity of
the Reconstruction regime. That campaign came to a climax, in
1875, when Dawson was indicted for criminal libel. In his campaign against crooked Reconstruction politicians he had written
that the Republican sheriff of Charleston County, former Congressman Christopher Columbus Bowen, was a "thief, forger
and murderer." Now, demanding $100,000 damages, Bowen was
out to kill the *News and Courier*.

Dawson was in a precarious position on his most serious
charge, that Bowen had brought about the murder of a fellow
officer in the Confederate Army. Then suddenly help came from
Bowen's discarded wife. She sent him word that Eli Grimes, the
young private Bowen had forced to do his killing, was living in
Lee County, Georgia. He was ready to talk but feared for his
safety.

The Democratic editor then found Republican aid. Governor
Daniel H. Chamberlain, whose election Dawson had opposed,
was now trying to clean up the mess in his own party. Chamberlain promised to pardon Grimes if he were convicted as result of
his testimony against Bowen. Jimmy Morgan was dispatched as
a special state constable to bring Grimes to Charleston. There the
soldier told to a startled courtroom his story of the murder
Bowen had ordered. Dawson won his case and damned his prosecutor to the satisfaction of the whole community, though one
henchman of the sheriff on the jury made the result a mistrial
instead of a straight not-guilty verdict.

A greater trial was approaching for the combative journalist, this time before the Democrats he had been leading. The *News and Courier* expressed complete approval of Chamberlain's efforts to clean up the state government. Counseling moderation and advocating compromise in a state with a Negro majority backed by Federal bayonets, he urged Chamberlain's re-election on a ticket containing some Negroes. Behind the leadership of old hotheads of South Carolina, now calling themselves Straightouts in a determination for all-out repudiation of Republican Reconstruction, whites turned on Dawson in indignation. He was accused of having been bribed with state printing. He was condemned as a dangerous stranger.

Colonel Rhett was called back from a place he had secured on the *Picayune* in New Orleans. In May 1876, he set up his *Journal of Commerce*. A stream of subscription cancellations poured in on the *News and Courier*. Bushel baskets full of new subscriptions came to the *Journal;* challenges to duels came to Dawson in a number almost equal to stop orders for his paper.

One arrived in all punctilio from the Straightout leader, tall, thin, profane General Martin Witherspoon Gary, known as the Bald Eagle of Edgefield. Not only in upcountry Edgefield County but throughout the state, Gary was recognized as a relentless antagonist. His dashing service in the Confederate cavalry had been crowned in South Carolina remembrance by his refusal to follow even Lee at Appomattox.

"South Carolinians never surrender," he announced then. That was his idea still.

Dawson was not dismayed. He wrote that Gary was "the champion of the shotgun policy." He called him a slanderer and a braggart. Though Gary in turn called him coward, he still declined to fight a duel. But Colonel Rhett of the *Journal,* pressing the resurgence of his new paper, did not mean to let the *News and Courier* editor avoid a meeting. Over his name in the *Journal* on August 10 he published a denunciation of his rival which under the code clearly called for a challenge. Dawson gave him equally violent verbal reply on August 11, mentioning his own war record and saying that while he fought for the South Rhett was "snugly ensconced in his newspaper office in Charleston through the war." Dawson's pen was the only weapon with which he meant to meet Rhett. Charleston awaited a collison between the two editors.

At the foot of Broad Street that August day the steps and portico of the Old Exchange building and the doors and windows of offices nearby were crowded with spectators. They saw Colonel Rhett come from his office on East Bay, turn the corner into Broad. With two of his assistant editors and two printers, all armed, he strolled up the north side of Broad. It was the hour at which Captain Dawson regularly went to his office at Broad Street and Gadsden's Alley. None of those watching doubted that he would come that day.

They saw him coming. Along the south side of Broad, the Captain moved as usual. He was accompanied only by Jimmy Morgan. He and Dawson walked calmly along the street. Rhett and his companions moved toward them. Only the width of the street separated Rhett and Dawson. At every pace the crowd expected a shot. Custom then required that Colonel Rhett, having given the original insult, allow Captain Dawson to resent it with his gun. The men moved closer to each other. No shot was fired. Dawson's refusal to resent the insult in the only manner which, under South Carolina tradition, it could be resented properly, brought him new and greater risk of contempt and ostracism. He moved on. Puzzled Charleston gentlemen, knowing Dawson's reputation for valor, differed as to which of the editors showed the greatest bravery that day.

Dawson could wear his badge of courage on Broad Street. Yet in the state where Red Shirts, unmasked successors of the outlawed Ku Klux Klan, galloped on errands of intimidation and stubborn Negro soldiers marched, increasing racial collisions left little ground for a moderate with counsels of compromise. A riot at the village of Hamburg between whites and Negro militia at first seemed to Dawson "bloody work" by the whites. Later reports convinced him he was wrong. So when a week after he and Rhett had tensely passed each other, the Democrats nominated Wade Hampton for Governor, Dawson's doubts as to what he should do disappeared.

He recanted with a ruffle of verbal drums and what modern writers of the *News and Courier* call "a touch of genius." His

editorial on the morning after the Hampton nomination was a
Democratic bugle blast. HAMPTON AND VICTORY he headed it. He
was clearly ready for the *News and Courier* to resume its role as
the leading Democratic voice. Some amusement but little scorn
greeted his retreat. Indeed, one historian of that Hampton
campaign declared that his swift shift was regarded as "an
audacious, masterly somersault at which everybody laughed, but
which everybody approved."

Actually Dawson's "somersault" was far more apparent
than real. Hampton, though the nominee of the Straightouts,
was a man closer to the moderation of Dawson than the violence
of Gary and Rhett. Indeed, it required the Negro voters won by
Hampton's persuasion as well as intimidation and trick by Red
Shirts and their associates to win that election. Few men contributed more to the victory than the converted captain and his
News and Courier. He fought in his paper. He moved among the
people. On election night, riding to polling places in the tense
city he received a bullet wound in his leg—a small price to pay
for triumph. And in the victory, as Dawson's power mounted in
Democratic councils and the *News and Courier*'s circulation
flourished, some of the Straightouts (who long nourished political violence) felt that the latecomer was too much the best
served.

Certainly trigger-readiness on fields of honor and grounds of
brawls did not disappear when the Democrats won. There was
need for Dawson's telling editorials against gun, knife, and
torch. They gave South Carolina, he insisted endlessly, a bad
name and less hope. Only order could serve as a basis for prosperity. He made his campaign against violence a part of his work
as the first conspicuous editorial figure in the postwar movement
to "bring the cotton mills to the cotton fields." It was part, too,
of his efforts to attract European farmers and artisans who
would help make the state less dependent on the North and West
for food and manufactured goods.

In their happy house at the corner of Lightwood Alley and
Meeting Street, Sarah worked with him. He found able men to
help him at the office. In an area supposedly reluctant to accept
newcomers, the English editor with a Louisiana wife procured as

his most dramatic aide young, handsome Narciso Gener Gonzales. He wrote of small things with lightness and grace. He could be deadly serious, too, in robust prose. Sometimes, indeed, when he wrote of cranks and scoundrels he put such impetuosity into his work that Dawson had to restrain him. In the old homogeneous state the Spanish half of Gonzales' blood set him a little apart.

Gonzales' father, a rebel against Spanish tyranny in Cuba, had married into the rich and distinguished Elliott family of the South Carolina Low Country. But when Narciso and his brothers, Ambrose and William Elliott, reached school age the family had fallen into the dignified destitution of Reconstruction. As men had earlier come into journalism as printers, Narciso (always called N. G.) and Ambrose moved into it as telegraph operators at little railway stations where they also became country newspaper correspondents. In the crowded year of 1876, N. G. startled Dawson when he sent a scoop about a riot to Rhett's opposition *Journal*. N. G. was then eighteen. Four years later Dawson hired him as traveling correspondent for his *News and Courier* with headquarters at Columbia.

Dawson dispatched Gonzales about the state to report the hard facts about the violence the editor deplored. Dawson damned not only the duel. He excused violence only, in the mood of his times, when it involved the rape of a white woman by a Negro. In 1880 the *News and Courier* gave publicity and approval, as a "cheering evidence of a quickening of the moral sense," to the establishment of an antidueling society in Camden. That brought cause to a climax.

Rich, irascible, and (according to his enemies) disreputable Colonel Ellerbe Boggan Crawford Cash of Camden loudly damned the society. He had been one of the most ardent of the Straightouts who had sneered at Dawson in 1876. Now he suggested the antidueling society had been formed as a protection for some whom in honor he wished to call to account. His name, he said, had been "closely associated with these movements." So he took up his pen as he might have aimed his pistol.

"I desire to notice them," he wrote, "but feel confident that were I to apply for use of the columns of the *News and Courier*, I would meet with refusal. No one will doubt that the editors of the *News and Courier* are in full sympathy with the antidueling movement. Their past records and private characters are such as not only to qualify them for full membership to such an association, but would justify their elevation to prominent positions in the same.''

Then he snorted at the society's members: ''These archangels take it upon themselves to denounce as 'criminal!' the acts of men who are as far their superiors as the eagle is the superior of the buzzard.''

The antidueling society did not prevent the meeting of Colonel Cash and Colonel William S. Shannon, on July 5, 1880, on the highland above DuBose's Bridge over Lynches River near Camden. Cash claimed that Shannon, described by antiduelists as an ''unoffending gentleman,'' had reflected on his mother's character in a lawsuit. Shannon fired first and his bullet fell harmless in the sand (deflected, said those who condemned Cash, by metal armor Cash secretly wore). Cash put his ball into Shannon's breast, killing him almost instantly. The last fatal duel had been fought, but the fury about it was just begun.

Dawson's indignation at the duel was spread in every issue of his paper which went each morning to doorsteps throughout the state. Other editors joined him. Cash cried that, with few exceptions, all South Carolina papers were inmates of Dawson's ''kennel, and with wagging tails are ever ready to howl response to their master's horn.'' The Colonel, in 1881, resorted to a pamphlet, ''The Cash–Shannon Duel.''

''The 'Charleston *News and Courier*,' '' he wrote, ''edited by an imported flunky and a notorious cuckold (for both of whom I have never sought to conceal my most boundless contempt), was now in a blaze of glory.''

He did not identify the alleged cuckold. But he elaborated his denunciation of Dawson.

''Since this paper war was commenced on me,'' he continued, ''I have endeavored to find out something of the antecedents of F. W. Dawson, who edits the 'News and Courier.' He appears to claim to be of English birth and if so, would be known in that country as 'Lackey' or 'Flunkey'; by others he is believed to be a Yankee vagabond who 'guessed' at his father's name and then made his way South during the war, and while acting as boxing master or hostler for a Confederate General, played spy for the Yankee army. Be this as it may, he is evidently a man of energy and decided smartness for although his intimate and villainous connection with the Radical Party ... and his shameless coward-ice and utter disregard for truth have been thoroughly venti-lated, he is now master of the situation and more completely rules poor, emasculated, Yankee-ised, South Carolina, than ever did our immortal Calhoun.''

Dawson had disregarded worse slurs from better men. Many leading men supported him now. But Cash as duelist got quick support from General Gary, the old Bald Eagle Dawson had declined to meet in 1876. Gary had repeatedly been defeated for office by the conservatives, including Dawson. Now he was old and sick but he drew steady aim on the Charleston editor.

''I have no respect,'' the old Red Shirt leader wrote, ''for the opinion of F. W. Dawson, who I am informed is a bastard, and who I know to be a liar, a bribe-taker, a coward and a blackguard.''

Such venomed words overshot their mark. They did not embitter the editor now living in a finer house on Bull Street where Sarah, with a son, Warrington, and a daughter, Ethel, served and defended serenity. Attacks did not shake the confi-dence of Dawson's friends and supporters. He did have the power, described as malignant by Cash, to secure the passage of a law outlawing dueling in South Carolina. Across America papers and people praised his efforts. From Rome came word that in recognition of his antidueling activities Pope Leo XIII had made the devout Catholic Dawson a Knight of the Order of St. Gregory the Great.

Violence was not ended in South Carolina. If Dawson was acclaimed, Cash was acquitted of any crime in connection with his duel. Indeed, that duel, which ended conflicts of honor, seemed to point up the bloody political feud. Cash claimed that the Dawson crowd, ''the Ring,'' the ''Bourbon Democracy'' moved from the denunciation of dueling to the arrangement of assassination. Certainly the Colonel, in 1882, had shifted from his role as Straightout Democrat to opposition even when it took him as a member of the Greenback or Independent Party into collaboration with Negroes and Republicans. One of Cash's associates in that revolt whom the Colonel regarded as "a man of honor and courage" was killed by Democrats in a political argument. Now, said a report attributed to the Charleston *Mercury* in a 1930 revision by Bessie Cash Irby of the Colonel's original pamphlet, Cash's removal also "became a political necessity" to "the Bourbons and their tools." But in his case "the game of shooting him ... was not quite so openly resorted to." The blow, it said, was aimed at his boy.

Boggan Cash had come home in 1876 from V.M.I. where he had been First Captain of the Corps, to ride as an erect, roaring captain of Red Shirts in the Straightout Campaign. According to those who condemned the Cashes long and late, he was pulled not only into dueling but into degeneracy by his father. They even said that he joined his father in incestuous relations with a mulatto girl, Juliana, his sister and his father's daughter. The better-verified fact the Cash family history reports is that as a part of Republican patronage young, belligerent Boggan was appointed U.S. Marshal under President Chester A. Arthur. Some South Carolinians then regarded such service under the party of the Yankees and the Negroes as scarcely less a sin.

Historians now can choose completely contradictory versions about the events that followed. *One:* Boggan, as U.S. Marshal, was the target of gunshots in the night when he investigated Democratic vote frauds. *Two:* Boggan became a "Cavalier outlaw," terrorizing the town of Cheraw with gunplay on drunken sprees. As a result of one or the other he was badly clubbed by the Cheraw town marshal. A few days later, his pride hurt as much as his head, he returned to the town. In vengeance or "self-defense," he put the bullets of his .38 Smith & Wesson into the marshal and a bystander. Leaving the dying men, he fled into hiding.

The *News and Courier* raised the hue and cry for his arrest. The Charleston *Mercury* editorial quoted in the Cash pamphlet, however, insisted that Boggan only went into hiding "because he knew that there was a certain gang belonging to the Bourbon

Democracy, urged on by the inflammatory articles in the State Organ, who were bent on killing him, if he placed himself in the power of the posse sent to secure his arrest, and if he had surrendered to the Sheriff before the meeting of the Court, bands of Border Ruffians would have been enrolled in various counties to lynch him.''

Dawson, editor of the Organ, scorned such charges. The Cashes were only items in his determined campaign against violence. The fact that he was a member of the State Executive Committee, which had been disturbed by the Independent revolt, was another matter. The Democratic Governor offered a reward for young Cash, who slipped into a swamp to elude the first officers sent after him. In that posse, according to one who regarded the Cashes as criminals, was ''the *News and Courier's* good looking Gonzales'' carrying a Springfield rifle.

Gonzales' stories of the case followed to its conclusion. A second posse, led by an informer, surrounded a barn where Boggan was hiding. In the dawn he rushed out loaded with arms. He was killed, members of the posse reported, in an exchange of fire. His body, said the Cashes, was kicked and stomped after he was dead. Colonel Cash rendered his bitter verdict in a communication to the Columbia *Register* with the editors of which Gonzales had had some ''personal difficulties'' and which resented the larger circulation of the *News and Courier* in its town.

The Colonel insisted that his boy ''was shot to death by the thugs and henchmen of the Ring.'' Boggan was twenty-eight when he died. The Colonel, then sixty-one, engraved upon his tombstone a line from Horace: *''Durum. Sed Levius Fit Patientia Quidquid Corrigere Est Nefas.''*

It was hard; it would have been a crime to correct it. But *patience* was a strange word for the Colonel to put in stone. Broken in heart but not in spirit, a descendant said, he died on his plantation on March 10, 1888, four years after he had put his boy into the graveyard to which he was borne.

South Carolina did not believe the Cash charges. The stature of Gonzales as a reporter grew as he covered other incidents of violence, digging up the facts as a basis for indignation and reform. In Charleston, Dawson moved as a knight of the Pope and a Democratic power in the city and the state. With his family he began to take more and more trips to the North and abroad. He had much more to concern him in the year in which Boggan Cash was killed than violence in Kershaw County, private or political. That year, moving from state to national concerns, he won a majority of the South Carolina delegation for the nomination of Grover Cleveland. With Cleveland's gratitude he gained appointment as consul-general to Australasia for Sarah's brother, James, who had walked along Broad Street with him the day Charleston expected Rhett-Dawson bullets. There were mutterings from some South Carolinians that Morgan had not always been a Democrat. Other opposition, Dawson said, came from those "who have always hated me because I have been successful in politics and otherwise, and have only lived about twenty years in the State."

Perhaps nothing less than the Charleston earthquake of August 31, 1886, could have made his acceptance final among his neighbors. Dawson barely missed being killed in the shaking city when part of his residence fell. But he was quickly back at his office as newsman and citizen to confront the disaster in which scores of people were killed and many buildings made uninhabitable. While its building trembled, the *News and Courier* went to press. Editors, printers, and reporters brought out the paper to a city in debris. In serious aftermath of the quake, homelessness, hunger, and danger had to be faced. The stricken city turned to the English-born editor for leadership. Then the representatives of the oldest families gave to the newcomer (by Charleston standards) the accolade of their appreciation and acceptance.

South Carolina, however, was not composed only of the Charleston elite. Dawson, now at the height of his personal and political power, had to meet rising charges about the domination of the state by the Bourbon Ring which the Columbia *Register* said "is on Dawson's little finger." Far more important than any such charges from a rival paper was the mounting agrarian opposition led by the brilliant, irascible, one-eyed Benjamin R.

Tillman from Edgefield. In rural invective Tillman referred to Dawson as a buzzard spreading its slime over him.

Dawson answered with courage and dignity, but as the mass protest against the Conservatives and Charleston aristocracy mounted he betrayed a class irritation which was to mark the fury of the gathering storm. From the heritage of Low Country scorn, he described the Tillmanites as "people who carry pistols in their hip pockets, who expectorate upon the floors, who have no tooth brushes, and comb their hair with their fingers." With that and similar language, he matched Tillman's invective in August 1888. The Captain was prepared to move forward fighting in the years ahead. Not quite as agile as he had been as a young war veteran, his weight had grown with his power. Now a square man, graying, he weighed 200 pounds. He was not to be pushed around, physically or politically.

Few men dealt with violence and violent politics with such seeming serenity. Yet he sought in his home, his son said later, a peace he did not find elsewhere. Often he took his place at the organ at the foot of the stairs and filled the big Bull Street house with music—lively, gentle, sometimes religious. His books were arranged with such preciseness that his young daughter Ethel could quickly find, as the third volume on the fourth row or the second on the fifth, the exact one he needed. He made a ceremony of family dinner, which came each day at four o'clock (not three, as later Charlestonians said). He left the discipline of the children to Sarah. But he was luckily and bravely with them one day to seize by the scruff of its neck and dispose of a large pet dog which suddenly went mad and came frothing and snarling toward his young son. On that occasion he did have a gun with which to kill the beast.

All seemed happy and secure when they came back from one of their trips to Europe bringing with them a dark-haired and dark-eyed young Swiss, Marie (or, as she was sometimes called, Hélène) Burdayron, to attend the children. Her status apparently was not exactly that of governess, but she violently resented it when she discovered that young Warrington wrote of her in a diary as "the French maid." Suddenly it appeared that she was being subjected to improper attentions by a Dr. T. B. McDow.

Dawson suspected that the doctor was the prowler who had been noticed about the house on Bull Street in the evenings while Sarah and the children were out of town and he was at the office. Also the editor had been publishing reports of an investigation of insurance claims among Negroes which involved McDow.

Sarah was confident of the virtue of the young Swiss. On the basis of reports of detectives Dawson had had shadow the doctor and the girl, Dawson could not have been sure. Though Dawson had rejected dueling, he did not cease to defend his household. Disregarding police warnings that McDow, though a small man, was dangerous, he called at the doctor's office on Rutledge Street nearby at four o'clock on the afternoon of March 12, 1889. In the office McDow shot him dead. At first it seemed that only the killer remained to tell what happened. He never explained why Dawson was, as the state contended, shot in the back or why he tried to bury his body. Only weeks after the trial did the Burdayron woman, in a fury over the label *French maid,* admit that she had known in advance that McDow planned to kill the editor. She was glad he had done it, she said. Sarah dismissed her but insisted that her story be kept secret. Sarah's son Warrington made it public only long after his mother's death. The story of the woman's confession, as related by the son, leaves much mystery still about the affair.

Angrily Charleston then cried "Murder!" but at the time only McDow could speak about what happened in his office. A *News and Courier* reporter, who interviewed him in a jail cell that night, gave his version.

"Here it is in a nutshell," the doctor insisted. "Captain Dawson entered my office, used abusive language and knocked me down with his cane. I got up and he was about to strike me again, when I shot him."

Crowds collecting around the jail were content with no such tale. A party of men gathered and moved toward the site of the prison on Magazine Street. Their purpose was to lynch the doctor. It "would not have been foiled," said a later editor of the *News and Courier.* But a few hundred yards from the jail a young Irishman who was leading the mob suddenly hesitated and halted.

"Boys," he said, "I believe we had better not do this. I have been thinking as we walked along about what the Captain has always said about lynching in the *News and Courier* and I don't think he would like it if he were here."

The mob dispersed. Charleston grieved as Dawson was buried on a day of beating wind and rain. Flags in the city hung sodden at half-mast. Mourners overflowed the church and filled the adjacent streets. McDow was tried by the law which Dawson always insisted must be upheld. The jury had on it seven Negroes and five white men. The sweep of a new generation of Straightouts had not yet prevailed. Negroes had been those who had been most served by the editor's steady insistence that law and not force or fury should prevail. Still there was resentment among them that in the case of rape of white women by Negroes he believed lynching was justified. McDow was acquitted on his claim of self-defense. Some believe that corruption helped shape the verdict. Certainly the failure of the young Swiss woman to tell the jury all she knew helped form it.

Gonzales did not succeed to the editorship as he had once been led to believe he would. The *News and Courier* became much milder in its causes than it was under Dawson. It preferred a less vigorous course than Gonzales would have followed—or Dawson, had he lived to face the new situation confronting the well-loved state of his adoption and his place and power in it. Lacking Dawson's position, the thirty-one-year-old reporter took his place in the fight against the rising tide of rural demands. With his brother in 1891 he established *The State* at Columbia. The followers of Ben Tillman said it was founded only to "keep alive prejudices and malice." Standing with the Conservatives, the paper did represent a continuity of principles and prejudices. Though a greater man and standing now for important causes, Tillman was in a sense the heir of the truculent General Gary whose partisan and protégé he had been.

Tied as Gonzales was by birth to the Low-Country gentry whose conservative members had constituted so much of the "Bourbon Democracy," his editorial opposition to Tillman was natural. He shared Tillman's concern for education, though he

did not always agree as to methods. But he was repelled by the
class hatreds and racial antagonisms stirred among Tillman's
artisan and farmer followers which too often mounted to renewed violence and bloodshed. Furthermore, Gonzales' association with the "aristocracy" against the "red necks" was
strengthened when the editor's sister Gertrude married Frank
Hampton, nephew of the great General, Governor, and Senator
whose name was a symbol for the state's old political regime. In
1890, in its sweeping proscription of "dudes, dandies and
snobs," as the Tillmanites called the Conservatives, even the
long-honored Hampton was refused re-election to the Senate.
Tillman's rise to power was revolutionary change in which a
relative of Colonel Cash would be promoted to the governorship.

Tillmanism was the Gonzales target. But the editor fought for
education, against the convict-lease system, for protections for
children laboring in the mills. He made his paper such a foe of
violence that his brother, Ambrose E. Gonzales, wrote that *The
State* under his brother's leadership "was the first Southern
newspaper to cry out against the cowardice and barbarity of
lynching—the first to denounce lynchers as murderers and to
denounce them here at home, where enemies are always to be
made." Perhaps that statement too swiftly dismissed the vigorous though limited opposition to mob violence by Dawson. Certainly *The State* did take the lead in that cause from the *News
and Courier,* now in softer hands than those which held Dawson's pen.

N. G. made enemies at home. To many of them, who felt
what Tillman called his "sneering pen," the editor became "No
Good" Gonzales and, because of his Cuban father, "the perfidious Spaniard." He had not forgotten his ties to that island,
from which tyranny long before had driven his father. Indeed,
while William Randolph Hearst, Joseph Pulitzer, and other
American journalists were making the Spanish-American War a
crusade for circulation as well as freedom, Gonzales at forty
went off to fight as a soldier with Cuban forces in the jungles of
the island.

He came back to the hardly less dangerous jungle of South
Carolina politics. By this time the powerful Tillman had won his

name "Pitchfork Ben" in torn radical-conservative Democratic politics by promising to stick his pitchfork into the ribs of Dawson's friend Grover Cleveland. In the new relentless mood of Palmetto politics, Gonzales walked in danger as Dawson had done before. He marched to its climax, in 1902, when he opposed Ben Tillman's nephew, James H. Tillman, for governor and undertook to expose his "dishonorable conduct."

Other editors had said worse things of this Tillman who, according to the biographer of the greater Tillman, "represented the Tillmans and Tillmanism at its worst." Jim had favored closing the Negro schools by denying licenses to Negro teachers and had in general appealed to the worst anti-Negro prejudices among men too ready to make the mobs.

The editor of the small Gaffney *Ledger* called Jim Tillman a drunkard and a gambler to his face on a speaker's stand. The Anderson *Daily Mail* declared that he "lives and breathes in a very atmosphere of falsehood." The Charleston *Evening Post* in comparing Jim Tillman with a political opponent, a conservative Spanish War veteran, used the words "The Soldier and the Swashbuckler, the Gentleman and the Blackguard." Gonzales listed ten of the eleven daily papers of the state which condemned and opposed Jim Tillman.

The State's editor was the chief voice of opposition. Ten years earlier he had privately denounced this Tillman as "unfit for association with gentlemen." Then Tillman, in defiance of the law passed after the Cash–Shannon meeting, challenged Gonzales to a duel. The editor ignored it with the hardly placating explanation that "so contemptible an object as this callow fellow" was beneath his notice. He noticed him in *The State* only to expose him to South Carolina voters. And he was effective in that.

Jim Tillman had a German Luger automatic pistol repaired. He also armed himself with a Colt revolver. On January 15, 1903, he waited for Gonzales to take his usual route home from the newspaper office. No expectant crowd waited this time, like that which attended the passing of Dawson and Rhett on Broad Street in Charleston nearly thirty years before. Only a lady met reserved and preoccupied Gonzales as he walked toward home.

She was about to speak to him. At that moment the waiting
Tillman fired with his Luger. The lady's scream brought others
to the scene. The shot had done its deadly work at the corner of
Main and Gervais streets at the heart of South Carolina in
Columbia. Across the street in the Capitol grounds the planted
palmettoes seemed little more symbol of the state of sad angers
and furies than the pistol which smoked in Tillman's hand.

The editor had been unarmed, but the politician was acquitted. Yet beyond the courthouse, as Benjamin Tillman's
biographer said, "the Gonzales family experienced a ghastly
vengeance: The ghost of the dead man pursued Jim Tillman the
rest of his unhappy days."

With the help of two editors who ironically died violently,
violence in South Carolina and the South around it became a
mark not of honor but of shame. The deaths of both men served
the cause for which they fought. Yet, as a final irony, Gonzales
at the last owned and kept a revolver. Though he did not carry
it, it was found locked in a drawer of his editorial desk after he
died. Obviously, though as reporter and editor he had fought
violence all his career, he was not sure that its dangers had
passed. Perhaps no fighting editor ever can be.

Sarah Dawson was living in Paris when Gonzales died. She
had lived in loneliness in the Bull Street house in Charleston
after her Captain died. She turned down at least two suitors.
Then she sold her interest in the *News and Courier* and took up
again her writing in the Faubourg Saint Germain. Her Civil
War diary was not published until after her death in 1909. The
tumult in its pages was far behind her. Contentment came to her
even beyond the memory of murder in South Carolina. She wrote
eagerly. Her best-received work related to a gentler postwar
South. It was *Les Aventures de Jeannot,* a French version of the
Uncle Remus Brer Rabbit stories written by the Georgia journalist Joel Chandler Harris. Little French children loved these
stories of the American South so well that *Jeannot* became a
textbook in their schools.

13

Yellow Genesis

John Albert Cockerill was a square, compactly built man of twenty-five when he arrived in Cincinnati in 1870. During the Civil War, in which his father had won admiration as a fighter as Colonel of the 24th Ohio Regiment, John had been only a printer's devil turned drummer boy, then bugler. Now on his first job as a reporter on the *Cincinnati Enquirer*, he began to grow the mustache later described as bristling. Also he loaded his language with rough soldier talk.

Nobody knew better than Cockerill that his newspaper experience had been limited to a boy's work in the shop of the *Scion of*

Temperance in little West Union, Ohio, and as printer on the Dayton *Empire.* In the composing room of the Copperhead organ, the *Empire,* he may have absorbed some of the combative tradition of that paper. Newspaper conflict during the war had been carried on with sticks and stones, not merely ink. One of the *Empire's* editors had been shot down on the street, touching off two years of rioting. In the tumult a mob of Copperheads had wrecked the office of the loyal Dayton *Journal.* Such furies were quieting when John went to work. But in Cincinnati he found the competition for circulation almost as sharp as the differences of war.

Neither he nor any of the other young newspapermen realized how much of the future patterns of the American press were being shaped in the sprawling city on the Ohio. Cincinnati was concerned with prosperity around great hogpens and with the development of music and the arts. The city was noted for good German beer and the bitter taste of its slum poverty, but it was soon to be the scene of even greater contrasts in the history of American journalism. There at one time a seldom-equaled body of the newspaper elite gathered to remake America and, all unnoticed under their elevated nostrils, obscure characters were about to remake the American press.

Cincinnati was a young newspaperman's town as the 1870s began. Five years earlier Henry Watterson had found himself at twenty-five, editor of the Republican Cincinnati *Evening Times.* Now he had gone to become the swashbuckling editor of the Louisville *Courier-Journal.* During the war handsome Whitelaw Reid had gone from the city editorship of the *Cincinnati Gazette* to become a celebrated war correspondent and friend of the great. Now one of the *Gazette's* owners, Reid was also first assistant to the great Horace Greeley on the *New York Tribune.* But Murat Halstead, classic reporter of the conventions which nominated Lincoln and tore the Democratic Party to pieces, was still on the ground as editor of the *Cincinnati Commercial.* When Cockerill became managing editor of the *Enquirer* in 1872, he was still relatively obscure in the journalism of the town and the country.

He seemed even more obscure when the Liberal Republican

convention in May 1872 brought to the Ohio metropolis so many newsmen that Watterson said the gathering might have been mistaken for an annual meeting of the Associated Press. In terms of press power it promised to be more than that. Its lofty editorial leaders were assembled to form a more decorous Union. And probably no more fastidious plotters ever met than the four editors who gathered in a private parlor in the St. Nicholas Hotel, where the convention had its headquarters.

That parlor was no "smoke-filled room," though in it the fervent, bright-eyed editors hoped to impose their guidance upon the swarm of malcontents, idealists, and politicians in the bars, streets, and halls below them. Certainly these journalists constituted no "conclave of cranks" as lesser newsmen had already called the body of delegates come together in determination to put an end to the regime of cigar-chomping Ulysses S. Grant. In a republic torn by Reconstruction and shaken by scandals, the aim of the gathering was to sweep out vindictiveness and venality with brooms of reunion and reform. The four editors in the parlor were sure they knew how to accomplish the required political change.

It did not occur to them—any more than to Cockerill at his *Enquirer* desk—that Cincinnati that year was the source of change in American journalism. As gentlemen of the press—for the men in the parlor the phrase was real, not rhetorical—they saw no need for change in American journalism as they represented it. If change was to occur, they did not expect it from such an interloper as young, dapper Whitelaw Reid. They hardly recognized the existence of some lesser scribblers in the city who would cause a series of changes—reporters like eccentric Lafcadio Hearn, profane John Cockerill, and domineering Joseph Pulitzer.

The four editors in the parlor called themselves the Quadrilateral. In erudition and self-confidence they had taken the name from four supposedly impregnable fortresses in the Italian Alps. The editorial quartet was impressive if not impregnable: Horace White of the *Chicago Tribune,* Samuel Bowles of the *Springfield Republican,* Watterson of the Louisville *Courier-Journal,* and the local luminary, Halstead of the *Cincinnati Commercial.* They had expanded the four to five to admit Senator Carl Schurz, of Missouri, onetime young German revolutionary who had become American journalist, diplomat, soldier, and politician but kept some of the stiffness of a German professor about him.

Their choice as Presidential candidate of the convention was Charles Francis Adams of Massachusetts, son of one President and grandson of another. It rather recommended him to them that Adams had indicated ''he would accept the nomination only if it were brought to him on a silver tray bearing no finger prints of the politician's grimy hand.'' All ''politicians'' seemed unacceptable to the editors in the parlor. And they put high in their distaste their own crusading colleague Greeley of the *Tribune*. They were shocked when Reid, as Horace's first assistant editor on the ''Great Moral Organ,'' came demanding admission to the Quadrilateral. Rather imperiously he accosted Watterson.

Why, he demanded, was *The Tribune* left out of the Quadrilateral?

Certainly Greeley's *Tribune* had beaten the drums which stirred the Liberal Republican revolt. But all too evidently the famous editor was ready to lead it now. There were many ready to wave the symbol of his old floppy white hat. But, to put it mildly, Greeley did not seem the serene and austere statesman the neater journalists of the Quadrilateral required. Still young Watterson argued. In the campaign ahead, the support of *The Tribune* would be indispensable. Greeley couldn't be nominated. So by taking in Reid, ''we both eat our cake and have it, too.''

It was as simple as that—or the editors were that simple. Reid was in, and in on all their plans. The morning of the voting in crowded *Saengerfest* Hall, Reid invited all his friends of the Quadrilateral to eat his cake or his dinner after the session. The hall to which they hastened was crowded with newsmen as well as delegates, banners, and bands.

Young Joseph Pulitzer, already a belligerent newspaperman and one of the proprietors of the *Westliche Post* of German-crowded St. Louis, was present as delegate and one of the secretaries of the convention. John Cockerill had his men arrayed in the hall. So did the Quadrilateral's Halstead of the *Cincinnati*

Commercial. White, Bowles, and Watterson assumed their roles as editorial correspondents as well as editorial conspirators. The election of Schurz as temporary chairman seemed a good sign for the fastidious forces behind Adams. But Reid was busy on the floor. On the sixth ballot an evidently carefully planned stampede set in for his boss. With economical brevity Reid wired Greeley in New York: NOMINATED. W. R. Then he went to greet his guests of the Quadrilateral at dinner.

"Horace White looked more than ever like an iceberg," Watterson wrote of the occasion. "Sam Bowles was diplomatic but ineffusive; Schurz was as a death's head at the board; Halstead and I, through sheer bravado, tried to enliven the feast. But they would have none of us, or it, and we separated early and sadly, reformers hoist by their own petard."

The journalists dispersed. Sam Bowles, expressing the general views of the Quadrilateral, wired his Massachusetts paper to support Greeley but "not to gush." More enthusiastic, Pulitzer went back to Missouri and made sixty speeches in German for Greeley's election. Reid went home to take the place of Candidate Greeley as editor of the *New York Tribune.* In the tough campaign the Republican stalwarts put on against the crusading editor as crank, traitor, and rustic comic, Greeley said he was sometimes not sure whether he was running for the Presidency or the penitentiary. And, in the month after he came home defeated to mental disintegration and death, it was not certain whether he had lost the *Tribune* editorship or Reid had taken it away from him.

Certainly the change in American journalism represented by *The Tribune* was clear. In the better clubs and at Delmonico's no journalist could deplore the appearance of the press as personified by Mr. Reid. Still, the change at Greeley's death was marked by universal mourning. Even President Grant, whom Greeley had opposed, moved in the funeral procession. And down the scale lesser folk, for whose causes Greeley had clamored, were saddened. Printers noted that he was almost the last of the great editors who had begun their careers at the type fonts. As the first president of their union, they erected a monument over his grave. But five years after the funeral Reid began his long quarrel with the printers which resulted in a boycott of his *Tribune*—and his Republican Party in large measure—by union labor. Whatever the grief and change, the appearance of the press, rescued for respectability, was improved. It was no longer a bumpkin in unpressed pants, shambling to concerns about everything and everybody under a rumpled old white hat. Neither was it to be a gentleman in a plug hat and a Prince Albert coat.

Not all the gentlemen of the press at the Cincinnati convention dispersed in triumph or disappointment. John Cockerill roared in increasing confidence at his reporters in the routine of Cincinnati news coverage. And in the month in which Greeley died, Cockerill had an unexpected caller. He looked up from his desk to see a quaint, dark-skinned little fellow, strangely diffident, with a manuscript in his hand. The visitor's name was Lafcadio Hearn.

Apparently none of Cockerill's brusqueness marked this meeting, though later Hearn was to describe the editor as a hard newsroom character he did not like very well but admired very much. Cockerill remembered the dark young man as "sensitive as a flower." On this occasion he must have been moved more by charity, which was as much a part of his character as his crustiness, than by expectation.

"In a soft shrinking voice," the editor wrote years after, "he asked if I ever paid for outside contributions. I informed him that I was somewhat restricted in the matter of expenditures, but that I would give consideration to whatever he had to offer."

He read the piece. He was astonished by it. He paid Hearn out of his own pocket. Later he remembered how "inadequately" he paid him then, and what a "ridiculously low" salary he paid him afterward. Certainly in Cockerill's own life and in terms of the journalism he was to help shape, he could not have made a better bargain.

Even in polyglot Cincinnati, filled with former slaves pushing up from the South and a variety of newcomers from Europe, Hearn was a special stranger. Born in 1850 on a Greek island,

son of an Irish surgeon-major in the British Army and a lovely
Greek girl, whose family probably had a strain of Arab and
Moorish blood, he seemed from the beginning a child nobody
wanted. His father, ordered to the West Indies, deposited wife
and son with relatives in Dublin. Then when he was seven
Lafcadio's mother ran off, supposedly with a lover, leaving the
boy with a bigoted Irish-Catholic aunt. She undertook to educate
him for the priesthood, but at the school to which he was sent he
first lost the sight of one eye in a game and then was expelled.
Later he ran away from a Jesuit school in France. His injured
eye was covered with a milky film. The other was swollen to
twice its size by the abuse of omnivorous reading. He was ugly.
He was not pliant for the old lady's pious purposes. The aunt
got rid of him by paying his passage to America, where he arrived in 1869 half-blind, friendless, and with a morbid obsession
about his physical repulsiveness.

Working at menial job after menial job, he somehow found his
way to Cincinnati. He slept in haylofts and rusty boilers in
vacant lots. He worked as messenger boy and sold mirrors for a
Syrian peddler. He got a job in the public library but lost it
because he neglected his duties while reading the books he was
supposed to distribute. A kindly old English printer, Henry
Watkin, gave him a job and let him sleep in the shop. Finally,
when he was twenty-two, he took his manuscript to Cockerill.

"Then," Cockerill wrote later, "he stole away like a dis-
torted brownie, leaving behind him an impression that was un-
canny and indescribable."

The piece the young man brought seems hardly likely to have
been one to pull money from an Ohio news editor's pocket. It
was a review of a recently published part of Tennyson's *Idylls
of the King*. Still Cockerill printed the piece and, though he had
no job for Hearn, let him have desk room. He sent him to interview local painters in a city growing conscious of the arts. Then
in 1873, Hearn got closer to sensational reporting in a vivid
piece about low-life activities in the river town. He interviewed a
gravedigger and wrote about pawnshops. Gradually he began to
write about Negroes. He gave dramatic quality to social concern
in a story he produced about the seamstresses of the city called

"Slow Starvation." He went on to ragpickers, night workers. He exposed fortune tellers and mediums. He wrote of conscienceless doctors, lunatics, opium addicts.

Cockerill put him on the payroll. The young fellow he had paid on a hunch turned out to be the producer of circulation-building copy. The editor turned him loose on the waterfront, in the narrow slum streets to write of policemen, of riverboat men, of barkeeps and prostitutes. He brought up the ugly, dirty, but vital life in the city's depths.

Cincinnati was shocked but eager, when he wrote of the murder of a seducer, a tanyard worker, who was beaten, stabbed with a pitchfork, and then crammed into a furnace and cremated. Hearn left out no simmering detail of the burned body. He described its fragments laid out for the coroner in an undertaking establishment on the "clean white lining of the coffin." It rather resembled, he wrote, "great shapeless lumps of half-burnt bituminous coal than aught else at the first hurried glance; and only a closer investigation could enable a strong-stomached observer to detect their ghastly character—masses of crumbling human bones, strung together by half-burnt sinews, or glued one upon another by a hideous adhesion of half-molten flesh, boiled brains and jellied blood mingled with coal. The skull had burst like a shell in the fierce furnace-heat; and the whole upper portion seemed as though it had been *blown out* by the steam from the boiling and bubbling brains."

This was strong stuff for Cincinnati breakfast tables, but it was apparently what Cincinnati and American newspaper readers wanted. The *Enquirer*'s circulation soared with this story and rose again with other Hearn contributions. Cockerill approved the copy. He had found what kind of journalism people wanted in Cincinnati. There were protests from the squeamish, as there were later about stories Cockerill brought to St. Louis and New York. "Beastly Cincinnati," Hearn called the city about which he wrote, but his stories of its squalor, stinks, sins, and crimes came out of fascination for the place. They fascinated *Enquirer* readers, too.

Then the young man's own personal story became less pleasing to his employers. In this city on the border of the South where Harriet Beecher Stowe had found the materials for her Uncle Tom and Little Eva, Hearn, who felt himself repulsive to others, found satisfaction and affection in a strong, handsome mulatto woman who worked as a servant in the miserable boardinghouse where he lived. Considered a Bohemian, friend of artists, writers, and musicians, his casual alliance might have been lightly dismissed. But Hearn, resentful of racial barriers then as always, determined to make something proper about his relationship with Mattie Foley, four years his senior. In a state with laws against miscegenation, he lied to get a marriage license. He finally found a Negro minister who performed the ceremony on the night of June 14, 1874.

Apparently little was said about the marriage at first. Cockerill gave him an increasingly free hand in finding sensational stories. Out of his prose rose the miasmic atmosphere of the sections by the slaughterhouses, the soap factories, the immense hogpens. His words vividly led his readers down the alleys, dark and filthy, which lost their width in tortuous curves and narrow twists and labyrinthine perplexity, to the ghoulish aroma of stink-factories and the sickening smell of hogpens. His twisting alleys were bringing Hearn to the end of his road with Cockerill.

In the summer of 1875, his employers learned beyond all doubt that Hearn was married to a Negro. Perhaps bachelor Cockerill did not care. The scandal, however, was being used by a group of city politicians to silence criticism of them. Hearn came into the city room and received peremptory dismissal instead of an assignment. His world seemed to have come to an end. He was prevented from jumping into the canal only by a friend, though there were those who said he would have committed suicide only if he could have written in full sensational detail the news story about himself and seen it headlined on the front page by Cockerill.

Apparently no resentment lingered between Hearn and Cockerill. Later the writer described his editor as "a sort of furious young man."

"He was," Hearn said, "a hard master, a tremendous worker, and a born journalist. I think none of us liked him, but we all

admired his ability to run things. He used to swear at us, work
us half to death (never sparing himself), and he had a rough
skill in sarcasm that we were all afraid of.''

And, Hearn added, taking no credit for himself, "In a few
years he had forced up the circulation of the paper to a very
large figure.''

Cockerill, after he and Hearn had both attained fame, recalled
his young reporter with evident appreciation:

> His eyes troubled him greatly in those days. An un-
> kind word from anybody was as serious to him as a cut
> from a whiplash, but I do not believe he was in any
> sense resentful. The classics were at his fingers' ends.
> He was poetic, and his whole nature seemed attuned to
> the beautiful, and he wrote beautiful things that were
> neither wholesome nor inspiring.

The wholesome and inspiring were not fixed as absolute limits.
The colors Hearn brought to journalism undoubtedly contained
the yellow which Cockerill helped turn into the yellow press.
Certainly the recognized value of sensationalism did not wait
upon New York's appreciation. Promptly after Cockerill fired
Hearn, the *Cincinnati Commercial,* edited by Murat Halstead,
hired him. That paper apparently was less fearful of the pressures of gossip about its staff. It took Hearn on at $20 a week.

The *Commercial* meant to get its money's worth. It pushed its
new reporter for sensational stories. Hearn's interest in literature sometimes seemed funny to his associates. His bosses had
little interest in his nonnewspaper work, then taking shape in his
first book, *One of Cleopatra's Nights,* a translation of six short
stories by Théophile Gautier. His marriage to Mattie Foley
shrank into an unhappy, ugly relationship. Many years later
Mattie said that she wearied of Hearn's peculiarities. Certainly
he was wearying of Cincinnati. In October 1877, he abruptly
announced to his managing editor on the *Commercial* that he
was leaving and going South.

Obviously his departure was regretted by the paper. Henry
Watkin, the old printer who had been his first friend, came to
the depot to tell him good-by. So did Edwin Henderson, Hearn's

managing editor, and—even more significantly—Murat Halstead himself. It was a departure not only from the city but, though he worked for a while on the New Orleans *Item,* it was also a departure from the kind of journalism he had helped Cockerill design on the *Enquirer.*

Cockerill did not see Hearn off. He had left his editorial desk a year before to go as correspondent for the *Enquirer* to the Russo-Turkish War. He had also left Cincinnati forever. When he returned to America he worked briefly for the *Washington Post* and later became managing editor of the *Baltimore Gazette.* Then the call came from the gaunt young German newspaperman who had served as secretary of the Liberal Republican Convention in 1872. Joseph Pulitzer, whose path had first crossed Cockerill's in Cincinnati, had purchased the bankrupt *St. Louis Dispatch* for $2500 at a sheriff's sale on December 9, 1878.

Pulitzer had been in little better shape, physically and financially, on his arrival in America in 1864 than Lafcadio Hearn when he came four years later. The frail but adventurous son of a Jew of Magyar descent and a Hungarian-Catholic mother, he had already been turned down as soldier by Austrian, French, and British military authorities before the less choosy recruitment officers of the Union signed him up in Hamburg in 1864. He was seventeen when he took the passage they provided, then slipped off the ship in Boston and swam ashore to collect his own enlistment bounty. Member of a regiment of Germans, he saw little service. Mustered out into the poverty of a land with more veterans than jobs, he made his way west to the Mississippi across from St. Louis. He did not have a cent. So he paid his ferry passage by firing the boilers, his face in blistering heat and his back in a freezing rain.

He got a job as a hostler. He worked on a river packet loaded with people dying of cholera. He was a stevedore for a while. And on the Mississippi waterfront, he saw the teeming violence and poverty of the city which Hearn confronted in Cincinnati. Pulitzer, however, was definitely not "sensitive as a flower." From the beginning he seems to have understood the value of the dollars he did not have. He was pushing up as a bookkeeper in a lumberyard, as a right-of-way agent for a railroad, as a young

German in the politics of the big German vote. Then suddenly, though he regarded himself almost a luckless boy of the streets, he got a job as reporter on the powerful German-language *Westliche Post,* edited by Emil Preetorius and Carl Schurz, both German revolutionary refugees and ardent advocates of democracy.

Despite jibes at his eccentric appearance, the scrawny, red-bearded young reporter showed himself a born crusader and newspaperman. He was also an energetic politician. In the year after he joined the paper, he was both its state-capitol correspondent and a member of the legislature, though technically too young to serve. A politician resented his charges of graft. After an exchange of epithets—"liar" and "puppy"—the politico received a bullet in his hip from the young reporter-legislator's gun. Pulitzer got off with a fine of $105, though his biographer says he was "plainly guilty of felonious assault." But friends rallied. Pulitzer was made a police commissioner in St. Louis. An ardent advocate of the Liberal Republican movement just turned twenty-five, he attended the convention in Cincinnati.

The nomination of Greeley not only put Reid into the editorship of *The Tribune;* Greeley's defeat brought Pulitzer to newspaper ownership. Some of the proprietors of the *Westliche Post,* he said, "became nervous, wanted to retire, thought the paper was ruined by the Greeley campaign, and sold me a proprietary interest in that paper on very liberal terms." Things did not turn out so badly as the older owners feared. They also found out that young Pulitzer was a little too high-geared for them. They bought back his interest for $30,000.

He took a trip back to Hungary. But he was not merely strutting in his luck. A shrewd businessman, in 1874 he bid in the bankrupt *Staats-Zeitung* of St. Louis for a song. Apparently no one else had noticed that, though financially on the rocks, the paper owned an Associated Press franchise. Pulitzer published it for one day, then sold its AP connection for $20,000. He picked up some more money for its machinery.

In December 1878, Pulitzer appeared to be making a similar deal for quick profit. At the Courthouse steps he bought for $2500 the *St. Louis Dispatch,* which an experienced newspaperman said was not "worth a damn." But it also had a press franchise which the knowing suggested he would sell immediately to the *Dispatch*'s limping competitor, the *Post*. Instead, three days later, the combined *Post-Dispatch* appeared. What might have been another quick bargain and sale became instead the foundation of a newspaper empire. Pulitzer called Cockerill, whose work he had watched in Cincinnati, to help him build it.

Then thirty-four, Cockerill's confidence matched his brusqueness. He was two years older than Pulitzer and, said the publisher's biographer, "had already achieved considerable eminence in his profession." He was regarded as likely to be the equal of redoubtable editorial competitors in St. Louis. Pulitzer knew Cockerill would be ready to "face the music on all occasions, no matter how loudly it played."

Often he played it very loudly. As editorial manager Cockerill could be highly agreeable or effectively repulsive—according to one who knew him—depending upon the occasion. As the paper's profits grew and Pulitzer's health began to trouble him, the publisher more and more left the general conduct of the paper to Cockerill. Then as always, Pulitzer had many outside interests. The year after Cockerill arrived he ran unsuccessfully for Congress. He was absent much in the summer and early fall of 1882.

Cockerill turned the paper's fire upon a candidate for Congress, Colonel James O. Broadhead of the law firm of Broadhead, Slayback and Haeussler. The *Post-Dispatch* printed that Broadhead, after accepting a $10,000 retainer from the city in a suit against the Laclede Gas Company, had later abandoned his client to defend the case against the corporation. The paper's articles struck at the whole law firm and one of its partners, Colonel Alonzo W. Slayback, became fighting mad.

In the Elks Club of which both were members, Colonel Slayback asked General Sherman about the editor now become "Colonel," too, on the staff of an Ohio governor. Sherman told Slayback that Cockerill's father had served with him in the Army. He was a fighter and his son would fight, too. The Colonel-lawyer and the Colonel-editor met in the club and, over a bottle of wine, seemed to settle their differences. But a week later in a speech Slayback called the *Post-Dispatch* a blackmailing sheet. The next day Cockerill reprinted an old charge reflecting on Slayback's courage. The lawyer announced his intention of going to the *Post-Dispatch* office, slapping Cockerill's face, and forcing him to retract.

He went. Witnesses differed as to what happened. Slayback shouted a few excited words. Cockerill took a pistol from his drawer and killed him. A friend who had accompanied Slayback said the lawyer was unarmed and was taking off his coat to fight with his fists. Cockerill insisted that Slayback was pointing a revolver at him when he shot. The coroner's jury dodged the issue, but a crowd gathered about the *Post-Dispatch* building. Some threatened to burn it. There were lynch cries. In the highly competitive town other papers gave great space to the story. Cockerill surrendered to the police and was bailed out. No criminal action was taken. But the circulation of the *Post-Dispatch* slumped. Feeling remained high. The "personal" character of the paper's editorial crusading was especially condemned.

Pulitzer, no longer the boy reporter with a gun himself, was shaken. He stood behind Cockerill. But it was agreed that the Colonel take a trip until angers subsided. In the meantime another editor was put in charge. Slowly the resentment diminished but Pulitzer, according to Don Seitz, his longtime associate and biographer, came to a feeling "which he never lost: that he was unwelcome in the town." His ill health increased. Doctors ordered him to take a long and complete rest. Obediently he set off for Europe. But he delayed in New York, where he sensed a bargain. Also, he saw possibility of the welcome he felt he had lost in St. Louis. There, on May 10, 1883, from Jay Gould, who had helped Whitelaw Reid buy control of *The Tribune,* he bought the New York *World* for $346,000. With his "Midas touch" he made it profitable from the start. But he needed Cockerill's news touch, too. Within a week of the purchase Cockerill was in town and in charge of the news of the paper.

Colonel Cockerill obviously had much to do with the "Pulitzer methods" which lifted circulation but scandalized the town.

The paper, as Oswald Garrison Villard wrote, "resorted to 'features,' to 'stunts,' to long stories, increasing headlines, cartoons, sketches, pictures, sensational exploitation of crime." That is oversimplification. Pulitzer and Cockerill brought ideas as well as sensation to the city. Pulitzer wrote his statement of purposes for a paper "dedicated to the cause of the people rather than to that of the purse potentates." Cockerill brought to the front page the "art of imparting nervous force to editorial expression." But the relationship of the two men was never better shown than a few days after they went to work. They prepared to cover the opening of the Brooklyn Bridge, just around the corner from *The World* plant at 32 Park Row, almost as if the bridge belonged to the new *World*. But a printers' strike over the provision of soap and ice in the composing room exploded just at the height of their preparations. Together Pulitzer and Cockerill adjourned to nearby Keenan's Café with John R. O'Donnell, president of Typographical Union No. 6. Not only were ice and soap details settled but a firm basis was established for labor support for *The World*.

The two men worked as "Joe" and "John." They occupied adjoining offices facing Park Row and the old Post Office. Together they made the crusades against boodling aldermen and others. Cockerill splashed crime stories and other colorful copy across the front page, but one of their great causes was the patriotic campaign which raised the funds for the pedestal of the Statue of Liberty. Pulitzer gave Grover Cleveland and the Democratic Party a strong, clear voice, one aspect of the paper's policy about which Cockerill did not always agree with him.

The publisher took a splendid residence on dignified Gramercy Square. Cockerill began his long tenancy of Room No. 1 in the old Astor House, just across City Hall Park from the paper, between Vesey and Barclay streets. Both worked around the clock, but busy Pulitzer in a foolish moment let himself be elected to Congress from a solidly Democratic district. As an inevitable result he was criticized for much absenteeism and resigned his place. No absenteeism slowed *The World*'s growth. Within three years after Pulitzer paid $360,000 for *The World* its year's profit was $500,000. When circulation passed the 100,000 mark a hundred guns were fired in City Hall Park. Every *World* employe was given a tall silk hat.

Greater responsibilities piled on Cockerill's thick shoulders. Five years after he and Pulitzer went to work on *The World,* the Colonel went into the publisher's adjoining office. He found his thin chief slumped in his chair.

"I can't see," he said. "My eyes have given out."

Actually this news came as no surprise. Pulitzer had been increasingly ill, though staying on his feet and on the job for a year. To nervousness and failing eyesight was added trouble with his lungs. He became morbidly sensitive about noise. The first frank announcement of his increasing incapacity was probably the letter of regret he sent, in February 1888, to the New York Press Club explaining his absence from a dinner honoring Cockerill as the club's president. His inability to come, Pulitzer wrote rather quaintly, deprived him of his "long cherished desire of paying tribute to Colonel Cockerill's high talents and charming amiabilities of character."

On October 16, 1890, he announced formally that he had "entirely withdrawn" from *The World*'s editorship because of his health. It was a strange retirement. It did not leave Cockerill in full command. He and George W. Turner, the business manager, were made parts of a regency triumvirate headed by Pulitzer's brother-in-law, Colonel William L. Davis. But on his yacht Pulitzer remained in cable-head command at ports all around the world. The publisher's plan of retirement turned out to be almost a design for chaos and conflict which only the blind man could resolve. Don Seitz associated the opening of the gold-domed new *World* Building in 1890 with the quarrels which followed its dedication.

"Death comes with the new house," he quoted.

There were no exterior signs of death under the gleaming dome. Indeed, as Pulitzer "retired" even the tart *New York Herald* saluted his success. His methods, it said, had been "queer and peculiar, but after all they have suited the present American public." The *Herald* only regretted, it declared, "that he did not encourage us in the new departure which he made, instead of

merely astonishing us, and, we may add—now that it is past—
perhaps a little bit disgusting us.''

The editorial pleased Pulitzer. And Cockerill, who had been
brought to New York to help create the ''new departure,'' had a
right to a share of satisfaction, too. Perhaps neither he nor Pulitzer then knew the directions being taken. Sensationalism, in
content and big headlines, was racing ahead in *The World.*
Obviously, however, with a blind man in the distance in command—and cables at high rates taking the place of ''Joe'' and
''John'' exchanges—Cockerill was himself something of a cap-
tive in the ''new journalism'' he had made. He needed able aides
as the paper grew. He was not always pleased with those he
found or Pulitzer provided.

Ballard Smith, an Indiana man who had acquired the grace
and temperament of a Kentucky gentleman on Watterson's
Courier-Journal, had been brought over from the *New York
Herald.* The acid New York *Sun* said that he was hired to aid
Pulitzer's social ambitions. Even before Pulitzer departed,
Smith and the Colonel were clashing. Smith was hastening the
''new departure'' onward beyond the limits which Cockerill had
set.

Smith hired a youth named Morrill Goddard who had trained
himself, after graduating from Dartmouth, in the New York
Morgue. He rose on *The World,* a reporter who slipped into a
carriage just behind the hearse at Grant's funeral and later
spied on the honeymoon of Grover Cleveland. Sunday Editor
Goddard was a master at dishing up sex, pseudo science, and
death to the taste of the masses. His sensationalism surpassed
anything Cockerill had discovered in Cincinnati.

There were irritations aplenty in his own editorial department. Cockerill roared at Smith and once silenced his answering
roars by banishing him to the Brooklyn office. William H. Merrill, on the editorial page, was getting his orders straight from
the ''retired'' editor on the yacht and rather enjoyed disregarding the Colonel. But the ''feud of the first magnitude'' in which
Cockerill became engaged was not with his supposed subordinates but with the other member of the regency, Business Manager Turner. Their quarrels over the size of the paper to be

published each day were perhaps conflicts standard in most newspaper offices. They arrayed themselves and their supporters against each other over other office details. But as Pulitzer's biographer Seitz said later, the basic quarrel was "as to who really was IT in the establishment." Yet with the real IT still commanding from cable-heads in Singapore or Yokohama or more distant and obscure ports, their quarreling moved from collision to futility to frustation.

"Neither was longer paying close attention to affairs," wrote Seitz, in possible reflection of a Pulitzer impression.

Turner had acquired a small yacht of his own. At sea and on shore he turned to other pleasures. And though it was just across City Hall Square from *The World,* Cockerill spent more and more of his time in his room at the Astor House. Some have suggested that there was often a bottle of bourbon on his table. Though Cockerill's salary was said to be the then-enormous sum of $15,000 a year, living at the old Astor did not constitute great luxury. His needs apparently were few. Much of his money went to young and poorer newspapermen, often given brusquely but with the same impulse which prompted him to pay for Hearn's first piece out of his own pocket long before.

Cockerill and Turner apparently agreed on one thing: that they had earned an interest in the property. But it was Turner who, late in the spring of 1891, as Seitz put it, "far overestimating his value to the paper," made a flat demand for a controlling share in it. Cockerill did not minimize his contribution to *The World.* Undoubtedly he felt that any share given Turner on demand should be matched by a grant to him. There was no discussion of that. Pulitzer instantly dismissed the business manager. Then, Seitz reported, "feeling that he might as well have a round up," the blind publisher ordered Cockerill back to the *Post-Dispatch* from which he had brought him to help build *The World* eight years before.

Cockerill was forty-six. He seemed a personage "upon whom the wear and tear of newspaper management made no abrasion." He was proud beneath his supposedly tough hide. He was no longer the obscure young man he had been in Cincinnati when shy Lafcadio Hearn had slipped in with the manuscript in his hand.

The Colonel declined to go back to St. Louis. Instead he left forever the towering *World* he had helped to build. Farewell to him from *The World* was only a curt paragraph by Editorial Writer Merrill to the effect that there were few indispensable men. Cockerill's part in the pattern of new vivid, often strident journalism was completed. Indeed, he got out before, many were to feel, that sensational development got out of hand. Experiments with color presses had already been going on before he left. But it was not until three years after his departure that there first appeared the "funny paper" in which Richard Outcault presented his "Yellow Kid." Only then did "yellow journalism" acquire its name. Cockerill had prepared the way for it. He escaped its label.

The Colonel got a paper of his own, *The Commercial Advertiser*, backed by Collis P. Huntington and Mark Hopkins, the railroad magnates. The publication did not prosper. Perhaps the Colonel had lost his touch. Possibly he was effective only under Pulitzer's guiding hand. Maybe, as he said when he left the *Advertiser* on September 24, 1894, the place under the railway magnates and their lawyers was not compatible to him. He joined the staff of *The Herald,* then run *in absentia,* too, by the younger James Gordon Bennett. In January 1895, he was assigned to the Far East, where he did notable work as a correspondent in China and Japan.

Early in 1896, he sent back an article from Japan where he had recently met—not for the first time—"a man who, in his way is as remarkable in literature as Goldsmith, Keats and Shelley." Lafcadio Hearn, then forty-six, had moved like a brilliant but uncertain meteor across the sky of letters. He had wandered and written, quarreled with editors, suffered under real and imagined humiliations, sought the tropics and strange people under its sun. He had spent some time in the New York which fascinated Cockerill and been appalled by its noise and immensity. Apparently he and Cockerill did not meet there, though the editor often heard of him "living in humble retire-

ment, enjoying his own rich thoughts and letting the world roll
on in its own whimsical way.''

But now as a sort of man in exile, too, though on a plush
payroll, Cockerill sought Hearn out in Japan. There the writer
had tried journalism and then become a Japanese citizen with a
Japanese wife, and a professor of English literature at the Impe-
rial University. When Cockerill came, Hearn had just published
his third Japanese book, *Kokoro*. In terms of literary history the
Herald correspondent wrote too little of the man he saw. He was
preoccupied with the man he remembered, the young man making literary forms who fashioned a new sort of literary form for
himself—and for Cockerill—in sensational journalism.

The Colonel sent his story about Hearn back to *The Herald*. It
was reprinted soon after in *Current Literature*. One of the last
pieces he wrote, he followed it homeward. At Shepheard's Hotel
in Cairo, he was stricken with apoplexy and died on April 11,
1896. *The Herald* praised its correspondent. So did *The World*.
Now its praises seem a little perfunctory. It remained for the
newspaper trade publication the *Journalist* to say at the time
that he was the true ''father'' of the new journalism. And even
he might not have recognized his child as the gap-toothed yellow
brat which New York newcomer Hearst and blind Pulitzer were,
many thought, competitively making a monster never equaled
for blatancy and brass.

14

"Words Can Kill"

Melville E. Stone was thirty-eight that grim May day in 1886 when he went to the Cook County Courthouse in Chicago to attend the inquest over the shattered bones and torn flesh which were all that remained of the body of Policeman Mathias Degan. He was present as editor of *The Chicago Daily News,* which he had led to circulation supremacy in a competitive decade. Along with other papers in the angry and terrified city then, it faced its biggest news story in the Haymarket bombing of the night before.

Stone had heard the explosion from his house on West Adams

Street. Soon he heard police wagons rolling by filled with
wounded and dying officers. The editor called William Pinkerton
of the detective agency—a group hated by labor as a tough corps
of strike-breaking industrial police. He instructed Pinkerton to
round up anarchists whom he knew and named. But next morning the coroner, the sheriff, and the state's attorney were per-
plexed. They had neither known bomb-thrower nor available
clue.

No matter, said Stone. "Words can kill," he declared later.

He went to a standing desk and wrote out what he believed a
proper indictment stating that Degan had been killed by a person or persons unknown acting in conspiracy with editors and
agitators of the racial labor movement. Some of these "Chicago
Anarchists" were already in the hands of the police. The net
was spread for more, including especially a slim, dark, thirty-
eight-year-old Texan named Albert Richard Parsons, whose radical views were certain but whose philosophical ideas about anarchism seemed often confused.

Stone was not the most violent reactionary in the capitalistic
journalism of Chicago. He had not gone so far as *The Chicago
Tribune* under the editorship of Joseph Medill, who had once
fought for freedom and the nomination of Abraham Lincoln.
That paper, as the 1880s advanced to the climax of unrest at the
Haymarket, a place where farmers came to sell their grain, had
an effective plan for those Parsons and others called the
proletariat. It suggested: "The simplest plan, probably, when
one is not a member of the Humane Society, is to put arsenic in
the supplies of food furnished the unemployed or the tramp."

On *The Daily News*, Stone was more concerned with reporters
than with such rhetoric. He was the son of a Methodist circuit
rider who added to his limited ministerial income by making
tools for sawmills. The younger Stone, after apprenticeship as a
reporter in Chicago, had become an iron founder. Burned out in
the great fire of 1871, he went back into newspaper work and in
1875 helped establish *The Chicago Daily News*. He built it rapidly on the basis of what he liked to call "detective journalism." In the roaring railroad strikes of 1877, he sent out reporters, some on horseback, some disguised as rioters, to bring back

the news. One was arrested because he was "in the front ranks of the mob." In 1886, as detective editor he had his list of anarchists before any bomb exploded; Parsons was high on the list.

His name was easy to read and remember. He was no foreign agitator in the linguistic babel and muttering melting pot Chicago had become. He was the product of the oldest and best American stock. Ironically, it appeared later, he began his career as a rebel in defense of Negro slavery. But his story ran—and runs—from the lingering frontier to the still-unfinished industrial revolution.

When Albert Parsons was born in Montgomery, Alabama, on June 24, 1848, his family, which had come there from Maine, could count its genealogy with as much pride as any plantation Southerners, and more than most Chicago plutocrats. His father, Samuel Parsons, who operated a shoe and leather factory, traced his line back to 1632, when his first American ancestor had arrived in Narragansett Bay.

Young Albert's philanthropic father and devout Methodist mother both died before he was five. The boy went to live with his oldest brother, William Henry Parsons, then editor and proprietor of the *Telegraph* in Tyler, Texas. The newspaper business was not flourishing in little Tyler. The Parsons moved westward to lands along the Brazos River. It was still a frontier country; buffalo and antelope abounded about the Parsons' lands, which were not near enough neighbors to "hear each other's dog bark or the cocks crow."

Albert may have been boasting when he said in recollection that, as a boy of ten or eleven, he became an expert with pistol and rifle at hunting and riding. He was only eleven in 1859 when he went to Waco to live with a sister whose husband, in a region where military titles became ubiquitous, was a Major Bird. They sent him to Galveston, where he was apprenticed for seven years to learn his trade as a printer on the *Galveston Daily News,* then the wealthiest and most influential paper in Texas.

Work as a printer's devil did not satisfy Albert when war came in 1861. He slipped off as a thirteen-year-old soldier with a local Confederate company. His master and guardian snatched him back. Still, though he afterward said he had been opposed to

slavery and spoke of the war as "the slave-holders' Rebellion,"
he became a "powder monkey" instead of a printer's devil in
the company of one brother and then joined the cavalry brigade
of which W. H. Parsons was the General. He was riding as one
of McInoly's Confederate Scouts when the war ended.

He was little more than a boy when he came home at seventeen. He had a good mule. He swapped it for the right to harvest
forty acres of corn, paying ex-slaves who helped him the first
wages they had ever received. From his profits he got enough
money for six months' tuition at Waco (now Baylor) University. Then in the mounting bitterness of Reconstruction, per-
versely it seemed to old friends and neighbors, he took the Re-
publican-Negro side in a weekly he established called the *Spectator*.

His sympathies for the Negroes, he said, had been stirred in
memory of "dear old 'Aunt Easter,' " whom other Southerners
would have called a Negro Mammy. Parsons was soon speaking
to shouting multitudes of freedom from cotton bales in torch-
light among their cabins in river bottoms, in crowded court-
houses where black audiences were ringed by menacing white
men. The Ku Klux Klan watched him. A banker hit him with a
piece of iron because he had helped elect a Negro to the legislature. The Waco *Spectator* folded. But Republican politicians got
him a job as secretary of the Texas state senate, later as a deputy
U.S. revenue collector. He traveled, too, by horseback as correspondent and agent of the *Houston Daily Telegraph*. On such
travels, he met "a charming young Spanish-Indian maiden" on
her uncle's ranch near Buffalo Creek.

The Associated Press, in reports about Parsons later, described this maiden, Lucy Eldine Gonzales, whom he married in
Austin on June 10, 1871, as his Negro wife. Apparently Lucy
disregarded this statement except to reprint the indignant report of a friend that she was "represented in the dailies with the
face of a negro and the retreating forehead of a monkey." Obviously the last was slander. She was a good-looking woman. The
picture, however, that she published of herself, in the book she
edited about her husband, bears out the possibility that she had
some Negro blood.

Undoubtedly she was a woman of force and ability. During her husband's trial she was called "a female tiger." Undoubtedly, also, Parsons loved her very much. Still, in terms of Texas attitudes toward miscegenation at the time, any suggestion that his wife was touched with the tar brush would have built hostility and inhospitality for him among Texans. And their position could have brought to him and to Lucy the passion of the proscribed.

Parsons seemed unequal to swaggering enmity. Small and thin, he never looked like a Texas scout. Indeed, he always appeared more dapper than daring. His clothes were exceptionally neat. His wide mustache was precisely trimmed. Even when he was a fugitive in a great American manhunt, a stout citizen who harbored him referred to him as a "dear little man." He was gentle, joking, convivial. Only when he took the pen or the platform did he grow to powerful, even terrifying, proportions.

He was not a man to be pushed around. As he described it, his departure from Texas was not flight. Indeed, he went North on an editorial excursion as representative of the *Texas Agriculturalist* of Austin as guest of the Missouri, Kansas & Texas Railway. Considering his involvement in labor troubles later, his free trip North as a railroad guest is another irony. Lucy joined him in Philadelphia. They decided to settle in Chicago. Many hoped for work there in the gallant and tumultuous rebuilding of the city from the ashes of the great fire of 1871. More substantial structures rose. There also rose, as a *Chicago Tribune* writer quoted by Parsons said later, whole streets of slums "where the possession of a cooking-stove was regarded as a badge of aristocracy, the holes of which were rented to other less wealthy neighbors for a few pennies per hour."

Albert became a member of Typographical Union No. 16. He "subbed" for a time on the *Inter-Ocean* ("Republican in everything; independent in nothing") on which Melville Stone, not yet ready to start his own paper, was a news executive. Then he went to work under "permit" on the *Times*, operated by elegant, sensation-mongering Wilbur Storey. No composing room job alone absorbed Parsons' energies, however. A year after he arrived he became, he said, interested in the "labor question."

Complaints had been made that great sums, which a charitable world had sent to incinerated Chicago, had gone not to the poor but to rings of speculators. He went on setting type while the newspapers quickly condemned the critics of those who handled these funds as "communists, robbers, loafers." Nevertheless, he decided that what white Texans had done to the Negroes was what Chicago employers were doing to workingmen there.

In 1876, at a workingmen's meeting in Pittsburgh, he watched a split between conservative and radical workers. He joined the radicals in forming the Workingmen's Party of the United States. In 1877, when the great railroad strike spread across the country, he had advanced in radicalism to the point where he was called to address 30,000 labor people assembled in Chicago. He eloquently urged the crowd to support the program of the Workingmen's Party which was to "exercise the sovereign ballot for the purpose of obtaining State control of all means of production, transportation, communication and exchange, thus taking these instruments of labor and wealth out of the hands or control of private individuals, corporations, monopolists and syndicates."

When the orator went to work as printer at the *Times* next day he found that his name had been stricken from the roll of employes. A day later he was picked up by the police and questioned roughly in a room lined with angry citizens. Parsons reported that while he calmly answered the questions there were mutterings around him—"Hang him," "Lynch him," "Lock him up." The police chief himself asked if he didn't "know better than to come up here from Texas and incite the working people to insurrection." The chief took Parsons' arm as he led him to the door to release him.

"Parsons," he told him, "your life is in danger. I advise you to leave the city at once. Beware. Everything you say or do is made known to me. I have men on your track who shadow you. Do you know you are liable to be assassinated any moment on the street?"

The thin Texan asked him by whom and what for.

"Why," said the chief, "those Board of Trade men would as leave hang you to a lamp-post as not."

Parsons went to *The Tribune* composing room "partly to get a night's work and partly to be near the men of my own craft, whom I instinctively felt sympathized with me." He got no work. Instead two strong men grabbed him, threatened him, and pushed him from the building. Excitement was left behind him. Joseph Medill himself, Parsons reported, came nervously and assured his printers that he had nothing to do with the incident. As Parsons walked the streets filled with wary police and soldiers, he realized that he was blacklisted by every big paper in Chicago.

He joined the Knights of Labor. The Workingmen's Party put up a full county ticket and nominated him for County Clerk. He ran ahead of the rest of the ticket, but his 7963 votes were far from enough. They were not enough when he campaigned for alderman, Congressman. Still he rose in labor ranks. He was delegate to the convention of the Workingmen's Party in Newark, New Jersey, in 1878, when its name was changed to the Socialist Labor Party. In the same year he organized the Trades Assembly of Chicago and became its first president. In 1879, the Socialist Labor Party in Allegheny City, Pennsylvania, nominated him as the Labor candidate for President of the United States. Parsons declined, but he always remembered that he was the first working man nominated by working men for the Presidency.

He had come a long way from Texas even if it seemed a dark and dangerous way. But he still had Lucy to support. They now had a boy and girl, Albert, Jr., and Lulu Eda. In 1876, Parsons became assistant editor of the weekly *Socialist*. But there were differences and dissensions in the Socialist organization over methods. Parsons began to feel that political reformation was a hopeless task. The politicians were stuffing the ballot boxes, he said. Better wages and more leisure were essential if the workers could even vote their convictions. So Parsons went to work, with the aid of labor organizations, pressing on workers in various parts of the country the necessity for an eight-hour day.

By 1884, he already considered himself an anarchist and in October of that year he joined in the founding in America of the International Working People's Association—the Black Inter-

national—which was already well established in Europe. The
International chose him as the editor of its weekly newspaper,
The Alarm, which began to sound its louder and louder warnings to workers on October 1, 1884. It was, however, no great
addition to a press of Chicago rising then to power and profits.
Governor John Peter Altgeld later described it as an obscure
little sheet. Parsons himself said the paper "belonged to the
organization."

"It was theirs," he declared. "They sent in articles—Tom,
Dick and Harry; everybody wanted to have something to say,
and I had no right to shut off anybody's complaint. *The Alarm*
was a labor paper, and it was specifically published for the purpose of allowing every human being who wore chains to clank
them in the columns of *The Alarm.*"

Still he edited it and built its appeal. He wrote much. Promot-
ing it and its cause, he traveled and spoke in many cities to big
audiences and to little ones huddled in crowded halls—many
dark and drafty, up rickety stairs, to rooms like one in Springfield, Illinois, which a "capitalistic" reporter said was as "cold
as a dead man's feet." Often he began by stating calmly it was
well known that he was an anarchist. The people to whom he
spoke and many others, who only fearfully heard reports of what
he said, were not exactly sure what an anarchist was. Parsons
himself never quite formulated his social philosophy. Often he
used the terms *socialism* and *anarchism* as if they were inter-
changeable. His statements concerning the use of violence were
contradictory. He had a notion, which sometimes seemed sinister,
that the invention of dynamite had rendered armies and police
corps powerless. All who listened to him, however, felt his passion for his cause. And those who knew him found him an often
gay and always friendly man.

No one was more eager than he about the general strike for the
eight-hour day which had been called by the Federation of Organized Trades and Labor Unions (forerunner of the American
Federation of Labor) on May 1, 1886. But when 38,000 men
struck in Chicago, he set out for Cincinnati, where he spoke on
Sunday, May 2. He was out of town on May 3, when, in a
collision of workers, scabs, and Pinkerton police near Cyrus H.

McCormick's reaper works, six workers (according to labor reports) were killed and others wounded.

Apparently he knew nothing about the clash when he got back to town. He did not know that his friend August Spies, co-editor of the anarchist *Arbeiter-Zeitung,* had issued a call for a giant protest rally near the Haymarket on Desplaines Street for the evening of May 4 "to denounce the latest atrocious act of the police." Instead, Parsons, when he got to town, put a notice in *The Chicago Daily News* of a meeting on the same night of the American Group of the International in a hall half a mile away. In the evening he set out for this meeting with his wife, their two small children, aged five and seven, and Mrs. Lizzie Holmes, who was his editorial assistant on *The Alarm.* On the way two reporters, old acquaintances, hailed him.

He told them he had not heard of the meeting near the Haymarket. He was in a good humor in a tense atmosphere. Playfully, he slapped one of the newsmen on the back and asked if he was armed.

The reporter countered: "Have you any dynamite about you?"

Parsons laughed.

"He's a very dangerous-looking man, isn't he?" Lucy Parsons said smiling beside her children.

They got on the streetcar headed for their small meeting. There the question before the group was the organization of the seamstresses of Chicago. A small appropriation was authorized to help in the work. But as the meeting adjourned, a messenger hurried in. August Spies sent word that there was a great need for speakers at the rally. The Parsons and Mrs. Holmes, with the children tagging along, walked half a mile to the Haymarket meeting where, from farm wagons, speakers on Desplaines Street were addressing crowds which packed the open space between Lake and Randolph streets.

Parsons reached the meeting while Spies was speaking. The German journalist talked on "Justice," referring to the murder of the strikers on the day before. Then Parsons left his wife and children in another wagon and mounted the one used as a rostrum. All agreed that he spoke rather statistically for nearly an hour on the eight-hour day. A stenographic reporter sent by *The Tribune* with instructions to take down only the most inflammatory utterances found little to jot down. One man in the crowd did shout that they should hang Jay Gould, exploiter of railroad men. But Parsons quickly disagreed.

"Kill Jay Gould," he replied, "and like a jack-in-a-box another or a hundred others like him will come up in his place under the existing social conditions. To kill the individual millionaire or capitalist would be like killing a flea upon a dog, whereas the purpose of Socialism is the destruction of the dog— the change of the existing system."

The children with Lucy and Lizzie in the other wagon must have been getting sleepy. Mayor Carter Harrison, who had come to the meeting fearful, apparently was getting bored. The weather was threatening. Samuel Fielden, an Englishman who had come to anarchism from the mills of Lancaster and Methodist lay preaching, spoke next. Then "a cloud, accompanied by a cold wind and with some threatenings of rain, swept up in the northern sky."

Parsons suggested adjournment to the hall over Zepf's Saloon about half a block away. But a man in the crowd said it was already occupied by a meeting of the Furniture Workers' Union. Fielden said he would cut his speech short. The crowd dwindled down to a few hundred. Mayor Harrison went to the police station nearby and told Inspector John Bonfield that no trouble loomed and he could release his reserves. Parsons left the speakers' wagon and joined his family. With the children he and Lucy went to Zepf's Saloon, later described as a sort of anarchist center but certainly in Chicago, which then retained many European customs, a place of family gatherings, too.

Suddenly at the disintegrating rally behind them hell broke loose. First Inspector Bonfield, disregarding the Mayor's suggestion, had rushed to the scene with a corps of cops. Loudly he ordered the company which was already scattering peaceably to disperse.

"But, captain, we are peaceable," replied Fielden.

Then from some hand, never to be known, the bomb was flung

into the contingent of nearly 200 police officers. There was no doubt about its lethal effect. The explosion not only killed men and shook buildings (Seven officers were fatally injured. Many more wounded. No certain count of the dead and wounded among the spectators was ever made.); the blast also created a lasting confusion as to what followed. Nevertheless, the Associated Press telegraphed to the nation that the police recovering from shock "gallantly" charged upon the "cowardly curs," shooting at every step. And it reported as fact, never afterward firmly established, that the Socialists returned the fire with guns obtained from the saloon to which Parsons and his family had gone.

The Associated Press required no judicial processes to fix the guilt as it reported the bombing. Before the smoke had blown away, in its May 5 dispatch from Chicago, it flatly stated: "The collision between the police and the anarchists was brought about by the leaders of the latter, August Spies, Sam Fielding [sic] and A. R. Parsons, endeavoring to incite a large mass meeting to riot and bloodshed."

Certainly Parsons had no reason to expect affection from what he consistently called the "monopolistic newspapers." In his Haymarket speech he had declared that in the interest of the corporations such papers had consistently blamed workingmen for disorder. He recalled that the *Chicago Times*, in 1877, had said that hand grenades ought to be thrown among striking sailors. That paper was the first dynamiter, he said. He mentioned *The Chicago Tribune*'s editorial suggesting that poison be put in bread given to the poor. He remembered that Frank Leslie's *Illustrated Weekly* had declared that "the American toiler must be driven to his task either by the slave-driver's lash or the immediate prospect of want." *The New York Herald,* he said, insisted that unemployed tramps should be given lead, not bread. He referred to Jay Gould, who owned newspapers as well as railroads and was charged by responsible editors with trying to control the Associated Press for stock-rigging purposes. Gould, he said, had hired thugs in East St. Louis to kill in cold blood nine unarmed men and women.

"Now, for years past the Associated Press, manipulated by Jay Gould and other traitors to the Republic, and their infamous minions, have been sowing the seeds of revolution."

If he mentioned Melville Stone, later to become the chief operator of a much changed Associated Press, it is not recorded. Stone's paper had grown. The year before the riot, 1885, he had borrowed gunners and a battery of artillery from an armory to salute on the lakefront on a summer day the fact that the circulation of his *News*, now publishing a morning as well as an afternoon edition, had reached 100,000, largest circulation of any American daily. He did not mean to let any other paper catch up. So he called the Pinkertons to make arrests and good copy, too.

Arrests were quickly made. Jailed promptly were Spies; Michael Schwab, assistant editor of the *Arbeiter-Zeitung;* Oscar Neebe, an organizer for the Beer Wagon Drivers' Union and owner of $2 worth of stock in the *Arbeiter-Zeitung;* Adolph Fischer, a printer on that paper; George Engel, a painter; and Louis Lingg, an organizer for the Carpenters' Union. Lingg, twenty-two or twenty-three, was the youngest of them all. As a German his English was limited. And even the Associated Press described him as handsome as Apollo. It also concluded that he was the most desperate anarchist of the lot and the man who made the bomb. But Parsons was not to be found. When the explosion came he was standing near the window at Zepf's looking out. With him in the room were Mrs. Parsons, the children, Lizzie Holmes, his editorial assistant, Fischer the printer, "and other comrades." Parsons turned to his companions.

"Don't be frightened," he said. "Don't be frightened."

"What is it?" Mrs. Holmes asked.

"I don't know. Maybe the Illinois regiments have brought up their Gatling guns."

Bullets whistled through the open door. People rushed in from the street. All moved for safety to a room at the back of the building. Someone shut the door and they were left in the dark and in doubt as to what had happened. Presently the door was opened. One after another the group moved cautiously into the street. Everything was quiet. No policemen were in sight. But as the Parsons group walked up the Desplaines Street viaduct headed homeward, Lizzie Holmes instinctively insisted that Parsons should leave the city for a few days at least.

Parsons hesitated, but agreed.

At the depot of the Chicago & Northwestern Railroad Mrs. Holmes bought him a ticket on the midnight train to Turner Junction. At that small place, less than forty miles from the city, he found a hotel room. Early next morning he arrived at the Holmes house in Geneva, a few miles away. William Holmes, his assistant's husband, sheltered him and went out to hear the reports from Chicago. Exaggerated rumors had already reached Geneva that over a score of dynamite bombs had been set off in Chicago. More reliable news in the papers indicated that the city was in a state of shock and anger. A network of detectives was seeking Parsons.

Obviously Holmes' house would soon be searched. Parsons shaved off his wide mustache. He took off his collar and neck scarf, tucked his pantaloons into his boots. He had come, Holmes said, a trim, neat city gentleman. He left looking like a respectable tramp. He went by the nearby village of St. Charles to the town of Elgin. There he took the train to Waukesha, Wisconsin, less than twenty miles west of Milwaukee. On May 10, he knocked on the door of a man he had never seen but who was a reader of *The Alarm*.

"When I heard this knock on the door," said Daniel Webster Hoan, a pumpmaker, "I felt that someone out of the common was there. I went and opened it myself.... 'Come in, and God bless you,' I said. 'The Lord sent you here—you've come to the right place.' I knew who it was, and I knew it was all right. I took him to the shop, and we talked it over. I told him he would be as safe as a child of my own, and that the Lord would preserve him to do his work yet. We got out some old clothes, a big gray coat, and a wide-brimmed hat. Then I brought him in and introduced him to the family as 'Mr. Jackson,' and said he would stay and work for me a while."

Despite the scorn he expressed for organized religion, Parsons rejoiced at this welcome in the Lord's name. He felt safe then, so safe that by roundabout ways he sent a defiant message in a letter to Melville Stone's *Daily News* to those trying to catch him.

In old clothes, with his hair and beard grown long, Parsons worked happily doing ornamental work on the Hoan house and as a hand in Hoan's factory which provided the pumps for Waukesha, then a fashionable resort around therapeutic springs. A month passed. But suddenly Annie, a young hired girl in the Hoan household, blurted to him.

"Say—they say you are Mr. Parsons—don't you think—" Parsons felt his face go cold and white.

"Is that so? Who says so?"

One man had told another that another man told him. The fugitive informed the old pumpmaker that he had better leave. Hoan went out, tracked down the story, and with "religious swear words" undertook to squelch the gossip of "a pack of fools."

Still it was obvious that Parsons could not hide forever. He began to feel that he ought to go back and join his comrades on trial. Lucy talked with defense attorneys in Chicago. Then on June 19, a month and a half after the riot, Parsons wrote a letter saying that he would return. Hoan slipped into Chicago and made arrangements. One of Hoan's boys (though probably not Daniel, Jr., who in a later changed time was socialist Mayor of Milwaukee and honorary chairman of the U.S. Conference of Mayors) drove Parsons in a light wagon to Milwaukee. A policeman looking for a thief stopped them there. He let them pass after joking conversation. Then as Parsons' train approached Chicago he decided to hop off at Kinzie Street where the engine slowed rather than risk being seen in the depot.

He slipped and fell. An Irish policeman picked him up. He scolded Parsons for his carelessness but, considering his appearance as a poorly dressed farmer, with unbarbered hair and beard and a market basket on his arm, he let him go on. By roundabout ways he reached the house of other friends named Ames. Avoiding detectives, Lucy joined him there. He was barbered and dressed in a "quiet suit of blue" to appear as the well-known, well-groomed anarchist. At two in the afternoon, he stepped from a hack at the courthouse door. A nervous defense attorney got him quickly before the bench of Judge Joseph E. Gary—just before Inspector Bonfield, who recognized him, could arrest him.

"I present myself for trial with my comrades, Your Honor."

Later an Associated Press reporter described him as tripping lightly into court and flippantly saying he was ready at once to be tried for his life. In her story Lucy set down as a sample of capitalistic reporting an article in which a newsman asked Parsons, described as the "arch-conspirator" and "the-much-sought-after-dynamiter," where he had been.

"He laughingly remarked, 'Oh, only rusticating at a fashionable western summer resort.'"

He had been in such a resort. But nobody knew better than Parsons that he was not involved in a laughing matter. It was clear that the strategy of the state was the plan of Melville Stone of the *Daily News* at the time of the inquest. Not the bomber, never found, but men who might have incited him were to be tried for their lives. And their trial began with the solemn statement of Police Captain M. J. Schaack that there had been an anarchist plot to "bomb and rack the city" on the night of the riot. The jury panel was carefully gathered by a bailiff intent upon conviction. And some of those who went on the jury, over defense objections, did so despite their admission that they had already expressed opinions of the defendants' guilt. In Parsons' case extracts from articles which had appeared in *The Alarm* over a number of years were admitted as evidence. The climax of the trial, *The Times* said, was Parsons' appearance on the witness stand when he repeated his Haymarket speech. He was "composed and eloquent," that paper reported, and in "measured tones he went on from eloquence to oratory, from oratory to logic, and from logic to argument."

No argument served. The jury gave the verdict expected by the angry city. Crowds around the courthouse cheered at the news. Before the jury retired the confident *Tribune* published proposals that $100,000 be raised to reward the jury for its arduous and patriotic labors. Parsons, Spies, Fielden, Engel, Schwab, Lingg, and Fischer were sentenced to death. Neebe, whose chief crime was that he owned $2 worth of stock in Spies' *Arbeiter-Zeitung,* was given fifteen years.

Order had triumphed over anarchy or, as Parsons put it, he and his comrades were doomed "that the wage slaves of Chicago and America may be horrified, terror-stricken, and driven like 'rats back to their holes,' to hunger, slavery, misery and death." But suddenly in the aftermath of the verdict many citizens were troubled. The case went up on appeal. Higher courts upheld the verdict. Then the disturbed consciences of many built a mounting demand for clemency. Stone of the *Daily News* was evidently concerned about Parsons' case.

There was special sympathy for Parsons. Even those who hated his ideas recognized his reputation as a brave, honest man passionately devoted to the cause of the oppressed. His voluntary surrender had been dramatic. Men had been moved by his eloquence. He was the only native American in the group. Under the law in Illinois, however, it was necessary that he apply to the Governor for clemency. Spies, Fielden, and Schwab signed their petitions. But Parsons not only wanted justice rather than mercy, he believed that if he asked for commutation, it would make it certain that Lingg, Engel, and Fischer would swing. He demanded, quoting Patrick Henry, liberty or death.

Two days before the scheduled hanging, Stone went to his cell. In his autobiography, *Fifty Years a Journalist,* the *Daily News* editor said Parsons asked him to come. He produced a note Parsons sent with his request: "M. E. Stone. Please bring along a box of good medium Havana's. P." Stone said that he made haste to comply with the request. But his version of the visit differed sharply from that told by Parsons to his friends.

"He at once began an appeal," Stone reported of his visit. "He urged me to intercede with the governor for a commutation of his sentence. We talked for two or three hours. I had no doubt then, as I had had no doubt from the beginning, of his honesty of purpose.... It was a very trying situation." Stone, the man who had called in the Pinkertons and drawn the charge, related that he told the prisoner he could not arrange a commutation or pardon, unless he was ready to admit his error.

"I longed for some chance to help him, and it was heartbreaking that our minds could not meet. It was inevitable that my respect for him was greatly increased by his steady refusal to yield in the slightest degree. But my sense of duty was equally compelling. Finally a fit of desperation seized him. He cried out that he could never leave his children a legacy of dishonour; that at least he was not a coward, and that I was responsible for his fate, and that all that was necessary to save him was that I should make an effort. When I replied that greatly as I grieved over it, I must follow the path which seemed to me to be right, he suddenly became violent and made an attack upon me. At that instant the door to his cell opened and a bailiff entered and seized him while I withdrew.''

Captain William P. Black, chief defense attorney, and Dyer D. Lum, Parsons' successor as editor of *The Alarm,* both declared Stone came uninvited. He sent word by a bailiff that he wanted to see Parsons in the prison library. Parsons refused to go. If Stone wanted to see him, he could come to his cell. Stone came to the cell door. Parsons insisted that if he wished to talk he must come inside. That was making it difficult for the more prominent editor. Parsons once said that his salary as editor of *The Alarm* was only $8 a week. Certainly it was an obscure paper. Stone soon was to receive $350,000 for his interest in the *News* plus a guarantee of $10,000 a year for ten years. The night he came to see Parsons his paper had more circulation than any other in the United States.

Stone entered the cell. Dyer Lum declared that the successful journalist pled with Parsons to "sign the retraction of his principles and live." Captain Black quoted his condemned client as saying that Stone "spent nearly two hours in my cell, urging me to sign a petition, and assuring me that if I would do so, I should have his influence and the influence of his paper in favor of the commutation of my sentence; and I know that means my sentence would be commuted.''

Perhaps as Lum said, Stone "with kindness, with sarcasm, with appeals to love for wife and children—with all the arts he knew so well to employ—'' beseeched Parsons "to sign, guaranteeing life as reward.'' The parting of the two editors may have been as harsh and dramatic as Lum described it.

Parsons was pictured as weary with Stone's importunities, pointing an accusing finger at him.

"You, Mr. Stone, are responsible for my fate. No one has done more than you to compass the iniquity under which I stand here awaiting Friday's deliverance. I courted trial, knowing my innocence; your venomous attacks condemned us in advance. I shall die with less fear and less regret than you will feel in living, for my blood is upon your head. I am through. Go!"

The sentences of Fielden and Schwab were commuted to life imprisonment. And young, handsome Lingg—"the bomb-maker," the AP called him—escaped the noose, too. One story is that his *maedchen* on a last visit gave him in a kiss a high explosive in a small case or cap. On the eve of the hanging, guards thought he was lighting a cigar with a candle when he lit the fuse of this "fulminating cap." Half of his handsome head was blown away.

Mile-long last minute petitions for clemency were being presented to the Governor in Springfield. William Penn Nixon, publisher of the strongly Republican *Inter-Ocean*, served as chairman of an amnesty committee. Potter Palmer, great merchant, and Marvin Hughitt, railroad president, put their names down with 40,000 other signers of a petition for clemency. But the routine of preparation for hanging went forward at the jail in Chicago. With four to hang, carpenters were extending a dull reddish-brown gallows originally built for the execution of three Italians who had killed a fellow countryman and shipped his body to Pittsburgh in a trunk.

Night fell on the jail. It was surrounded by police and soldiers and a corps of reporters who noted every minute detail. Indeed, *The Chicago Tribune* on the execution eve charged that an opposition "morning paper" was inventing as well as recording. It said that paper was making up stories about threats of riots by workers sympathetic with the condemned. Such press irresponsibility, it declared, was calculated to cause serious trouble in the already almost hysterical city. It did not name the paper or its "professional liar," but the morning edition of the *Daily News* was the competitor *The Tribune* most resented.

Inside the city prison that night the only sounds were the tramp and low talk of guards and the mewing of the jailhouse cat. All the anarchists slept soundly, though a peering AP reporter noted that Parsons at times stirred uneasily as if dreams were coursing through his mind. Once he awoke to complain of the hum of conversation in the jailor's office which was disturbing his sleep. The door of the jailor's office was shut. The mewing cat was put in the basement. Still, roused, Parsons in a low voice sang an anarchist song, "Marching to Liberty," to the tune of the "Marseillaise." Then, the AP man put it, he "had the nerve to entertain his guard with a song." This time he selected "Annie Laurie." He sang the sweet song, the reporter said, entirely through, rested his head on his hands for a moment, and then sang it again. "His fortitude was the wonder of all who heard him."

Bailiff Hanks suggested that he ought to try to get a little sleep. Parsons answered in a joking way.

"How can a fellow go to sleep with the music made by putting up the gallows?"

He and the others were ready in the morning. The doomed men could hear the gallows being tested with heavy bags of sand. Parsons declined a glass of wine but took a cup of coffee. He was the last of the four—all already wearing their white shrouds—to come on the platform in the prison yard. All behaved courageously. Spies, said a reporter, did not appear to regard the noose as of any more consequence than a new linen collar. Fischer showed almost too much bravado. Though unflinching, Engel with his stupid face made a hideous contrast to Parsons.

"The once jaunty, vivacious Texan" seemed to have aged twenty years since he had come voluntarily into court twelve months before, one who watched him wrote. He still caught the admiration of this newspaperman, whose basic story was that the men were "throttled by the law, the self-same law they had hoped to throttle."

"Only he—the one American—" he wrote of Parsons, "seemed to realize that he must die in a manner to impress, if possible, on all future generations the thought that he was a martyr. No tragedian that has paced the stage in America ever made a more marvelous presentation of a self-chosen part, perfect in every detail. The upturn of his eyes, his distant, far away look and above all the attitude of apparent complete resignation that every fold of the awkward shroud only seemed to make more distinct, was by far the most striking feature of the entire gallows picture.''

White caps were deftly slipped upon the heads of the four.

Spies cried, ''There will come a time when our silence will be more powerful than the voices they are strangling to death.''

Engel shouted, ''Hurrah for the Anarchists. This is the happiest moment of my life.''

''May I be allowed to speak?'' Parsons asked.

The yard crowded with 200 witnesses was hushed.

''Will you let me speak?''

Then at the last: ''Let the voice of the people be heard.''

But the ropes were cut. The hemp could ''be seen slowly tightening about the necks that, between the caps and the shrouds, could be noticed blackening and purpling.'' Plain black coffins, with silver screwheads for ornaments, were awaiting the dead.

The story of course did not end there. It did not end when the strictly regulated and police-guarded funeral procession—no banners, no arms, no music save dirges—moved with its mass of mourners to Waldheim Cemetery. It did not end with the funeral oration of Captain Black, the defense attorney, who closed with what he said were the last words spoken by Parsons. Those words made five verses. The central one said:

> Insult not my dust with your pity,
> Ye who're left on this desolate shore
> Still to suffer and lose and deplore.
> 'Tis I should, as I do,
> Pity you.

Parsons wrote much in the Chicago jail. From the time of his conviction he seemed to have little doubt about his execution. He wrote at the last a touching letter to his children:

As I write I blot your name with a tear. We never meet again. Oh, my children, how deeply, dearly your Papa loves you. We show our love by living *for* our loved ones, we also *prove* our love by dying when necessary for them. Of my life and the cause of my unnatu-

ral and cruel death, you will learn from others. *Your
Father is a self-offered Sacrifice upon the Altar of Liberty and Happiness.* To you I leave the legacy of an
honest name and duty done. Preserve it, emulate it. Be
true to yourselves, you cannot then be false to others.
Be industrious, sober and cheerful. Your Mother! Ah,
she is the grandest, noblest of women. Love, honor and
obey her.

My children, my precious ones, I request you to read
this parting message on each recurring anniversary of
my Death in remembrance of him who dies not alone for
you, but for the children yet unborn. Bless you, my
Darlings. Farewell;

Your Father,

Albert R. Parsons.

To Lucy he had written. "You I bequeath to the people, a
woman of the people. I have one request to make of you: Commit
no rash act to yourself when I am gone, but take up the great
cause of Socialism where I am compelled to lay it down."

He had reason to fear that Lucy might be rash. She was dis-
traught and dramatic. Early on the morning of the execution she
came from her apartment on the upper floor at 785 Milwaukee
Avenue to the tight police lines drawn about the jail. With her
were her two children and the ever-present Mrs. Holmes of *The
Alarm,* all dressed in deep mourning. Lucy insisted that she had
been promised that she and the children could see her husband.
But officers passed her along from one closed gate to another.
Then, uttering cries of rage and despair, she tried to push under
the ropes and past the police. A patrol wagon was called. Bodily
she and her children were lifted in it and carried to the Chicago
Avenue Station. Lucy's story of the morning as she told it to a
Tribune reporter was almost incoherent. Her friend supplied the
details.

"We were locked up in separate cells," Mrs. Holmes told
him, "stripped to the skin by the matron and thoroughly
searched. That was where Mrs. Parsons was when her husband
was executed. Instead of being surrounded by loving friends she

was caged in a filthy cell, insulted and degraded until her great heart was broken.''

Beyond that day of the official ''murder spree,'' as she called it, Lucy painstakingly collected the story of her husband's life and the trial of the anarchists. In effect she pled his cause to posterity. But she was no broken, resigned woman when she published her book two years after her husband's death about ''the vile conspiracy conducted by the wild howls of the millionaire rabble.'' She helped bring the facts together which added to the load on the conscience of Illinois—and America.

Men who hated radicalism remained disturbed about the case. It was undoubtedly only coincidence, in the year after Parsons died and in which Lucy was preparing her book, that Melville Stone (who was to live many long, productive years after that), unexpectedly sold his interest in the *News*. His paper was doing excellently. On the day of Parsons' execution the *News* sold 482,843 copies—a one-day increase of 180 per cent.

At forty—the age Parsons would have been if he had lived— Stone's health was bad. Friends who met him traveling about Europe found him ''far from well.'' He did not seem much interested when in Paris Milton A. McRae, one of the founders of the Scripps–McRae chain of papers, told him he had made a financial mistake. In his memoirs, published nearly half a century after Parsons was hanged, Melville Stone said he had no regrets for his part in the ''tragedy'' of the anarchists, as he described it. He died honored as the longtime head of the Associated Press. And his bones lie with the great in the crypt of the National Cathedral in Washington.

Other people had regrets. Among the relatively obscure citizens in Chicago who watched the trial of the anarchists was an ugly German-born lawyer just a year older than Parsons. In the year of the anarchist trial John Peter Altgeld was elected to the bench of the Superior Court of Cook County. He was chief justice of this court when he resigned in 1891. When, in 1892, was elected the Democratic Governor of Illinois he found the case of all the anarchists waiting for him in petitions for the pardon of Neebe, Schwab, and Fielden who were still in prison.

Altgeld had been cursed as practically an anarchist himself

because of his friendship for farm and labor elements, yet he could have pardoned these men without too much political pain. Conservatives were prepared to grant them clemency along the lines Stone had approved before. But just as Parsons had declined to ask merely for mercy in the death house, Altgeld insisted upon acting on the basis of justice now.

He not only turned the three men loose; he also condemned the processes by which all the anarchists, the dead and the living, had been convicted. His pardon message was an indignant essay on police methods, prejudice and pressure, jury packing and judicial misconduct. It was an indictment of the whole process Stone designed. The Governor must have known that he was asking for the furies, just as Parsons seemed obstinately—even insanely—insistent on the noose.

Altgeld was driven out of public life but not, despite Vachel Lindsay's much-quoted poem, *The Eagle That Is Forgotten*, out of public recollection. Eaglelike, his hope for humanity and justice has mounted since. Perhaps even Albert Parsons deserves a place in the same image of manhood and martyrdom.

15

Emporia to Prinkipo

There have been few more instructive journeys made by an American journalist than the generally happy, always lively way William Allen White went from Emporia toward the vision of Prinkipo. White's Emporia in Kansas was not unlike the place in that state from which Dorothy, with the help of a cyclone, set out for Oz. And Prinkipo, the tall island of exiles and expectations off Constantinople, was the scene where White, despite some ''cyclonic gusts,'' was prepared to confront Revolution as Dorothy confronted the Wizard. He differed from Dorothy, since he rather expected the Bolsheviks to be something

253

like the Wizard Dorothy found to her surprise in Oz to be only a
balloonist who had strayed from Omaha.

All his life White was much like a figure in an Oz book, zestful
in adventures in a strange world but ever eager to get back to
Kansas. He was never really the Scarecrow or the Tin Woodman,
though he sometimes looked like them. He was not quite the
Cowardly Lion. But he was a plump, charming, whimsical character who might have been labeled the Reluctant Revolutionary.
Despite his own efforts and those of some journalistic admirers
and interpreters, he was not a fictitious character. He came into
the world quite normally with a lusty cry on a February day in
1868.

The first railroad was then being built to connect Emporia
with the world. And sometimes White made it seem uncertain
whether the town was connected with the world or the world was
merely an adjunct of Emporia. He created that uncertainty
about himself, too. Sometimes at home, as a man whose neighbors
were nationwide, he seemed as he came and went almost a mysterious stranger. Certainly in great cities and capitals he wore
Emporia almost like a mask. In his national fame as country
editor perhaps he was a happy hypocrite. Nothing he ever wrote
was accomplished with such literary precision as the far-from-
simple picture he drew of himself.

He began quite consciously to draw it in 1895, when he came
home to Emporia to be editor-owner of the *Gazette*. All his life
was marked by careful contrasts between himself and other
newspapermen—newspapermen as different among themselves as
predatory press lords and such a Lucifer of the journalism of
revolution as John Reed, then a lighthearted cornstalk of a boy
in a happy, substantial American home. The coincidence has not
often been noted that the year he came to the *Gazette* was the
same as that in which Mr. William Randolph Hearst arrived in
metropolitan Manhattan. At twenty-eight, Hearst, with much of
his father's mining millions in his bank account and a spectacu-
lar success with the San Francisco *Examiner* behind him, had
paid $180,000 for the faltering New York *Journal*. Ready to
match money and sensation with Joseph Pulitzer's soaring
World, the horse-faced Californian on Park Row descended im-

perially from his carriage. In Emporia, the question for White
was whether or not he could afford to take a hack.

He was twenty-seven, plump, pink-cheeked, friendly as a
puppy. He had seemed "fat, freckled-faced and flippant" at
Kansas University where he became an ever-loyal Phi Delta
Theta. Yet he had a cocky confidence justified by his work on the
Star and *Journal* in Kansas City. By a series of notes and mort-
gages he had acquired the *Gazette,* with its rickety plant and
doubtful good will, for $3000. But when he arrived in the little
Kansas town with pretty, smart Sallie Lindsay, whom he had
married two years before, his available cash totaled $1.25. Before
familiar, staring faces at the depot, he stood undecided. Should
he lug their heavy baggage across town to their boardinghouse
and establish a reputation as a frugal, thrifty young publisher?
Or should he establish his credit in the community by going in a
hack? The hack cost a quarter. He piled bride and baggage into
it. A good front, he decided then, is more to be chosen than great
riches.

Largely because he felt that as an editor he ought to be a
Democrat or a Republican young White joined the more respectable, dominant Republican Party. He was ready to spread that
party's doctrines in the *Gazette.* But his journalistic opposition
was not impressed. Its editor was the Republican satrap of the
section. In announcing White's purchase of its competitor, the
older editor added the barbershop cry "Next!" as if it expected
White soon to be out of his editorial chair.

The *Gazette* (the "Willie silly-Billy paper" to its opposition) had fewer than 600 subscribers in a county of 20,000 people. Without ever relinquishing his editor's desk, White did not
stick tight to it. He had written poetry. He wanted to write
books. A year after he came home, perhaps to eke out his income,
he was off to St. Louis to cover the National Republican Convention for the Kansas City *World.*

He saw a dull, ultraconservative convention nominate William
McKinley as the candidate Mark Hanna and his big-business
associates felt was required. But he enjoyed himself with Edgar
W. Howe, editor of the Atchison *Globe.* Ed Howe had done the
two things Bill wanted to do. Ten years White's senior, Howe

had not only made a success of the *Globe,* which he had started
on a $200 shoestring; he was also famous as the author of *The
Story of a Country Town.* The drab, bare village of that novel,
full of "dull, boastful, discontented people," was a sharp contrast to the image of Emporia White was already building.
Howe's son wrote later that his father was the most wretchedly
unhappy man he ever knew, but the blithe White found him
good company—perhaps a good guide.

It was not an entirely happy time for country boys. The great
panic which had begun in 1893 had broken banks and built the
mass of the unemployed. Revolution or fear of it stalked city
streets in dirty shirts. Among frayed farmers economic distress
spread greater devastation than drought and grasshoppers.
Lamentation and anger moved across Kansas. And when White
went back to Emporia he found private trouble, too. Doctors had
told Sallie that she had a spot on a lung. Fortunately, railroad
passes to high, dry Colorado were easy to get then. White took
Sallie there. He came home lonely. His paper seemed politically
besieged. He sat by the telegraph desk when the news of William
Jennings Bryan's tremendous, poetic protest in his "Cross of
Gold" speech came over the wires from Chicago. It produced
what seemed revolution to many respectable, propertied people.
Though sometimes down to a dollar and a quarter in cash, *Gazette* editor-owner White was confidently one of them.

"The ardor of Kansas," he recalled, "was more than a fever.
It was a consuming flame."

The Democrats, cried someone in his presence, had nominated
Murat! Young White confronted the revolution when he was all
dressed up in his best "bib and tucker," ready to take a train to
Sallie and Colorado. The proofs of his first book, *The Real Issue,*
a collection of stories, had just come in. Proud and impatient to
be off, he was in no mood for a meeting on the street with a
crowd of argumentative and angry Populists and Democrats.

Their resentment had risen with the epithets *Socialists, anarchists, nihilists,* Republicans had flung at them. They were older
men than he, shabbily dressed, struggling with poverty, White
recalled later. And he "was rather spick-and-span, particularly
offensive in the gaudy neckties for which I have had unfortunate

weakness." The crowd hooted. White's anger flamed in his round face. He pushed through the crowd and to his pen.

"What's the Matter with Kansas?" he wrote. Then he let go. In terms of his Populist neighbors he drew a picture, which pleased stalwart Republicans everywhere, of the cast of characters fighting the "money power" in America. They included, he wrote, "an old mossback who snorts and howls because there is a bathtub in the State House ... a shabby, wild-eyed, rattle-brained fanatic who has said openly in a dozen speeches that 'the rights of the user are paramount to the rights of the owner' ... an old human hoop skirt who has failed as a businessman, who has failed as an editor, who has failed as a preacher ... a kid without a law practice ... and three or four harpies out lecturing, telling the people that Kansas is raising hell and letting the corn go to weed."

With sharpening sarcasm he went on: "We don't need population, we don't need wealth, we don't need well-dressed men on the streets, we don't need cities on the fertile prairies; you bet we don't! What we are after is the money power. Because we have become poorer and ornerier and meaner than a spavined, distempered mule, we, the people of Kansas, propose to kick; we don't care to build up, we wish to tear down. . . .

"Whoop it up for the ragged trousers; put the lazy, greasy fizzle, who can't pay his debts, on the altar, and bow down and worship him. Let the state ideal be high. What we need is not the respect of our fellow men, but the chance to get something for nothing. . . ."

He went on and on. He slammed the editorial on the hook and set off for Colorado. His staff did not like it. The big Irish foreman, who sometimes liked the bottle too well, called it "this damn thing." A woman printer devoted to Bryan set it in bristling anger. When it appeared in the *Gazette* and then quickly in wide reprinting in greater papers, it was read with both delight and fury. The editor came back from Colorado to fame.

The editorial blast helped elect McKinley. The publicity about it served the sale of White's first book. He was petted by Mark Hanna, first politician of the plutocrats. Republican desire to reward him threatened him with appointment as postmaster of

Emporia. Definitely, even then, he did not want to be stuck as close to the town as a stamp. So, early in 1897, he hurried East to forestall the Washington appointment and to meet suddenly interested New York editors.

It was a trip of transformation. In the capital of the Republic which had been saved from the Populists and Democrats, White met Theodore Roosevelt. Then a voluble, restive thirty-nine-year-old Assistant Secretary of the Navy, Roosevelt was far from complacent about the old order which had triumphed. In a long luncheon session at the Army and Navy Club, White became TR's devoted man. Then in New York he was welcomed by Samuel S. McClure, who was contemplating for his *McClure's Magazine* exposures of American problems which, his biographer said, "would capture a vision of the whole Republic, venal and splendid, craven and doughty, genteel and vulgar and fearful."

The politician and the publisher represented aspects of one movement. Perhaps revolution had been put down when McKinley beat Bryan. Still, Roosevelt and McClure were focuses of a mounting discontent which could not be left to the Populists but required attention nevertheless. Meeting Roosevelt was an almost evangelical experience for White. And McClure eagerly provided the place for the talents of White as a sudden convert to reform.

Other writers had been putting words and Roosevelt together. The swift rise of the aristocratic, literate New Yorker had been served by Jacob Riis, police reporter of the New York *Sun*. Riis described TR's enthusiastic work as metropolitan police commissioner. He had led and followed the young, bespectacled, big-toothed commissioner to discovery of the lowest level of slum conditions and to understanding of the alliance of graft, politics and crime. Riis had introduced Roosevelt to Lincoln Steffens, the "gentleman reporter" covering police for the New York *Evening Post*.

Steffens, who was to follow and expose the slimy trails of some American politicians, often seemed stuffy to White, although Steffens spoke his scorn of the conventional professional newspapermen of the time. Many of them were drunken cynics, he

said, who would do well to walk to the river and off the dock.
Gentleman Steffens talked of Harvard and Princeton men, poets,
aspiring novelists as the kind of reporters needed. He did not
specifically mention a plump, bright-eyed young man from Kansas. But opportunity was being prepared for White, with
Steffens and others, on *McClure's*.

Sam McClure, born in Ireland, raised in Indiana, had advanced on a succession of shoestrings as operator of an early
newspaper syndicate and literary agent for such writers as Robert Louis Stevenson and Rudyard Kipling. He had read
"What's the Matter with Kansas?" and when White's book
appeared he got permission to print two of its stories in his
magazine. Then with an opulence which dazzled Sallie and Bill
in Emporia, he ordered five more stories at $500 each. Still
thrilled by the pyrotechnic conversation of Roosevelt, White came
to New York—which made his country eyes, he said, "bug out
with excitement."

Ida M. Tarbell, already working for *McClure's,* though not
yet the great student of American corporate ruthlessness she
would become, was one of those who welcomed White. He was,
she said, "a little city-shy, or wanted us to think so"; no one
then or later was ever quite sure which. Certainly he was city-
pleased. The *McClure's* staff introduced him to celebrated literary figures. They fed him in a fancy restaurant near Grant's
Tomb. He went home to Kansas, pockets filled with more assignments.

His fiction, said McClure's biographer later, was "puerile
stuff." But his sketches of leading American politicians were
popular and provocative. Checks from *McClure's* poured with
happy regularity into Emporia and the *Gazette*'s editor was
increasingly away collecting his material. In 1900, the editor
who had arrived doubtful about hack fare bought Red Rocks, one
of the finest houses in town. It was a big, two-story structure of
Colorado sandstone with Victorian gables and dormer windows.
White surprised his banker when he improved the *Gazette* plant.
Then that year McClure assigned him to a story about Senator
Thomas Platt, Republican boss of the state of New York. White
turned to his friend Theodore Roosevelt for aid.

TR was glad to give it. In New York politics Roosevelt and
Platt were upstart and ogre to one another. The popularity of
his Spanish War service had pushed the younger man ahead.
Platt had been unable to prevent Roosevelt's election as Governor of New York. He had not been able to control the Rough
Rider in Albany even when TR's legislative program, including
the taxation of corporation franchises, seemed "Populist notions" to the old manipulator. But the old Boss, in what he
thought was shrewdness, had been able to sidetrack the young
Governor into the Republican nomination for the Vice-Presi-
dency. When White asked him for aid he was on the Vice-
Presidential bench—or shelf. He was happy to make appointments for the Kansas editor, White reported later, "with some
ancient and some recent enemies of Platt who had once been his
intimates." Then McKinley was assassinated in September 1901.
As men of Platt's political ideas saw it, that "damned cowboy,"
that "madman," was President of the United States.

White's article punctuated Platt's pain. It appeared in the
December 1901 issue of *McClure's*. It was "fairly obvious," as
White said later, that much of his information must have come
from TR or from TR's friends. The man from Emporia, however, solemnly denied that at the time. Later he said that he was
careful to credit the things Roosevelt told him to other sources:
"Generally he told me where to find the other source. For he
loved intrigue." But if the words were White's, the new President's feelings were expressed in the story about the Boss as "a
dwarf on stilts."

More important to White than his literary assassination of
Platt was his discovery by way of Platt that the Populists had
not been entirely fanatic and demagogic in their revolt against
the "money power." Platt was only one of those who controlled
politics through the manipulation of the upper-middle class in
the interest of the men of the top crust. His cohorts and henchmen, White found, "were well-bred, white-collared, kid-gloved,
silk-stockinged, plug-hatted." Something was the matter with
the country which had not been explained by a burlesque of
angry men in Kansas.

In much the same kind of language he had used about the

Populists in 1896, White described Platt in 1901 as "a little old
mangy rat in his nest." Rat or not, the Boss was no fool, though
his powers were waning. He went straight to the White House.
There he accused Roosevelt of abetting the story. He demanded
that White never again be admitted to the Executive offices.
Apparently Roosevelt was willing to placate the Senator from
his state. Later he let White, whom Platt did not recognize, sit in
his office when Platt came for an appointment. Roosevelt enjoyed
the joke when White marched out on Platt's heels before amused
reporters.

Afterward that was a merry memory. At the time the article
appeared, *McClure's* was pleased with the publicity of a Platt
threat to sue for a six-figure libel verdict. White also gaily told
his book publishers that they should take advantage of the news
reports and editorial comment on Platt's plan to get his scalp as
a means of selling his new book. Gaily he collected cartoons of
Platt on the warpath with his tomahawk. Actually, when White
learned eight days before Christmas of Platt's threat to sue, he
was much shaken by the result of his first foray against a captain
of the political-business regime.

"It scared me to death," he wrote, "and by Christmastime I
was going into nervous exhaustion."

The facts prove his remembered fears. In Emporia he was
unable to work. He got his old friend Ed Howe to announce first
in his Atchison *Globe* that White's health required him to leave
Kansas for a long rest. Others could carry on *McClure's* campaign against American political and social evils. When Steffens
began, in 1902, to expose the political-business shame of American cities, it was suggested that White take on the same job with
the states. He declined. But the exposures increased. Miss Tarbell relentlessly described the ruthless growth of the great
Standard Oil Company of the reigning Rockefellers. Other
writers were at work on the railroads, the scandalous, stinking
meat-packing industry, the dirt in food and the dangers in
drugs. They followed paths of corruption which ran even to the
Senate and at last close to some eminent gentlemen who were
TR's friends and supporters.

Roosevelt was apparently almost as appalled as White had

been when Platt threatened to sue. He was no longer summoning
writers to expose and point evils. They were stirring the people,
and the President "was being dragged ... by the popular magazines." The Roosevelt temper was wearing thin when, in March
1906, he wrote the man who was to be his hand-picked successor,
William Howard Taft.

TR repeated his feelings about the "dull, purblind folly" of
certain rich men. But the writers, he added, were "building up a
revolutionary feeling which will most probably take the form of
a political campaign...." Two days later he had similar things
to say about the probing journalists at a dinner of the Gridiron
Club, composed of leading Washington newsmen, many of them
correspondents for conservative newspapers. That reporters' organization preserved the tradition that no "reporters are ever
present at its dinners." Nevertheless the Roosevelt irritations
leaked. Some of the writers had obviously touched a sensitive
nerve. They were proclaimed "the muckrakers" when he spoke
publicly soon afterward at the laying of the cornerstone of the
House Office Building.

"In Bunyan's *Pilgrim's Progress*," he said, "you may recall
the description of the Man with the Muck-Rake, the man who
could look no way but downward, with the muck-rake in his
hands; who was offered a celestial crown for his muck-rake, but
who would neither look up nor regard the crown he was offered,
but continued to rake to himself the filth of the floor."

In the applause of conservative businessmen, politicians, and
journalists, apparently no one noticed that in the original Bunyan version the muck-raker was raking up money, not the un-
pleasant facts about its accumulation. Also, though the Roosevelt broadside seemed all-inclusive, he quietly and quickly
denied to writer after writer that he had meant him. And to
White, whom he had first helped with his rake, Roosevelt wrote
in special affection: "I miss you."

White was conscious then of changes in his ideas about things
he had written, too. He was speculating aloud about alterations
in his thinking since he had become famous by denouncing the
Populists as fanatics and demagogues. In the *Gazette* he admitted to his home folks that they had been right in much but

they were "out too early in the season" and their "views got frost bitten."

"This is a funny world," he wrote. "About all we can do is to move with it, and grow with it. Those who do not move are dead in the shell."

He had become, he thought, "a bleeding reformer." But while he looked for a respectable revolution, he carefully arranged his protective coloration. He had become the American image of the country editor at the bucolic best as he more and more became a national figure exposed to national ideas. In Emporia he was no longer the "spick-and-span" young man with a taste for gaudy ties. He dressed himself and reform in rustic fashion. Observers noted that as Emporia prospered and White flourished as its first citizen, he seemed to adopt for himself the shabby dress which poverty had put on the Populists. One of his neighbors said that his clothes looked as if "they had been planned and cut out by the town tinner." He wore pants that were patched and a battered hat that was crushed down on his head of sandy hair. He usually drove around town in an old two-seated buggy, drawn by a feeble old horse, though he could easily have afforded an automobile.

Evidently he had similar ideas about the costume reform should wear in America. Soon after Roosevelt's blast at the muckrakers, some of them were fussing among themselves. Ida Tarbell, Steffens, Ray Stannard Baker (able reporter out of Chicago who was to become Woodrow Wilson's aide and biographer), and others withdrew from *McClure's* to staff the *American Magazine*. White moved with them, cautiously.

"It seems to me," he wrote in the summer of 1906, "the great danger before you is that of being too purposeful. People will expect the pale drawn face; the set lips and a general line of emotional insanity. You should fool 'em. Give 'em something like 'Pigs is Pigs.' From the prospectus they will judge that you are going to produce a 'Thin red line of heroes,' and instead of which you should have the sharp claque of the slap stick and the rattle of broken glass down the sky-light to indicate the course of the Dutchman's journey."

He was ready for serious revolt, however, from the reactionary

Republicanism of his youth. His hopes were high when Roosevelt
came home from big-game hunting in Africa to rebuke the reaction which he felt had attended the administration of his hand-
chosen Taft. The Emporia editor listened in Chicago when big-
toothed TR on a Bull Moose rampage shouted to those seceding
with him from the Republican Party, "We stand at Armageddon, and we battle for the Lord." This did not seem emotional
insanity. Somehow, afterward, it did not seem purposeful
enough. With a partner of the House of Morgan "fluttering
around headquarters, smiling and simpering like a sinister
spectre," the Roosevelt revolt turned out to be, as White saw it,
only a "circumspect middle-class Armageddon."

Young new writers admired White but were not quite sure of
the image he presented. Since he had burlesqued the Populists,
he had written in his novel *A Certain Rich Young Man* of his
fears about new economic powers threatening village virtues.
Young Harry Kemp, "The Tramp Poet of Kansas," left an
appealing picture of the moon-faced editor he had visited. He
was not quite certain, however, whether White's almost bumpkin appearance "was sincere or affected." Later a more dramatic young writer, already on his way to revolution, quite
frankly assumed that White was a sort of sly purveyor of revolutionary ideas.

John Reed wrote the Emporia editor in a burst of enthusiasm
about an article striking at selfishness which White wrote for
The Saturday Evening Post.

"How on earth did the *Post* consent?" asked Reed. "I have a
theory that it was so damned transcendentally well done that
they couldn't refuse. . . . The way you stuck to life. . . . It's true
dispassionate life, how well understood, how deeply sympathet-
ically interpreted."

Though Theodore Roosevelt liked the same article, John
Reed's praise suggested that White had come a long way from
his anti-Populist fame. Reed had been one of the young writers
found for the *American Magazine* as White had been found for
McClure's more than a decade before. Steffens had discovered
him in Boston, where he had gone by invitation of leading citizens to investigate if not expose that city. Among graduates of

the celebrated Harvard class of 1910 (which also included Heywood Broun, T. S. Eliot, Alan Seegar), Steffens found Reed and
Walter Lippmann, who had been members of the Socialist Club.
Lippmann, soon to be famous as one of the enlightened new
intellectuals, had then only edited a thin book of poems by a
dead friend. Steffens kept him as secretary and assistant.
Lippmann must have been then solemn and able, as Steffens
always seemed to White. Reed was more like a gay counterpart
of White as young man. He had written a play which was produced by the Hasty Pudding Club and had been made ivy orator
and poet.

Like White, Reed came out of the West, but the greater dis-
tance from Oregon. There was nothing bucolic about him, however, then or later. His native Portland was a greater city than
Emporia. Harvard was not Kansas U. And though Reed did not
make one of the social clubs at Harvard as White had made Phi
Delt, he was cheerfully involved in almost every other activity.
He wrote for the *Lampoon* and the *Harvard Monthly*. In New
York he worked with Miss Tarbell and other of the old muckrakers. At first he seemed more merry than socially concerned.
With two other recent Harvard graduates he settled in some
back rooms in a Greenwich Village then just becoming the low-
rent, high-spirited colony of the insurgents in arts and ideas. It
had no similarity to Emporia. Reed described his quarters there
in a poem called "Forty-Two Washington Square":

> In winter the water is frigid,
> In summer the water is hot;
> And we're forming a club for controlling the tub
> For there's only one bath to the lot.
> You shave in unlathering Croton,
> If there's water at all, which is rare—
> But the life isn't bad for a talented lad
> At Forty-two Washington Square!
>
> The dust it flies in at the window,
> The smells they come in at the door,
> Our trousers lie meek where we threw 'em last week

Bestrewing the maculate floor.
The gas isn't all that it should be,
It flickers—and yet I declare
There's pleasure or near it for young men of spirit
At Forty-two Washington Square!

But nobody questions your morals,
And nobody asks for the rent—
There's no one to pry if we're tight, you and I,
Or demand how our evenings are spent.
The furniture's ancient but plenty,
The linen is spotless and fair,
O life is a joy to a broth of a boy
At Forty-two Washington Square!

Change in Reed showed in 1913 when he joined the staff of the Socialist organ, *The Masses,* edited by Max Eastman. Reed's extreme extracurricular activities brought on his arrest when he tried to speak for the strikers in the silk mills of Paterson, New Jersey. For them he put on a greater and certainly more moving show than any Hasty Pudding production in ''The Pageant of the Paterson Strike'' in Madison Square Garden. Poet of protest, there was no Emporia for Reed's recurrent retreat. His town was his world, his neighbors mankind. For the *Metropolitan Magazine* he went to report the Mexican revolution.

In his exuberant middle twenties then, Reed did not go to Mexico to find ''the good, kind darkness'' which Hearst's great sardonic reporter, Ambrose Bierce, sought there. Far from disappearing, as Bierce rather hoped to do, by ''being stood up against a Mexican stone wall and shot to rags,'' Reed found hope and excitement. Perhaps he overromanticized the stirring peons as White had overridiculed the Populists. For four months he shared the perils of Pancho Villa's army. His brilliant, sympathetic articles brought him national reputation, increased by their republication in his book, *Insurgent Mexico.* Perhaps more significant than his feeling about the exciting rise of the Mexican masses in fixing his ideas was his visit on the way home to Ludlow, Colorado.

On April 21, 1914, company detectives of the Rockefeller-dominated Colorado Fuel & Iron Company, using explosive bullets, had machine-gunned and set fire to the tent city of striking miners and their families who had been expelled from company villages. Thirteen women and children were burned to death, five men and a boy were killed in the fighting. Reed was not alone in protest. The "Ludlow Massacre" shocked the country. Young William Chenery, of the Denver *Rocky Mountain News,* hammered out his editorial "The Massacre of the Innocents," calling for federal intervention. Wilson's ear, he wrote, had heard "the wail of the innocent, outraged and dying Mexico. Cannot the President give heed to the sufferings of his own people?"

That editorial, a historian of the *Rocky Mountain News* wrote later, "rattled windows in the White House." Troops were sent. Peace was restored. The Rockefellers, whom White called "the clan of predatory respectability," first threatened a $500,000 libel suit. It was never brought to trial. But what John Reed saw was not only brutality in the mines but also cowardice in American press ownership. The then-owner of the paper, John C. Shaffer, of Chicago, a financier who paraded his philanthropy and religious activities, sent word to Chenery to "pursue a milder line." His staff was shamed. Instead of softening his blows, Chenery promptly resigned, went East to become editor of the New York *Globe* and then for twenty-five years editor and publisher of *Collier's.*

Reed came East to go on to Europe to cover the first phases of the European war for the *Metropolitan.* But years later when he wrote of revolution in Russia he remembered and wrote of the crime in Colorado and reminded the Communists of it. He was still poet as well as reporter with the armies of Germany, Serbia, Bulgaria, Romania, and Russia. His book about the war and his *Tamburlaine and Other Poems* both appeared in the same year. He was writing them when he wrote his enthusiastic letter to White. He came home from the battlefronts sick and disillusioned with this "clash of traders" regardless of the lives of people. He underwent an operation for the removal of a kidney at Johns Hopkins. That made him ineligible for conscription when America entered the war and saved him from the fate of being a conscientious objector. In 1917, when he was not quite thirty and America joined the Allies, he had come a long way from happy days at Harvard. If he had ever been a playboy of revolution, as some called him, that play was over.

White held back from TR's belligerent anger with Woodrow Wilson in the first years of war abroad. He told *Gazette* readers that American profits on war in Europe had brought them to the time "when our God was our belly and we minded earthly things!" He came slowly and at last enthusiastically with Wilson to the decision for American entry into the war. And in 1917, too old and too fat for service, he happily accepted appointment to go to Europe, in a uniform bulging if not a military, to investigate the operations of the Red Cross.

White and Reed sailed for Europe during the same month, August 1917. White, accompanied by his equally roly-poly friend Henry J. Allen, editor of the Wichita *Daily Beacon*, set out in gala fashion. The New York *Sun* headlined a story about them WHITE AND ALLEN OFF TO WIN WAR. And in even more facetious fashion it added: *Leaders of Kan. Will Kan Kaiser if They Don't Kan-Kan Among Sea Fish*. In this interview White said, though jokingly, he was sorry he was headed for France instead of Russia.

No such good-natured press farewell attended Reed's departure. With his wife Louise Bryant, a fellow journalist who never took his name, he set out for Russia in serious mood. They reached the torn nation in time to be enthusiastic observers of the October revolution in Petrograd. Soon Reed won the friendship of Lenin. He wrote much of the Bolshevik propaganda which was dropped over the German lines, but he remained good reporter to the Russians as well as among them. In January 1918, he told delegates to the All-Russian Soviet convention not to count on an immediate revolution in the United States. Also he began the collection of the documents, which were to help make a classic story of the revolution, for his book *Ten Days That Shook the World*.

There was nothing earth-shaking about White's adventures or his report on them. Writing as a humorist even in the war zone, in *The Martial Adventures of Henry and Me* he told of their travels and experiences. The book was a superficial report of a brief visit. It amused many. It also won the praise of Max Eastman, for whose paper Reed was writing from the Russian scene.

"I am more grateful than I can tell you for your charming book," Eastman wrote. "There are two special reasons: one is that I sadly need something just now to make me take things not too seriously (yet seriously enough), the other is that I like especially to think that I have a few friends like you when our queerly promiscuous government is so unfriendly."

One reason it was unfriendly was the tone of the articles which Reed had been sending back to *The Masses* from Russia. They had been instrumental in bringing an indictment against the magazine for sedition. One was headed "Knit a straight-jacket for your soldier boy." Absent at the first hearing, which ended in a mistrial, Reed came back for the second. It resulted in a divided jury, too, but he was indicted again for an alleged incendiary speech in the Bronx. This time he was released without trial. His papers had been seized, which delayed the writing and publication of *Ten Days* until 1919.

Early in 1919, White returned to Paris as a newspaper correspondent. He had tried and failed to get a place on the American peace delegation. He could still pretend, tongue in fat cheek, that he was just a country editor, but Dorothy Canfield Fisher noted that "he was wholly at home in the Hotel Crillon on the Place de la Concorde." Many of White's old friends were in Paris. He suffered no hardships. One fellow reporter described him as enjoying "much good French food, supplemented by big boxes of Kansas cakes, made by the subtle hand of Sallie." Miss Tarbell, Ray Stannard Baker—now aiding Wilson as much as he would be aided with the press—and others gave the Emporia editor a special dinner on his fifty-first birthday, the first he had spent away from Sallie in twenty-five years.

The party celebrated more than a birthday. Just before the party, President Wilson, at Baker's suggestion, had appointed White a delegate to a proposed conference with Soviet Russia at Prinkipo, an island resort just off Constantinople in the little sea between the Bosphorus and the Dardanelles. The place had a romantic sound. A resort in a mild and salubrious climate, it had once figured in Byzantine history as a place where such wicked or unfortunate Empresses as Irene, Zoe, and Euphrosyne had been exiled. Now there was a promise there of other great if less decorative personages. Wilson and Lloyd George had persuaded the French to agree to a conference there to which Lenin and Trotsky would send envoys or go themselves. The idea was to bring small eastern European nations to an agreement with the Bolsheviks which would guarantee the peace of the Baltic and could serve the peace of the world.

White was fascinated at the prospect. A month earlier, Baker had spoken to him about going to Russia for the American peace delegation and attempting to establish diplomatic relations with the Soviets. He had made modest protestations about his ignorance. But he did not feel himself to be the only brash American in Paris. With other newspapermen he listened in the Crillon lobby to Lincoln Steffens pontificating on his recent trip to Russia as an American observer. Though old acquaintances, White and Steffens were not absolute admirers of each other. Both belittled the other in their autobiographies. White found Steffens "bug-eyed with wonder" about the results of the revolution, but other of the listening reporters wearied of his talk.

"I have seen the future, and it works," he proclaimed.

Then, White remembered, Steffens offered final evidence of the Utopia he had observed.

"Gentlemen," he declared, "I tell you they have abolished prostitution!"

White was delighted by the interruption of an irreverent correspondent.

"My God, Steff! What did you do!"

And Steffens, said the editor from Emporia, rose "and trotted away, for he was too small to stalk." But the rotund White was to have his solemn Russian troubles, too. He was delighted by his assignment to Prinkipo. He cabled Sallie, back home running the *Gazette*.

"Come on," he wrote her, "take the boat for Constantinople. . . . It's once in a lifetime."

There would be problems, of course. Some statesmen were quite content that the revolutionary government remain unrep-

resented in Paris or recognized anywhere. The French held much
of the debt of Czarist Russia and still somehow hoped to collect
it. Russian refugees from revolution in Paris opposed any conference with the Reds. So did many Americans at home. But
White spoke up the day after his appointment. The Bolsheviks,
he declared, should be permitted to develop their regime in Russia without interference from other nations. He had backing in
the American delegation. Also, though he later deprecated his
qualifications, he was confident that progress for world peace,
perhaps a better world, could be made at Prinkipo. The Red
dragon might be tamed. Perhaps even revolution could be made
respectable.

"The difference between world politics and Kansas politics,"
he told Sallie, "is not much. You simply play the same game on
the same board with bigger checkers. Topeka and Paris are the
same kinds of towns."

The board was big; sometimes it was hard to see all the checkers. The game was complicated not merely by European complex-
ities but also by a storm which blew about a man from White's
own Middle West. Later he wrote of "the little cyclonic gust of
wind that moved across our plans for a conference at Prinkipo." Part of it came from the appointment of the other American delegate to the proposed conference. He was Professor
George D. Herron, a fifty-six-year-old American expatriate with
a square French beard, a soft insistent voice, and utterly humor-
less self-assurance.

Though White recognized Herron's erudition, he later said
that his colleague's sense that he was playing a Messianic role
made him "one of God's pedestal dwellers, always moving about
in bronze or marble . . . yet a kindly and some way sweet and
gentle soul withal." Maybe White had no Messianic moment of
his own, but he certainly worked as a sort of Messianic assistant
in trying to make the conference a certainty. Yet he wrote Sallie,
"Herron is forever seeing ghosts and goblins and is so serious
that I shall go mad if I am cooped up with him on a train or
ship."

Though he had lived long in Europe, Herron was a country
character, almost a world image of an 1896 Kansas Populist as

drawn by White. As a radical Congregational minister in Minnesota he had attracted the attention of conservatives before the Kansas editor damned the Populists. As a college professor in Iowa, he had deserted his wife to marry a rich woman, been defrocked, and moved to Europe to live and write. Along the way, however, as a professor he had known Wilson. In the war and the plans for the peace, he had turned up as one willing to advise the President and, as it turned out, to embarrass both him and White.

On the day of the Kansas editor's birthday party, *The New York Times* let go with a two-column editorial with regard to the Prinkipo appointments. Of Herron it declared: "As a teacher of the extreme doctrines of socialism and of the loose view of the marriage relation which many Socialists hold, Mr. Herron has been in close sympathy with the principles which have guided Lenin and Trotsky in their war upon capitalism and upon society."

The New York paper approved White's appointment. It gave him a belated dividend on "What's the Matter with Kansas?" The Emporia editor, it said, had opposed Populism, "a milder form of Bolshevism"!

White was saddened. But it never occurred to him to write anything called "What's the Matter with Paris?" He labored in conferences and cafés trying to meet the objections of those opposed to the Prinkipo meeting. Eagerly he added jest and comradeship and persuasion to Herron's erudition in urging that the conference be held. But when even organized labor in America joined newspapers and preachers in opposing this meeting with the Reds, White's hopes faded. He offered to resign as delegate if that would make it easier for Herron to agree to remove himself, too. The once-in-a-lifetime opportunity was slipping away. Still he hung on to hope, but with homesickness.

"I'd give all my hopes of Prinkipo," he wrote Sallie, "for one minute of Emporia."

The hopes of Prinkipo were no longer much to give for anything, let alone a minute in Emporia. There was to be no "once in a lifetime" for White on the island of empresses and exiles. All possibilities of any agreements with the Russians were fading. Soon Allied forces would be sent belligerently against the Reds. Blockade would ring the revolutionists. White stayed watching the greater conference in Paris, where any final lasting peace seemed precarious, too. He held to some hopes. He wrote praising President Wilson, but that did not mean necessarily the approval of the appointment of Herron or promise that he would not scurry soon back to the security of Republican regularity in Kansas. He was still the irrepressible man. On his way home he stopped in London. He had a gay time in a troubled world. He bought what he considered a debonair hat. And he sent a poem about it back to journalistic colleagues still in Paris. One verse ended:

And if I'm middle aged and bald and slow and rather fat—
You should see me in my new straw hat!

John Reed was not quite so tractable to his times. He confronted them with that hostility which not only makes good rebels but sometimes makes clear-seeing journalists, too. There was no chance that on the Russian side he might have met White on the island in the Sea of Marmora. At the time that the conference was to be held he and his wife were hailed before a Senate investigating committee in Washington. He was still in America when White got home. Harassed by Senators and police, he was also expelled by the more conservative members from the National Socialist Convention in the United States in August 1919. As the leader of the left-wing Communist Labor Party, he wrote its manifesto and edited its paper, *The Voice of Labor*. Right-wing Marxists called him "Jack the Liar."

Once more Reed was indicted for sedition. This time flight was imperative. Working his way as a stoker with a forged passport, he got to Finland, where he was jailed. For twelve weeks he was forced to subsist on a diet of frozen fish. Then he was released to Russia in an exchange of prisoners. The American government was still engaged in a nationwide hunt for him after he arrived and began making speeches in Moscow. He was famed and loved in the Soviet world then. His *Ten Days That Shook the World* was widely read and was translated into Russian by Lenin's wife. Lenin himself was later to write a laudatory introduction.

Then he went to Baku. That industrial and petroleum center
on the Caspian Sea is, even by plane, a long way from Prinkipo.
The tenor of the Communist Congress of Oriental Nations to
which Reed went was even more removed from White's "hopes
of Prinkipo." Much myth and mystery has grown about this
time in Reed's life. The unlikeliest legend is that he renounced
the revolution. All reports are that his speech at Baku roused the
delegates to the Conference there to revolutionary fury. But
there or on the 1500-mile way back to Moscow, he ate unwashed
fruit which bore the deadly typhus germ. He was taken to a
hospital and given the best medical attention, though perhaps
the embargo now imposed by the Allies even on medical supplies
to the Bolsheviks may have kept saving drugs from him. He died
on October 19, 1920. Guarded by soldiers of the Red Army, his
body lay in state. Then on October 24, proclaimed as a holiday in
Moscow, he was buried in Red Square. He was only three days
less than thirty-three years old when he died.

By then Bill White was back snug in Emporia. The town was
as charming as he always elsewhere gave the impression it was.
If there were troubles in the world, somehow they could be repaired. When Red Rocks burned that year, it was rebuilt on
broad and comfortable lines. Frank Lloyd Wright helped design
the new house. Fat and fifty-two, White looked ahead from a life
that was already full. In the years ahead he would know more
Presidents, fight the Ku Klux Klan, be denounced as a Red,
write more books and editorials for the *Gazette,* help build the
mass reading of books, and at last lead the movement for another
American crusade to aid freedom in the world as chairman of the
Committee to Defend America by Aiding the Allies.

To the last he felt that the format for reform must be something like his proposal to friends when they formed the *American Magazine.* There must always be laughter as well as the pale
drawn face, the set lips, the too-purposeful appearance. Yet his
serious concerns were never hidden by an attitude of witty non-
pretentiousness.

White hated reactionary editors. He declined even to let
Hearst buy his syndicated articles. Maybe he was, as he said, a
little rough on Frank Munsey, who bought, consolidated, and

often killed great newspapers. Still, he felt that the proper obituary for Munsey in the *Gazette* was to say that he brought to American journalism the talent of a meat packer, the morals of a moneychanger, and the manners of an undertaker. Later he said of Colonel Robert R. McCormick of the *Chicago Tribune* ("The World's Greatest Newspaper") that he should end up in jail before he wrecked the country.

Bill White could sting. He could play the man of jests and quips and he could never quite go all the headlong way of folly for faith. He was not a man to die far from home by the Kremlin. But even in his beloved Emporia there was always a vision of Prinkipo, a vision of revolution—tamed perhaps, never thwarted.

White understood better than almost any editor of his generation that the country journalist or any other newspaperman worthy of the name has the world as his circulation area. The crusader may die a martyr and outcast or go, amid popular applause, by a big funeral to his grave. In the guise of a rebel or in the ill-fitting costume of a Rotarian his task is the same.

16

The Death of *The World*

On February 27, 1931, the death of the New York *World* got almost equal play in its final issue as the murder of Vivian Gordon. That young woman, who had offered to tell investigators about police connections with vice, was found strangled in Van Cortlandt Park in the Bronx. On Park Row *The World* seemed almost as suddenly and horridly dead. It had been sold, disregarding injunctions in the last will and testament of Joseph Pulitzer that his heirs never let it go, to dapper Roy Howard of the Scripps–Howard chain. Despite elaborate inquests in both cases the killers have never been quite determined.

Neither fatality was unique in New York. Enough battered bodies of pretty, promiscuous girls had been found in the sleazy, lively decade of the Twenties to satisfy every greed for sensation of the new tabloids which began to flourish with the establishment of the *Daily News* (with *Chicago Tribune* money) on June 26, 1919. Hearst had followed with his *Daily Mirror*. Physical culturist Bernarr Macfadden ("Body-Love Macfadden," the new newsmagazine *Time* called him) set up the *Daily Graphic*. The war of "gutter journalism," said the fastidious Oswald Garrison Villard, had succeeded the tamer, tawdry "yellow journalism" of a quarter-century before.

The death of old newspapers provided drama less grisly than tabloid readers wanted, and the sudden death of journals was no longer news. Frank A. Munsey, whom William Allen White called the press's meat packer, moneychanger, and undertaker, had been on the scene with notions about newspapers no more romantic than about any other merchandise. He alone, cutting competition, reduced the number of metropolitan dailies from fourteen to nine. When he killed all of the old *Herald* except a name tagged onto the title of the *Tribune,* old *Herald* men held a wake. At the end of an evening of songs and bottles, laughter and oratory, a bugler played Taps sadly and almost loud enough for the elder and younger James Gordon Bennetts to hear it in their graves.

Perhaps even then, rigor mortis had set in unnoticed under *The World*'s golden dome, where crusading had been like the pulsing circulation of the blood. Finding it dead in 1931 was like discovering in a park the body of a pretty girl who had been eager and talkative the day before. Vivian Gordon's murder is still an unsolved case. But *The World* was no blabbing trollop, no ordinary newspaper. It had developed the "new journalism" under Joseph Pulitzer and John Cockerill. In competition with Hearst it had joined in "yellow journalism" without stultifying its editorial aims. Many wished for its crusading spirit the immortality old J. P. had seemed to guarantee for the paper property in his will. After its sad death a quick quest for culprits began. Its last city editor, James W. Barrett, angrily arrayed the evidence in a book, *THE WORLD The Flesh and*

Messrs. Pulitzer. He found suspects aplenty. He counted many accomplices. Despite his enthusiastic efforts, some mystery remains in the matter.

The man closest to all the clues was Ralph Pulitzer, the great J. P.'s oldest son. He did not look like a killer. Irvin S. Cobb, a Kentucky-born reporter then on the *Evening World* staff, described Ralph as he looked shortly before his father's death on the yacht, where J. P. found the quietness he required and from which he sent explosive cables to *The World.* Ralph then seemed "a bookish, kindly, retiring gentleman, more fitted, I think, for the life of a poet happily scribbling pastoral verses in the proverbial garret, than to be a cog in the racketing, grinding powerhouses of a great newspaper shop."

Cobb may have been prejudiced. He believed that "the Time of the Great Editor" had waned and faded. "The Time of the Great Reporter," which undoubtedly included Cobb, had succeeded it. The Kentuckian had never seen the elder Pulitzer. Only once had he heard his voice. That was when as reporter Cobb had simply and directly done a chore which Pulitzer's imperious directions and the overelaborate response of his subordinates had complicated and confused. Old blind Joe was amazed. Over the phone Cobb heard his comment in a tone which was high-pitched but just a bit gutteral on certain syllables and with the slightest possible slurring of accent.

"Well, I wish I might be God-damned!" said the builder of *The World.*

Ralph was born in St. Louis on June 11, 1879, a year after his father had put two struggling papers together to make the *Post-Dispatch.* The boy had been educated by private tutors in New York after J. P. in 1883 had bought *The World* for $346,000. More of his education was acquired in travel abroad with his peripatetic parent and at Harvard, where he got his A.B. in 1900.

Then Joseph Pulitzer had been "formally withdrawn" from the paper's editorship ten years. Though blind, he watched with prehensile vigilance as Ralph went first into the business office and then to the news staff. He was pleased that as an apprentice editorial writer Ralph showed a "sense of irony" and "delicacy of touch.'' He showed confidence in his son. When he made a will in 1904, he made the promising son, then the only one of his three boys who had come of age, a trustee of his estate. In 1906, Ralph became vice-president of the Press Publishing Company, operator of the morning, evening, and Sunday *Worlds*, and of the Pulitzer Publishing Company, which published the *St. Louis Post-Dispatch*.

This certainly did not suggest, as some *World* men believed later, that the Old Man was displeased by Ralph's marriage, on October 5, 1905, to Frederica Vanderbilt Webb, granddaughter of William H. Vanderbilt. The wedding in Burlington, Vermont, as Hearst's *Evening Journal* reported it, might have stirred some of the blind publisher's scorn for the ostentatious rich. The *Journal* reported that the gifts totaled nearly a million dollars in value. Mrs. Cornelius Vanderbilt, Sr., was there. So were Twombleys, Sloans, Waterburys, Biddles. A corps of chefs and servants was brought up from Sherry's in New York. The Bishop of Vermont performed the ceremony. Ralph and his bride rode off in a richly decorated coach drawn by gaily caparisoned horses; they sailed for their honeymoon on the bride's father's yacht.

Socially the Pulitzers had come far fast. Apparently, however, Ralph was not being captured by ''Society.'' In 1910, before his father's death, he wrote a satirical book, *New York Society on Parade*. It stirred the social world into which he had entered by marriage, a Pulitzer editor wrote later, because of its definition of society as ''an aristocracy whose membership is largely arbitrary.'' Still, whatever J. P. thought of the marriage or the book, he clearly was not pushing his boy quickly to editorial control of *The World*.

Through emissaries in 1904 he found Frank I. Cobb, no kin of Irvin Cobb on the news staff. Then thirty-five, Frank Cobb had not been richly reared. His farmer father, moving from New York state to Kansas, had been driven farther westward by a plague of grasshoppers. In the wilds of Michigan his son grew up among the rough men of a lumber camp. With limited formal education, young Cobb sought a job as a schoolteacher, then as a school principal before he was twenty-one. His self-confidence had matured early.

"We expected a man of at least thirty," said the school authorities.

"If I were thirty," Cobb told them, "I wouldn't work for you at fifteen hundred dollars a year."

He walked out to take a job as a reporter at $6 a week on the *Grand Rapids Herald.* Swiftly he became city editor, then moved over to the rival *Grand Rapids Daily Eagle.* In his middle twenties, he joined the staff of the Detroit *News.* That paper had been founded and was operated by James E. Scripps, brother of E. W. Scripps, who built the Scripps newspaper chain which as the Scripps–Howard papers bought *The World.* Cobb arrived in Detroit at a time when James Scripps, after supporting Bryan in 1896, was scurrying back to Republicanism and profits.

When Pulitzer reached for his editor to the Scripps Detroit *News,* he may have forgotten that twenty-five years before E. W. Scripps and his brothers had bought the St. Louis *Evening Chronicle.* Then E. W. found the competition of the Pulitzer *Post-Dispatch* too much for him. He was almost lost to the American newspaper story. His health failed. He traveled abroad. Two years later he returned to the United States to begin building the chain of newspapers bearing his name.

"Cobb will do," the elder Pulitzer decided. "He knows American history better than any man I have ever found. He has the damnable Roosevelt obsession; he must learn to be brief. But I think we can make a real editor of him in time."

The new editorial writer was goaded and prodded with alternate praise and blame, said one who knew him, by "the ever-watchful Founder." He plunged into *The World*'s crusades against corruption in the insurance business and malfeasance in municipal affairs. Soon, though the old man kept the title of editor for himself, he put Cobb in charge of the editorial page and of the policies of the paper. *In charge* did not mean in command. From the time of his retirement J. P.'s suspicions grew along with his blindness. He almost deliberately divided authority on the paper in such a way, a *World* executive wrote, as to set one man watching another.

Even his son Ralph was inevitably one of those watched and watching. Somehow, that seemed still true when the news came of his father's death on his yacht in the harbor of Charleston,

South Carolina, on October 29, 1911. It was incredible that the great Pulitzer was dead.

In his will J. P. made provisions for his wife and daughters. He dreamed up journalistic education, prizes, scholarships, concerts, memorials to himself. He left advice and admonitions. He had arranged and rearranged the shares of his sons in his newspapers.

Ralph at the time of his father's death was thirty-two, Joseph, Jr., was twenty-six, and Herbert not quite sixteen. In the final will and codicils Pulitzer left the largest share to his youngest son. By accident or design the final will did not include the name of Ralph as one of the trustees of the estate. The father provided that Joseph, then already engaged in the successful operation of the *Post-Dispatch,* should become a trustee when he reached thirty and Herbert when he became twenty-five. Ralph, ignored, came hurt into his inheritance.

"The only possible inference to be drawn from this omission of my name, if left unexplained, would be lack of confidence in me on his part," he said. Such an inference he could not accept.

"Therefore, in justice to my father, as well as to my own reputation," he insisted, "I wish to state that my father lived and died in the conviction that he had designated me in his will, not only as one of the guardians of my brother, Herbert, but as one of the executors and trustees of the estate."

With the agreement of all the brothers, old J. P.'s written directions were rearranged. It was presumed that, despite the blind man's many and costly lawyers and secretaries, Ralph's name had been inadvertently omitted. For a man who had hired the brightest eyes to watch for him that was, indeed, a strange typographical oversight.

None of the brothers, however, questioned the will's central provision that they could not sell "under any circumstances whatsoever" stock in the company which published *The World.* Obviously Joseph Pulitzer felt that his greatest monument was the paper "to the maintenance and upbuilding of which I have sacrificed my health and strength." This was no whim of a sick blind man. There was about it something of a whine in farewell.

The World remained the great *World* even if the telegraph lines to the blind man's yacht were cut forever. Now its strongest voice was clearly that of Frank Cobb, habitually wearing a shabby office coat in his open-doored suite on the fifteenth floor of the *World* building on Park Row. He became, according to last City Editor Barrett, "the guiding genius of *The World*, so far as its public character and inspiration were concerned." In his greatest triumph, despite great odds in New York and the nation, he put *The World* effectually behind the nomination and election of Woodrow Wilson. Old J. P. would have liked this evidence that Cobb had escaped from his "Roosevelt obsession." Wilson was so grateful that he offered the editor a place in his Cabinet. Cobb declined.

"That kind of power is merely temporary anyhow," he told his wife, "and I have as much as I want on *The World*."

All power, as even the elder Pulitzer seemed not quite to believe, was temporary. "Cobb of *The World*" added to the paper's reputation. He never lacked the support of Ralph as president of the company. The younger man never desired to compete with Cobb's strong, lucid words. He preferred to write poetry. His chief public notice in the decade after his father's death came when he went abroad as the European war began and published, in 1915, his second book, *Over the Front in an Airplane*. Business was good. Life was pleasant. The war passed. Troubled peace came. The Ku Kluxers marched in their sheets. Scandals shook the Harding administration in Washington. Then, on December 21, 1923, Frank Cobb died.

A new *World* had been slowly preparing while he lived. Ralph's trip to the war zone in 1914 had undoubtedly increased his admiration for one of the paper's great reporters, Herbert Bayard Swope, a lively red-headed Missourian. Three years younger than Ralph, he was a man who had no intention of remaining in any shadow. Born in St. Louis, Swope had begun his newspaper career on the *Post-Dispatch*. Then he had moved to *The World* by way of stints on the *Chicago Tribune* and the *New York Herald*. He had been responsible for a large part of *The World*'s magnificent coverage of the *Titanic* disaster in 1912. He had reported the sensational Becker-Rosenthal story involving murder and police corruption. When the European war broke out he was in the Azores watching for *The World* an early attempted flight across the Atlantic.

FORGET IT! the office cabled him. PROCEED TO GERMANY. His reports attracted attention and delighted Ralph. Returning to the United States, Swope received a quick invitation to visit Ralph's mansion in Manhassett, Long Island; a lasting friendship began. The reporter was transferred to a very special city editorship commanding more than usual pay. Some colleagues thought he showed less talent at the desk than on reporting assignments. Perhaps in this period he invented what Barrett, who came to that job later, called "the system of running *The World* from the Belmont Race Track." Restless on the desk, Swope was sent to Germany when that nation began its relentless submarine campaign.

Swope was the first New York staffer to get into Germany at that phase of the war. His stories won him the $1000 prize for superior reporting which old J. P. had provided in his will. They made a book, *Inside the German Empire*. His performance pulled him to Washington when America entered the war, as an associate member of the War Industries Board and special assistant to its chairman, Bernard M. Baruch, who was on his way to statesmanship via Wall Street speculation.

At the war's end Swope came back to Park Row, tall, handsome, and exuding confidence. He covered the Peace Conference in Paris. Then he was given a special office downstairs in the *World* building with the official title of "consulting editor." That was something new and strange in newspaper organization. Between Ralph and the regular news editors, he intervened and, some thought, interfered. He and the managing editor were soon in each other's hair. The managing editor quit. Swope put a new sign EXECUTIVE EDITOR on the door of special offices he had built for himself in the editorial suite of the morning *World*.

"The beginning of his executive editorship," wrote Barrett later, "marks the beginning of the transition from the old to the new tradition for *The World*."

Ralph had at last adopted for himself the title of editor when Cobb died. But his duties as president of the company remained. In times in which both costs and competition were rising, old office contentions—which J. P. had seemed to foster—grew under Ralph. Some business associates had more taste for economies than the old Pulitzer doctrine of "get the news first, no matter what it costs." Their tightfistedness put a crimp into Swope's style. And, said Barrett in hurt hindsight, "His own never-to-be-sufficiently-goddamned habit of giving his office absent treatment or administering it from the race track only gave the business office more ammunition."

Still Swope did illuminate the old *World* prestige. The Ku Klux campaign took place under his direction. The paper exposed plans for sweet profits by sugar interests under proposed tariff hikes. It hammered at the hypocrisies of prohibition. Swope and *The World* got credit for bringing the interminable 1924 Democratic National Convention to New York City. Temporarily that wrangling political gathering nearly destroyed the Democratic Party, nor did it help *The World*.

By a stroke of genius it seemed at the time, Swope found a device which could serve prestige and economies, too. He invented the "op. ed.," the opposite editorial page. The editorial page had always been the Pulitzer pride. *The World* brought Walter Lippmann to it without giving him the title of editor. On the "op. ed." page among other luminaries (Franklin P. Adams, Alexander Woollcott, Deems Taylor, Harry Hansen included) was Heywood Broun.

In different ways, the impeccable Lippmann and the disheveled Broun represented a new day in American journalism. Both were New York boys of well-to-do families. Both were members of the celebrated Harvard class of 1910. Lippmann had finished his undergraduate work in three years; Broun gave so much time to the Boston Red Sox, poker playing, and the theater that he failed to get his degree.

Some old city-room pros were not impressed by Lippmann. Barrett, as chief coroner of complaint after *The World*'s death, was irreverent about the young man whose liberalism had been uniformed in military intelligence in the war and somehow put into the dark coat and striped pants of diplomacy in the negotiations for the peace. Lippmann, Barrett said, was "regarded as the spokesman of the 'socially minded intellectuals of Amer-

ica.' '' Then he added a parenthesis: "(whoever in hell they
are)." More seriously he added, "Lippmann was not a Cobb—
that was clear.... Cobb was always hot in the wake of *The
World* news—Lippmann liked to think things over first and also
see what *The Times* and the *Herald-Tribune* had to say about it
before sounding any bugle calls. As a matter of fact, he sounded
no bugle calls at all.''

Broun blew a shriller blast than Ralph Pulitzer required. He
had been something of a maverick in his first job after Harvard.
He was fired by *The New York Morning Telegraph* when he
asked for a raise. Then after desultory travels he rose as a
luminary on *The Tribune* as a sports writer, war correspondent,
and literary critic. In 1921 his column, "It Seems to Me," was
set up on *The World*'s "op. ed." page. It alternated from
whimsy to whiplash. He called for the pardon of Socialist
Eugene Debs in jail for "sedition" in wartime. He joined joyously in *The World*'s crusade against the Ku Klux Klan. He
struck hard blows at literary censorship, and in that cause in
1927 he collaborated on a book, *Anthony Comstock: Rounds-
man of the Lord.*

His co-author was Margaret Kernochan Leech. Later to become famous as the author of *Reveille in Washington* and other
works, she had graduated from Vassar in 1915. She had already
written two novels. She and Broun were working on the story of
Comstock, the much-ridiculed and reviled regulator of books,
prints, and public morals in general, in 1926. That year Ralph
sent to all employes, with the Christmas bonus, a suggestion that
they contribute 10 per cent of it to the building of New York's
Episcopal Cathedral of St. John the Divine.

In 1927, though America was moving into the stock-market
boom, there was no bonus and no charitable suggestion. Under
business-office pressure, Ralph Pulitzer had increased the price
of *The World* from two to three cents in 1925. *The Times* and the
Herald-Tribune stuck to two cents. They picked up upper-
echelon circulation and the new tabloids struck at *The World*
from below. In something approximating panic the two-cent
price was restored in 1927. The Pulitzers were troubled. And
young Herbert Pulitzer, who, after brief service on *The World*,

had lived idly abroad from 1919 through 1927, prepared to come home.

The troubles of *The World* seemed to have no connection with the troubles of Nicola Sacco, a shoemaker, and Bartolomeo Vanzetti, a fish peddler, who were finally sentenced to die on April 9, 1927, for the alleged murder of a factory paymaster. The kind of people who read and wrote *The World* were concerned. With other ardent liberals, Broun believed that the two men were victims of anti-Red hysteria. In his column on the "op. ed." page he savagely attacked eminent Massachusetts citizens who had recommended against a new trial for the men. Many shared his views. In one demonstration before the State House in Boston 150 persons, including writers, artists, and intellectuals, were arrested. Many people, not all members of the conservative community of wealth and status, disagreed. Barrett on the city desk thought Sacco and Vanzetti were "guilty as hell." Ralph, already restive about many things, was disturbed when Broun wrote with bitter eloquence of a committee of elder citizens officially named to investigate the trial. Its eminent members, including the president of Harvard, reported that the two Italians had properly been found guilty. Broun lashed out at the "tight minds . . . of old men."

Ralph let two violent columns pass. Then he ordered the column suspended until Broun could write on other subjects. The columnist took a "witch's sabbatical." Sacco and Vanzetti were electrocuted. On May 4, 1928, in the *Nation* Broun wrote accusing *The World* of timidity and inconsistency. Ralph, who had often shown courage in crises before, acted with petulant promptness. With his brother Herbert at hand, he fired Broun for "disloyalty."

The World was making news, not merely covering it. Broun basked in martyrdom. And Barrett, the chief carper in retrospect, put his memory of the incident away for a later snort.

"And of all the tum-tum damfool blunders," he wrote, "the firing of Broun was the worst. It made him a national character . . . made him a radio as well as a newspaper personality . . . and made a damn fool out of *The World*."

Loyalties on the paper seemed strange and shifting. Soon after

Broun was fired Swope phoned the city desk to add a new
woman reporter to the staff who would cover the Democratic and
Republican conventions in Houston and Kansas City that year.
She was Broun's collaborator, the brilliant, thirty-four-year-old
Margaret Leech. It took a lot of wire-pulling to get press-box
space for her. *The World*'s coverage of the conventions that year
was, however, romantic as well as political. Ralph Pulitzer, now
forty-nine, who had been divorced in Paris in 1924 from his first
wife of the Vanderbilt clan, came along. And in *The World* shop
it was news equal in interest to the nominations of Herbert
Hoover and Al Smith when in August Swope phoned and gave
exact and elaborate instructions about the coverage of the story
of the wedding of Ralph Pulitzer and Margaret Leech.

The newlyweds sailed on the *Paris* for Europe. On board they
met the flashily dressed, diminutive, driving Roy Howard of the
Scripps–Howard papers. Howard, building circulation for the
New York Telegram, which he had bought two years before, had
quickly hired Ralph's old employe and Margaret's old friend
Broun. Apparently that incident troubled no one. Ralph and
Roy were more than fellow publishers. Both were inheritors of
the traditions of strong old men who had spent much time at sea
on their yachts.

It had been seventeen years since old J. P.'s death on his
yacht in Charleston harbor. E. W. Scripps, who had built the
Scripps–Howard chain, had come to the end of his tough journalistic life only two years before on his yacht in Monrovia Bay, off
the coast of Liberia. He had been deliberately less cultured in his
steady crusading than Pulitzer. He was held in less journalistic
awe. But his crusading for the masses—the "95 per cent," the
common people—had been realistic on stages less metropolitan
than New York and St. Louis.

Scripps rather cultivated the impression that he was uncouth.
Before his marriage he had had many mistresses and made less
than a secret of it. Perhaps he boasted a little when he said that
when he stopped drinking in 1900 he had been consuming a
gallon of whiskey a day. But he did not mind if many thought he
was a "damned old crank." That gave color to his crusading.
He cared less than Pulitzer about what people thought of him.

He wanted reporting not intimidated by the respectables of politics or finance. He brought a searching scorn to stuffed shirts.

Coming from a brilliant newspaper family, he quarreled with his half-brothers and his eldest son. But Scripps learned, as the elder Pulitzer never quite did, to trust other men. He gave local authority to the editors of his papers and demanded local initiative. Finally, though he had first snorted at his puniness, he found in Roy Howard in his plumage clothes a cocky, able, "terrier-busy" assistant.

Howard had come strutting up from poverty to dominate city rooms. He was ready when he was twenty-three to become the dominant factor in building the United Press Association. In that job he had survived even the monumental blooper of a premature announcement of the Armistice in World War I. At thirty-seven, in 1920, he was assistant chairman of the board of the Scripps company. Three years later old Scripps retired. Howard, at forty, was not only in command; his name had been added to the Scripps–Howard name. He was buying more papers, spreading the old Scripps empire. Behind his dazzling dress and the personal brass which matched it, he had charm for many and the admiration of all. He could joke and slug. Some did regard him as "a little son of a bitch." Nobody judged his powers by his physical size.

Ralph Pulitzer was subdued in appearance if not colorless beside him. It may have seemed presumptuous to Ralph that as they sailed and talked Howard, who had only come into New York journalism two years before, asked about the possibility— and the rumors—that the great old *World* might be for sale. He would be interested. Evidently the conversation was of the nature of "Well, no" and "Well, if ever."

The situation on Park Row was not improved when the bridegroom came home in the early fall. Barrett wrote that Swope was so depressed at the time that he did not even go to Saratoga for the races. No miracles had been wrought by Herbert Pulitzer, who had arrived in *The World* office—in a red-leather-upholstered suite—in January. Indeed, he seemed designed to be like Howard, though in a Bond Street way, a pictorial scapegoat for those who liked Ralph even when they despaired of him. Herbert wore very full double-breasted coats buttoned very high on the second button, causing many folds. His hair was seldom cropped. He smoked perfumed cigarettes. He was polite but distant to the staff. He was referred to by *World* reporters as the "Young Marster."

Rumor spread that old masters were departing. When Ralph returned, Swope resigned. There were reports that Ralph was retiring; these were denied. Still there was some of the sadness and some of the irritation of disintegration at farewell dinners given for Swope.

Nineteen twenty-nine seemed at its start lucky for everybody. The stock market, which sometimes interested Swope as much as the horse races, was soaring. And even when it came tumbling down in October Roy Howard, returning from a trip around the world, seemed as dazzling as ever. He found the rumors about the sale of *The World* increasing. He wrote to Herbert Pulitzer, who seemed more and more active in management. He got a polite note back that under the elder Pulitzer's will the trustees could not consider any proposals. But Herbert added that if the brothers ever did decide to sell they would communicate with Mr. Howard.

Ralph Pulitzer resigned his executive duties on *The World* because of ill health in February 1930. Other men then did not have jobs to give up. Some who did hung on to them tightly, fearful as they passed the unemployed on the streets. On Howard's *Telegram* Broun took time from his columning to run unsuccessfully for Congress on the Socialist ticket. In his column he conducted a "Give a Job until June" campaign. To assist unemployed actors he produced a musical, *Shoot the Works*. Big, fat, rumpled Broun danced and sang on the stage until he almost collapsed from exhaustion.

The great drama of *The World* moved on no spotlit stage. Indeed, the negotiations for its sale as 1930 moved into 1931 were so secret that the paper's city editor, who was supposed to keep on top of all the news in good old Pulitzer fashion, only learned about them on February 16, 1931. Then his news was denied. He had gone into the office of the managing editor to discuss some details about *The World*'s perennial coal fund for the poor. There would be a little money to carry over to the next year.

"There won't be any next year," he was told abruptly. "The show is over. After forty years on this paper—"

The editor did not finish the sentence.

"Scripps–Howard," he said more calmly, "have bought the whole thing."

This was denied by Herbert's office. He would not, he said, dignify the reports by bulletin-board denial. For their own information reporters resorted to tactics which they had sometimes used in covering politicians for the Pulitzers. The story was true enough. Howard had his contract to buy the papers for $5 million. It was only necessary to get a ruling from the surrogate court that, considering *The World*'s financial condition, old J. P.'s provision that the paper never be sold could be set aside.

Other publishers were suddenly eager to get a chance to bid. Barrett and others on the staff hastily tried to buy and save the paper for its employes. Their eagerness mounted; sympathy for them soared. The management of the Astor Hotel happily gave them a ballroom for their meeting. Their prospects seemed hopeful—certainly exciting. Printers were ready with their savings. Reporters offered to hock future earnings. One shift in the composing room pledged at least $50,000. Friends offered to help. Newpapermen all over the country and many overseas wired support.

Howard had his cash and his contract. At the final hearing he looked very snappy in a brown double-breasted suit with accentuated tailoring. The whole business had been arranged. Able lawyers took apart the provision in the will which Pulitzer's able lawyers had put together. The surrogate ruled. It was clear at last that Howard planned to combine the *Evening World* with his *Telegram*. *The Sunday World* would be discontinued. The morning *World,* the institution, the paper of tradition, would be killed.

The old paper operated on its last day as on every day before. Reporters worked as if they would be on the grisly story to its end covering the details of the death of poor, strangled Vivian Gordon. The last paper carried the news that the House of Representatives had overwhelmingly overridden President Hoover's veto of the veterans' bonus. Charlie Chaplin and George Bernard Shaw were exchanging jokes. Two hundred and fifty people were dead in the track of a typhoon in the Fiji Islands. And there was the news of the sale of *The World,* which seemed clearly edited in the business office.

"The thought uppermost in the minds of our associates, Robert P. Scripps and myself," announced Roy Howard, "is that the consolidation means not the death of the New York *World* but its rebirth. . . ."

Walter Lippmann's approving comment on the sale was run under the headline EDITOR EXTOLS COURAGE AND SINCERITY OF NEW OWNERS OF THE WORLD.

"The Scripps–Howard chain of newspapers is a powerful influence in American life," Lippmann wrote in unexceptional prose. "Their courage, sincerity, independence and sympathy have been tested and proved. While all mergers of newspapers have in them an element of chance, it seems to me that this merger is logical and appropriate."

As to his own future, Mr. Lippmann said, "My personal plans have not been affected by the sale of *The World.* My contract is almost completed and last summer I told Mr. Herbert Pulitzer that when it expired I did not wish to continue as editor any longer than he might think was necessary to assist in the plan of reorganization which was then contemplated. I told him that, after seven years of continuous responsibility for the editorial page of *The World,* an intermission seemed to be in order, and that I had planned to travel and then to settle down to do some writing."

It did not seem an intermission to others. James Barrett, the last city editor, typified the pain and the surprise which spread like panic under *The World*'s golden dome. As he worked to put out the last editions he led the futile movement to make it possible for the men who had produced *The World* every day to possess it in the days ahead. After fifteen years on the paper, nine as city editor, it is easy to understand his pain. His surprise is not quite so comprehensible. He had come to New York journalism when the *Denver Times,* on which he was the star re-

porter, was sold like any other property. He had "seen newspapers bought and sold without a whimper from readers or
editors." *The World*'s death was the only one, he said, which
made grimy printers and cynical reporters cry.

In his anguish he undertook to assess the blame. As first
defender of a torn tradition he set up old Joseph Pulitzer
as his journalistic Jehovah and made the Pulitzer will his
Ark of the Covenant. He rather forgave Ralph and his brother,
Joseph, Jr. He believed they were sorry after the sale of *The
World*. He poured out his prejudice against Herbert, who only
came into the operating picture after Barrett himself said it was
"plain as a pikestaff that the ship was going to sink." Still he
struck at all the heirs of old J. P.

He arraigned them for "betrayal of the trust ... for the scut-
tling of the sacred ship because there was rough weather....
merely because seven lean years succeeded seven exceedingly fat
and prosperous years ... , merely because the flesh was tired."
(The dots are Barrett's.)

That anger is history now. *World* men dispersed and disappeared and died. And less emotional men than James Barrett
have seen that Founder Joseph Pulitzer himself killed *The
World* he loved. He began to kill it when in suspicious blindness
he set up such a divided control in his own lifetime that real
direction could come only from him on his yacht. He played
employe against employe. Then in the changing of wills he
seemed to play son against son. Certainly if the omission of
Ralph's name as a trustee was a typographical error in the will,
J. P. was capable of other errors in his blind day-to-day domination of the paper while he lived.

He did not die suddenly. He had been dead to the sight of his
subordinates while he jealously controlled *The World* from in-
sulated chambers onshore and at sea. When he actually died the
divisions and the distrusts and some of his own deviousness had
pervaded *The World*. Frank Cobb was, Barrett said, "moulded
... by the ever-watchful Founder." Ralph Pulitzer was ruled
by the extension of his father's dead hand in the person of Cobb
until 1923. The fact is not altered because Cobb was brilliant. A
gentle, bookish man, Ralph did not find the force behind him

upon which he had been long taught to depend in the often-absent Swope and the intellectually elegant Lippmann. Because Ralph could not lead he almost courted the crusading insubordination of Broun.

In tragic measure *The World* had ceased to be *The World* long before February 1931. Its news coverage had declined. The thunder of its editorial policy was muted. The addition of the "op. ed." page made the paper more intellectually entertaining than morally invigorating. The institution had become only a tradition. The time had come for the arrival of brash, busy, bedazzling Roy Howard. He was no villain in the death of *The World*. He was no upstart in the higher precincts of the press. Actually, even as a pint-sized peacock in power, he was as tragic a figure in the history of American journalism as any or all of the Messrs. Pulitzer.

Lippmann was correct in his statement that the Scripps–Howard papers had represented as true and strong a crusading spirit as did *The World*. Indeed, cranky, crusading E. W. Scripps was as much a fighting personality of the press as Joseph Pulitzer. Both could only have heirs to their powers. Pulitzer's boys let *The World* lapse. And under Roy Howard's direction, according to careful, objective Frank Luther Mott in his history *American Journalism,* "the old rough-and-tumble fights for the underdog elements . . . became less characteristic of Scripps–Howard than a dignified liberalism." Mott added: "Critics allege a decline in the chain's crusading spirit."

The tragedy in the death of *The World* was not that the *World-Telegram* swallowed it. It was that the loss of something vital on both sides was marked by the combination. Even as a skyrocketing dandy Roy Howard had come to a dominant, rich place in the newspaper business. Wealthy and respectable, Ralph Pulitzer was incapable of assault on eminent old men like those Broun damned. A certain audacity and hostility in confronting public affairs had been lost which old Pulitzer and old Scripps both had possessed. They were not transferable by wills or codicils or bargain and sale. Howard could not buy what Pulitzer tried to leave—and hold at the same time. And *The World* died not because it was hard up but because it was no longer really ready to be roughneck when occasion required. In a sense it was killed by dignity, decorum, charm without challenge, and the lack of any sense of vital destination or direction.

Swope, who had departed early, found a prosperous place for himself on the boards of large corporations, keeping his journalistic hand in only as director of a polo magazine. Lippmann became the noted, lucid, syndicated columnist referred to by some as the "other State Department," by others as a man subdued by "the aristocratic embrace." Only Broun became more and more liberal—radical, many believed.

After the death of *The World* he helped organize the American Newspaper Guild as a union of newspaper employes. Howard, who had welcomed him to the *Telegram* when Ralph Pulitzer fired him, didn't like the Guild. He began to be more and more restive about Broun. In July 1939, some of Broun's columns for the *World-Telegram* were edited. Others were omitted. The fat, disheveled columnist anticipated the end of his contract by inserting a Situation Wanted advertisement in New York newspapers.

There would, of course, always be a place for his words. But Broun realized that he was no more immortal than *The World*. He worried about death. Suddenly, in May, he had become a Roman Catholic. About the same time Ralph Pulitzer, a man in retirement, underwent an operation for abdominal cancer. He died in June, younger than his father had been when death came to him.

Broun survived Ralph Pulitzer by five months. Perhaps, as some historians say, Ralph presided over the end of the crusading journalism *The World* represented. Broun, as crusader, set the pattern for the signed syndicated column of opinion, not necessarily in agreement with the editorial policies of the papers in which it appeared. Broun also may have written the best epitaph of Ralph Pulitzer when he observed that if Ralph put *The World* in the red, to his great credit he took it out of the yellow. Maybe there was some gain for journalism in that. There could be none if the yeast was lost with the yellow.

17

Continental Divide

Greater than the distance between them on two sides of a continent were the differences between Adolph S. Ochs, publisher of *The New York Times,* and Fremont Older, editor of the San Francisco *Bulletin.* Earnest, energetic Ochs was eager to be loved; Older was always ready to be hated. Yet their lives coincided almost exactly. They were among the last of printers who came to editorial power. And in the same year both came to crises in classic cases of the recurrent impatience with the press on the part of the public—or at least a part of the public which assumes the right to speak loudly and righteously for the whole.

That year was 1918, when home furies almost matched World War horrors. Popular feeling was almost as high as in 1867 when Horace Greeley, after a gesture of forgiveness to the South, felt the roar of unpopularity in the Union which had put down rebellion and meant to keep Rebels down, too. Then Greeley had been ready to defy even such "men of substance and standing" as members of the Union League Club of New York. In 1918, Older was ready still—deliberately—to confront similar men. Ochs, caught almost by accident in superpatriotic and plutocratic impatience with his paper, was distressed by the possibility of their disapproval.

Greeley had been an idol of Ochs since young Adolph had turned up as a blue-eyed fourteen-year-old with dark moist curls seeking a job in the shop of *The Knoxville Chronicle* in 1872. The boy began as printer's devil building legends of how well he swept the ink-stained floor and how brightly he polished the editor's lamp. Grave as he was energetic, he was given the nickname "Mooley," farm term for any hornless steer or cow. He did seem more timid than equipped for combat. In his later years, he said, he learned his trade well because he hung around the shop after his work was done so that on his walk home by a graveyard he would be accompanied by the foreman.

Ochs moved on fast from sorting type and cleaning cuspidors. More than superstitious fear of a cemetery kept him hard at work. In the household of his scholarly but impractical father and his dominant mother, both German-Jewish immigrants, he was the chief support. Before he was old enough to vote he acquired the controlling interest in *The Chattanooga Times* with $250 of borrowed money. The paper was regarded as pretty much of a wreck. Ochs bought debts as well as prospects. Though the payroll was often a problem, the paper employed six men in the composing room, two Negro printers, four delivery boys, one reporter, and an editor complete with the title of Colonel. In staff it seems to have been a fairly substantial shoestring in the hands of a boy. And as the paper grew and prospered Ochs seemed only to extend and enlarge his shoestrings.

Steadily borrowing more and more for real estate speculation as well as news plant expansion, his story in these Chattanooga years seems almost a race with the moneylenders by a man advancing to success on bigger and bigger debts. Disaster seemed always close at his heels. Yellow fever came up the rivers to empty Chattanooga of readers and advertisers. In energetic promotion of the industrial and economic life of his town, he was overpersuaded by his own paper's pieces on ever-rising real estate values. But, though land losses came and debts piled up, Ochs brought the first linotype machine to the South. He built a fine plant with a golden dome. He met prominent people, including President Cleveland, developers, promoters, financiers who had in their portfolios investments in the press. He came to New York with a rising reputation but in the city, looking for greater opportunity as a means of paying greater debts, he was more impressive than opulent.

The sagging *New York Times* was, he saw, his chance to soar. And he convinced important people in one way or another interested in it that he provided *The Times'* hope, too. In a night-long talk he won the enthusiastic support of the paper's worried editor, Charles R. Miller. Miller had come to the staff under George Jones, who had fought the Tammany Tiger. With others he had acquired the property from the Jones heirs. Now he introduced Ochs to personages concerned about the paper's poor prospects. And with push, charm, and glittering self-confidence Ochs won the support of Charles Flint who, in this era of emerging monopolies, was called "the Father of Trusts." He moved on to others—J. P. Morgan, August Belmont, Jacob Schiff—who had investments, if they could still be so called, in the foundering newspaper.

Ochs interested all these gentlemen in the new objective journalism, eschewing partisan violence, he had developed in Tennessee. As Ochs talked to them, "sound money" seemed threatened by Populist and Democratic talk of "free silver." Ochs himself—as publisher, not philosopher—had recently appeared willing to come into New York as publisher of a free-silver newspaper though in Tennessee his paper had been a strong advocate of "sound money." He wrote his wife that he really didn't understand the question. Neither did millions of other Americans, though all were excited one way or the other

about it. The financiers with whom Ochs talked of *The Times*
had no doubts. Bryan was a menace. Free silver was soaking the
rich to serve the poor. As the negotiations for his control of the
paper progressed Ochs wired his editor in Tennessee to intensify
fire on Bryan.

To the very last Ochs was afraid he would not get his chance
to run *The Times*. He turned down offers from its owners to run
it on a salary. He wanted ownership. Then there were rumors of
a wide variety of richer seekers for the old paper. Finally, however, a new company was formed and with $75,000, mostly bor-
rowed, the thirty-eight-year-old Southerner secured the control—or the chance to control if he fulfilled his promises of
profit. Those were large promises about a paper with only 9000
circulation, losing at the rate of $1000 a day. It was a tremen-
dous gamble for a man self-described as ''a country newspaperman burdened with debt,'' even if he did have the beneficent
wishes of powerful people.

William Randolph Hearst had arrived the year before with his
pockets full of money to contend with Pulitzer's *World* in the
competitive creation of yellow journalism. If Ochs had wished,
he could not have afforded to match the costly pyrotechnic journalism of Hearst and Pulitzer—even the cost of its limited
coverage of the Spanish War almost broke *The Times*. Nevertheless, its steady, objective news reporting brought it more and
more readers who objected to the yellow journals. And Editor
Miller, freed of debt worries, became a sometimes eloquent, always pleasing pillar of strength and scholarly respectability.

Ochs' crusade was for respectable journalism. His plan was
immediately embodied in the famous motto ''All The News
That's Fit To Print.'' Under it, shrewdly, perhaps intuitively,
and in his lifelong disinclination to offend, he maintained his
appeal to those repelled by the rising roar of the popular press.
Despite some cynical sneers from other newsmen, the idea paid
off. Solid, often sober news was presented. And as time went on,
it was remarkable what did turn out to be fit to print on the
paper's decorous pages. Sin and shame were not kept entirely
secret from *Times* readers, though they might have to look on
inside pages to find them. Somehow the impression was made

that when *The Times* gave extensive coverage to crime and violence, its reports were not sensationalism but sociology. The
reader got what he wanted, but with a sense of greater dignity
when he read it in *The Times*.

The money began to roll in. When America entered World
War I the cable costs alone of *The Times* amounted to more than
$750,000 a year—ten times Ochs' original investment in his now
prestigious, profitable paper. And Ochs had almost similarly
mounted in position and respect. Though he directed policy, he
happily depended for editorial expression on Miller. Still *The
Times* was Ochs and, as everybody knew, Ochs was *The Times*.
Perhaps, as Meyer Berger said in his history of the paper, in
Tennessee and in New York Ochs "took the personal slant out of
journalism." *He* was, as no one was ever allowed to forget, its
personality. When Miller wrote, Ochs was heard. That was especially true as Allied sentiment grew in financial and other circles
after the outbreak of war in Europe in 1914. In an editorial in
December of that year, Miller for Ochs added prophecy to *The
Times'* strong Allied support:

> Germany is doomed to sure defeat. Bankrupt in states-
> manship, overmatched in arms, under the moral condemna-
> tion of the civilized world, befriended only by the Austrian
> and the Turk, two backward-looking and dying nations,
> desperately battling against the hosts of three great powers
> to which help and reinforcement from States now neu-
> tral will certainly come should the decision be long de-
> ferred, she pours out the blood of her heroic subjects and
> wastes her diminishing substance in a hopeless struggle
> that postpones but cannot alter the final decree.

The sentence was long but the paper's policy was clear. It
remained clear—and was cheered first by Preparedness patriots
and then by Americans generally. Perhaps its very vehemence
led to the sudden shock of many readers and to what Ochs and all
his biographers have depicted as the dark hour of humiliation in
his life. The publisher was at the fine summer home he had built
for himself at Lake George in the foothills of the Adirondacks on
Saturday afternoon, September 15, 1918. He was called to the

phone. Cables had brought to *The Times* newsroom the word that
Austria had put out a peace bid. Jubilantly Ochs received the
news. He asked if Editor Miller had been informed so that he
might write an editorial. He was told that Miller had been informed and was telephoning his comments from his place on
Long Island. That satisfied Ochs. The always-dependable Miller
wrote his editorial in enthusiasm—and to an explosion.

In retrospect the editorial seems sound and sensible enough.
Then, however, Miller's advice that the Austrian proposal for a
nonbinding discussion of peace terms be accepted roused violent
reaction. It seemed almost treason to fevered patriots. In advocating anything less than unconditional surrender, they suggested, *The Times* was suddenly running up the white flag.

Ochs had not seen the editorial until it appeared. It is not
apparent that he came down from the Adirondacks in agitation
about it. But when he arrived at his office his desk was piled with
denunciatory telegrams. Even in his newsroom some staff members were muttering in anger about it. Then the crowning blow
came. The Union League Club, the plush and patriotic embodiment of the respectable readership at which Ochs had always
aimed, called a meeting to consider barring *The Times* from its
reading room as well as a public denunciation of the paper.

Ochs appeared "utterly bludgeoned," said one of his own
writers. He was "like a man dazed by a head blow." From his
desk piled deep with abusive messages, he wandered about the
shop into the newsroom, the composing room. He even suggested
to a friend that perhaps in view of the evident public antagonism he ought to retire and turn the paper over to trustees. It
never occurred to him to reach, as Greeley had done when the
Union League questioned his conduct, for a pugnacious pen.

Instead, prominent friends were mobilized. Chauncey M.
Depew, great orator and railroad spokesman, declined to attend
the Union League meeting and accompanied his refusal with
praise of *The Times* despite its "unfortunate" editorial. Other
Union League members rallied to *The Times:* the famous Elihu
Root, dime-store magnate Frank W. Woolworth. Miller secured a
friendly statement from President Eliot of Harvard. Ochs appealed personally to Woodrow Wilson's friend Colonel E. M.

House. And while some newspapers had joined the hue and cry against Ochs and *The Times,* support came from the unexpected source of Frank Munsey. That publisher, who seemed more a meat packer than a newspaperman to William Allen White, put a piece in *The Sun* declaring the editorial to be honest, sincere, and not unpatriotic. Ochs was almost pathetically grateful for it.

An able corps of authorized biographers have made much of the fact that despite his state of shock Ochs stood by Miller. The publisher said that he had been given credit for much of Miller's contribution to the paper. He himself was responsible for the paper as a whole. They had worked together then for nearly a quarter of a century. Yet because he did not punish or repudiate his editor, one of his biographers thought he became "a hero to the craft" in newspaper offices all over the country. That throws more light on the precarious tenure of the craft then than on the temperament of Ochs. Yet the same biographer wrote that in offices throughout America newspaper workers Ochs had never seen or heard of cried:

"What a man!"

Ochs did stand, though so shaken that after the excitement subsided he spent some time under the care of psychiatrists. He did not damn or dodge his longtime, dependable editor. But in command at *The Times* he was not quite George Jones beset by the Tiger and Tammany's millionaire friends. He precipitated no riotous session in the rich and powerful Union League Club by defiance and disdain as Greeley had done. In terms of hazard faced and met, he was not the crusading equivalent of Fremont Older—beset at almost the same time a continent away by similar forces of opulent superpatriotism.

The coincidence pointed sharply the contrast in the men. Ochs was well-groomed, affable, expansive in his tall Times Square building, which had become the center of metropolis. Older, in the shabby *Bulletin* building in San Francisco, seemed less amiable. He was careless of his appearance. An avowed pessimist, he was ready to fight where an optimist would not have dared. The impeccability Ochs undertook to bring to the press found no echo in the *Bulletin* as Older shaped it.

The San Francisco editor flamboyantly played up crime and
scandals—and the sadness and horror of San Francisco, as
Lafcadio Hearn had done in Cincinnati. He put seven-column
streamers over stories of violence, sin, and corruption. But he
had ample place as well on his pages for issues of tolerance and
decency. A significant difference between the two men also was
that while Ochs' *Times* had cheered on the cause of the Allies,
popular with plutocratic patriots, Older had been deeply distressed by a war he considered only a waste of life and resources.
But Older like Ochs had built impressive readership from similar sagging 9000 circulations.

Born in a poverty at least equal to that of Ochs' childhood,
Older had soon been left fatherless. As a means of livelihood his
mother peddled books. One was a life of Horace Greeley, the
reading of which made Greeley the hero of young Older in the
West as he had been of Ochs in the South. Older began his
career as a devil in a printshop. By the time he was eighteen he
was a composing-room foreman on a San Francisco paper, learning also about the collection of news. But he was thirty-nine,
with editorial experience, when he was made managing editor of
the limping *Bulletin*.

At the outset Older crusaded with the primary idea of attract-
ing attention and getting circulation. The paper had been able to
struggle along only because the politically powerful Southern
Pacific Railroad slipped to it, as it did to some other sheets,
monthly "good will" payments for its "friendliness." But,
struggling with a small staff, Older decided that the railroad was
his best target in his efforts to attract readers. He set out to
break railroad domination of California.

Converted by his own crusade, Older not only forced his publisher to give up similar subsidies from gas, utility, and other
corporate interests, he also went after the city boss. With a reluctant publisher behind him, Older engaged in violent battle.
Once his life was said to have been saved when a man hired to
kidnap and kill him lost his nerve. Older himself arranged the
abduction of a Chinaman from whom he hoped to extract evidence about graft. His support helped elect Hiram W. Johnson

as reform governor and built the paper's circulation toward the 100,000 it attained under his editorial direction.

Older seemed almost swept along by the causes he served. Soon after he succeeded in sending San Francisco boss Abraham Ruef to prison in 1908 on a charge of extortion, he decided that the fault was not the man but the system which "made money our measure of sucess." He campaigned now for Ruef's parole.

"Fremont Older has gone suddenly soft ... , " said an article in *Collier's Weekly*. "He was the nemesis of the crooks. He has become their best friend."

As prison reformer, he indeed seemed to be. He published in the *Bulletin* one convict's story of his prison life which attracted national attention. He established a bureau in the *Bulletin* office to aid ex-convicts. Fallen men and women became his deepest concern and the paper's best copy. His new social views with regard to those he considered oppressed led him to encouragement of labor unions and to the sympathy he expressed for the International Workers of the World and William D. Haywood, its founder, who fled to Russia after conviction for sedition.

Criticism grew around Older. It increased when he wrote with tolerance even of the McNamara brothers, who pled guilty to bombing the antiunion *Los Angeles Times*. But conservative indignation boiled over when he crusaded for the reprieve and later the pardon of labor leader Tom Mooney who, Older believed, had been "framed" in the trial for bombing the Preparedness Day parade in San Francisco on July 22, 1916, in which ten people were killed.

That parade was not merely designed to support American preparedness for war. Twelve days before the parade, 2000 San Francisco businessmen, obviously the "men of substance and standing" of the Golden Gate, met at the Chamber of Commerce. Unanimously they declared that "intolerable conditions prevailed in the industrial life of San Francisco." In the face of efforts of Mooney and others to organize labor, notably railroad workers, they formed a "Law and Order Committee" to back the chamber's antiunion policy. The committee meant business.

Employers let their workers know that they were expected to march in the parade—or else! Some thought of the old Vigilantes of James King of William's time. Older's young editorial writer, R. L. Duffus, who later joined the staff of Ochs' *Times,* recalled a saying about rich San Franciscans that "the nob's boiled linen covered the red shirt of the former miner."

Such men were not pleased with Older's crusade for justice for Mooney, who had actually been half a mile away when the bomb went off. Advertisers withdrew their business. Pressure intensified on the paper's publisher, elderly, heavy-drinking R. A. Crothers, whom Older's circulation-building had enriched. There was response to the pressure, particularly from Crothers' pushing nephew and heir, Loring Pickering. Though young Pickering had other faults—like pomposity—his real weakness was, Duffus thought, "his desire to be liked and admired by the right people."

"What Loring did not seem to see was that if a newspaper publisher really did what a small number of his most important advertisers wanted him to do he ran the risk of producing a dull newspaper. And there is no way in a relatively free country to make anybody read a dull newspaper."

That was the essence of Older's understanding, though a social sense stirred by his own causes took him far beyond it. But the *Bulletin* business office was tired of crusades. Older was ordered to drop the Mooney case. Word of his trouble got around. Hearst, who had added the *Call* to the San Francisco anchor of his growing chain in 1913, had moved to wider fields the year Older began on the *Bulletin,* but he knew what the troubled editor had done for the *Bulletin*'s circulation. He invited Older, now sixty-two and with no wealth except limited savings from his salary, to become editor of the *Call* and, as Older reported, "to bring the Mooney case with me."

Older wrote to Crothers on July 16, 1918, just two months before Ochs was made desolate by the reaction to Miller's editorial. It was a sad rather than an angry farewell:

"It may be that the old policies of the paper, which were so dear to me, were only dreams, but they have taken such a firm hold upon my imagination that I must cling to them to the end.

I have gone too far to turn back. I should get lost on the way.''

Perhaps afterward he took some rueful satisfaction in the fact that the *Bulletin* he had built began swiftly to go downhill. His biographer wrote that before long the paper was losing $125,000 a month, a lot of money even behind the Golden Gate. It represented a terrible tide for the timid. Hearst bought the paper, adding it to his *Call,* and made Older president as well as editor of the *Call-Bulletin.*

In so secure a position Older lived long enough to see the judge who had tried Mooney and ten survivors of the jury which had convicted him favor his release. Indeed, the judge declared that the conviction of the labor organizer was ''one of the dirtiest jobs ever put over and I resent the fact that my court was used for such a contemptible piece of work.'' But the hard spirit of the reactionaries who had railroaded Mooney receded slowly in California. It was not until four years after the tall, strong Older died in 1935 that the Governor of California crowned the editor's long crusade by granting an unconditional pardon to Mooney. Older was not on hand to see the big parade the pardoned Mooney then led along the same route as that of the Preparedness Parade of nineteen years before nor to hear the cheers on the sidewalks above the siren on the Ferry Building shrieking as shrilly as it had when it proclaimed the bombing.

The Hearst years, Older said, were the happiest of his newspaper career. Perhaps that accounted for his judgment that Hearst's ''record of progressive achievements'' made him ''unparalleled in American journalism.'' Many who shared no such view of Hearst regarded Older as a great, maybe the last, crusading editor. Oswald Garrison Villard, whose abolitionist grandfather had founded *The Liberator* and whose rich father had bought the distinguished *New York Evening Post,* felt so.

''In a period when personality and even personal force are disappearing from journalism,'' Villard wrote, ''one turns with joy to such a character, difficult as it is to analyze, great as are its contradictions.''

On March 3, 1935, Older had begun an editorial on Montaigne's essay on death just before he got into his automobile, which at seventy-seven he drove back and forth between his office and his Santa Clara County ranch. His death came quickly after a heart attack at the steering wheel. His grave was marked by a heap of rocks brought from far and near by friends, some of whom might have been friendless except for him.

It was a time for the exit of old men. A month after Older collapsed, Ochs was visiting in his home town Chattanooga, where he had begun his efforts to mute the rowdiness and stress the objectivity of the press. He had come by this time, an appointed historian of his paper said, to a "deep stony-floored valley of melancholy, in much the same condition as that in which he had fallen ... when the Austrian peace editorial and readers' subsequent anger had buffeted and bewildered him."

In New York he no longer answered calls from the paper. But the Tennessee visit seemed to bring a glimpse of light at the last. He was almost gay in Chattanooga. He visited *The Chattanooga Times*, where his newspaper management had begun. But at luncheon on April 8, 1935, he failed to answer a question as to what he would have. There would be no more for him. He was dead. "From all the civliized world," his paper's chronicler said, "men wrote in tribute." Not stones but flowers were brought to his grave.

In their separate ways, Ochs and Older were both crusaders. Ochs was always carefully concerned for the decency of his paper and Older was more explosively concerned for the decency of the world around his. Neither cause can be spared.

18

Crusaders All

The crusading editor in "personal journalism" has always been a man about to disappear. Horace Greeley had some such notion himself as early as 1841, when he was only beginning to be the great tempestuous, eccentric, and influential editor he became. And by 1855 *Putnam's Monthly* was confidently declaring that "the great journals are now rather corporate institutions than individual organs; and hence the former autocratic influence of men like Horace Greeley is on the decline." Then, of course, many were sure when Greeley died in 1872 "that the day for personal journalism is gone by, and that impersonal journalism will take its place."

"A great deal of twaddle," said Charles A. Dana, editor of *The New York Sun,* who could be both charming and caustic and in his own lifetime changed from idealistic socialist to extreme conservative.

"Whenever in the newspaper profession," said Dana, "a man rises up who is original, strong, and bold enough to make his opinions a matter of consequence to the public, there will be personal journalism; and whenever newspapers are conducted only by commonplace individuals whose views are of no consequence to anybody, there will be nothing but impersonal journalism.

"And this is the essence of the whole question."

Charles A. Dana applied the word *profession* to journalism. Greeley had doubted that it was a separate profession. William Cullen Bryant, whose great career as editor of *The New York Evening Post* has been obscured by his lesser activities as poet, thought that the press was accorded no such status. Often its practitioners did not seem quite respectable.

There was a growing journalistic hunger to be respectable. Sometimes there was a ready and rough disposition by editors to prove the gentility of their position at the pen even if they had to do it with cane, cowhide, or pistol. Joseph Pulitzer, after he had competed and collaborated with Hearst in creating yellow journalism, left millions to add the patina of professionally educated men to editorial staffs. More elegant journalists had been disturbed by rowdier elements in the craft. Their protests became almost a crusade, too, when the yelling yellows of Hearst and Pulitzer helped push America into the newsful war with Spain.

Edwin L. Godkin, who regarded himself a moral censor of the press, declared in *The New York Evening Post* that the behavior of *The World* and the *Journal* in that journalistic jingoism was more disgraceful than anything known in the history of American journalism.

"It is a crying shame," he cried, "that men should work such mischief in order to sell more papers."

The Tribune was disdainfully sarcastic. Its owner, Whitelaw Reid, had advanced far from his beginnings in Xenia, Ohio.

With Greeley's *Tribune* and an heiress wife, he had become an ambassador and a Republican candidate for Vice-President. He lived in a massive Florentine mansion behind St. Patrick's Cathedral. A few weeks after the destruction of the *Maine,* his paper declared that the war had been "a glorious success, as will be seen by the billboard announcements of the increased circulation of the newspapers which have carried it in ... the greatest triumph ever achieved by large type and a liberty-loving press."

Some other crusades were less than universally popular. As a result of one, Theodore Roosevelt called the elder Pulitzer a liar who ought to be in jail. The public welfare was not necessarily served when Hearst made one of the great crusades of his papers his campaign to make his mistress a movie star. To some crusading editors other editors sometimes seemed irresponsible and disreputable. Sometimes they were. That feeling undoubtedly prompted the meeting in New York City in 1922 of many who sincerely wanted to be gentlemen of the press to form the American Society of Newspaper Editors. Two men were particularly prominent in the movement. One was Frank Cobb of *The World* of Pulitzer, who had brought his ripsnorting readability out of St. Louis. The other was Casper S. Yost of the *St. Louis Globe-Democrat.* The *Globe-Democrat* had grown in crusading competition with Pulitzer's *Post-Dispatch.*

One apocryphal tale of sensationalism was about Yost's great predecessor, J. B. McCullagh. An assistant brought to Editor McCullagh some huge wooden type for a proposed head over a story of an 1896 tornado in St. Louis.

"Wonderful!" McCullagh is supposed to have said. "A great head! But really, I was saving that type for the Second Coming of Christ!"

Many did not wait for that story. In heads and editorials and news stories, their causes, crusades, and sensations screamed. Cobb, Yost, and others hoped that something could be done to put an ethical lid on often-boiling journalism. They organized. Yost was elected president. Cobb was made vice-president and director. A committee was appointed to draw up "Canons of Journalism" to be presented at a first general meeting the following year. One of its canons was to read "A journalist who uses his power for any selfish or unworthy purpose is faithless to high trust."

The timing of the determination to provide such tenets was unconsciously well-chosen. This was the year Harry H. Tammen and Fred G. Bonfils of the *Denver Post* sent a star reporter into New Mexico. On a tip from an alert editor, Carl Magee, he went to investigate rumors that oil millionaires and high government officials were conspiring in corruption to loot the people and property of the United States. In itself the journalistic errand was worthy, though any errand of Tammen and Bonfils, called by their biographer Gene Fowler "the Katzenjammer Kids" of Rocky Mountain journalism, was suspect.

In 1919 Magee, a Tulsa, Oklahoma, Democratic lawyer, had moved to the dry New Mexican climate when his wife developed tuberculosis. He had always wanted to be an editor. Now forty-five, wanting something to do, he tried to buy the Albuquerque *Morning Journal*. Republican U.S. Senator Albert B. Fall, one of its owners, stopped the sale. But by February 1920, Fall, who a year later was to become Secretary of the Interior in Harding's Cabinet, needed money so badly that he entertained Magee at his ranch, arranged for a quick cash sale. Fall told Magee that he was so poor that he couldn't pay the taxes on his ranch. He was going to resign from the Senate to rebuild his fortunes.

Then suddenly, early in 1922, Magee and a reporter on his *Journal*, Clinton P. Anderson, later United States Senator, noticed sudden strange signs of opulence at the Fall ranch. Back taxes were paid. A fine racehorse and blooded cattle were brought in a special railroad car from somewhere in the East. The newspapermen made inquiries to other papers, including the *Denver Post*. Bonfils and Tammen, with no light to shed on the mystery, showed interest. They sent a staff man named Stackelback, to New Mexico to look into Fall's affairs.

From the station agent at Three Rivers near Fall's place, he managed to get the bill of lading and receipts for the racehorse and cattle. They had come from the Rancocas Farm in New Jersey of Harry F. Sinclair, the big oil man. Suddenly Stackelback was threatened with violence unless he left New Mexico.

But Magee and Anderson began publishing all they could without danger of libel. As early as April 1922, the Albuquerque *Journal* began exposing what was to become the Teapot Dome scandal.

Secretary Fall marched into Magee's office.

"I'll put you on the rack and break you," he threatened.

"Fasten your hat on tight and get out," said Magee.

Fall was not threatening idly. Magee's bank loans were suddenly called. An advertising boycott began. Social ostracism was imposed on Magee and his wife. Criminal libel actions were brought against him. Other suits were brought to harass him and exhaust his resources. A judge friendly to Fall remarked in open court that he preferred horse thieves to editors like Magee; he put the editor in jail for two days for contempt. Friends brought his food in fear that he would be poisoned. Obviously the former Senator and Secretary of Interior was no man to fool with. He stalked again into the *Journal* office.

"Who is the son of a bitch who is writing those lies about me?"

Young Anderson rose tall.

"I'm the son of a bitch and I don't write lies."

Fall left the office quickly. In April 1922, the month in which the Teapot Dome lease of the oil lands, long reserved and protected for the Navy, was signed, Magee was forced to sell his newspaper to the First National Bank of Albuquerque. The bank was controlled by a crony of President Harding's and a friend of Fall's, James G. McNary, who later failed of confirmation when the President appointed him Comptroller of the Currency. This bank also owned the *Herald*, Albuquerque's other paper. Silence ensued until the dispossessed editor started *Magee's Independent*. He took his information to Senatorial investigators. Later, though not until the Senate had taken over the crusade, he turned his weekly into the *New Mexico State Tribune*.

Bonfils and Tammen, owners of the *Denver Post* in 1922, took a more practical view of the crusade against the corrupt Fall-Sinclair deal than Magee had. Tammen was a fat former bartender who never took much trouble concealing the fact that he

was a rogue. Bonfils, a handsome, mustachioed, well-dressed
man, was a second-generation Corsican. He was said always to
feel that Denver should honor him while he robbed it. Roly-poly
Tammen brought to the paper the understanding of human
weakness he had learned on the back side of the bar. Tall Bonfils
brought the boldness and the capital he had required as crooked
gambler often operating under aliases back in the Kansas City
area. They made their paper a circus of continual sensations.
They crusaded. Though their gaudily painted office was called
the Bucket of Blood, Bonfils inscribed on the newspaper building's façade, "O Justice, When Expelled from Other Habita-
tions, Make This Thy Dwelling Place." A cartoonist on the
opposition *News* suggested that they would not know the blind
goddess if they saw the lady. The two vaudevillian journalists
could see talent: They hired the cartoonist.

Against staid and startled opposition they built the *Denver
Post* from a newspaper ruin they had acquired for $12,500. As
its circulation rose they intimidated advertisers and others.
Regardless of their reputations, their paper was read. They grew
rich, but not beyond greediness. And the Teapot Dome scandal
provided the proof (though no conviction) of the charge of
blackmail often made against them.

In its pious role of protector of the people the *Post* (self-
named "The Paper with a Heart and Soul") began publishing
editorials based on the information which Stackelback had
brought back from New Mexico. The actual information they
kept locked in the office safe. In its front-page editorial feature,
headed in large red letters SO THE PEOPLE MAY KNOW, the *Post*
expressed, as the Republic's protector, its protest of the oil
leases.

"A few such arbitrary and autocratic deals as this," the
paper said on April 27, 1922, of the lease to Sinclair, "will set the
country aflame with protests against these kinds of methods,
these kinds of deals, and this kind of favoritism of the Government for the powerful and already completely entrenched oil
monopoly."

The *Post*'s indignation mounted and then suddenly subsided.
Some months later Bonfils was called to Washington by the

Senate committee investigating the oil lease. It had discovered that Bonfils had arranged a secret million-dollar shut-up settlement with Harry Sinclair, then decided that there was nothing the people should know after all. Before the Senate investigators he denied any wrongdoing. Also, characteristically, he used the committee forum to put in a plug for the *Post*.

"The *Denver Post* has the greatest circulation per capita of its publication city of any newspaper in the history of the world."

A Senator said, "I suppose Mr. Sinclair knew all that."

Back in Denver, the Tammen-Bonfils opposition on the *Rocky Mountain News* was elated. Next day, as the investigation proceeded, the elation evaporated. The owner of the *News,* John C. Shaffer, was an insistent exemplar of clean journalism. One story is that he told Tammen he was going to edit the *News* as Jesus Christ would edit it. The *Post* referred to him as John "Clean" Shaffer. Grain speculator, oil millionaire, and owner of the *Chicago Evening Post* and a string of Indiana papers, Shaffer liked it when biographers mentioned his long service as a Sunday School superintendent. Now it turned out that, with some inside dope, too, he had demanded and taken his own shut-up payoff. And it humiliated his already disgusted employes on the *News* that as usual in Denver, in comparison with Bonfils, Shaffer had only got a cut-rate share.

After Magee's first efforts, the part of the press in this greatest American crusade against top-level corruption was worse than limited. Some reporters, notably the erratic, heavy-drinking Paul Y. Anderson, who had left a position on the *St. Louis Post-Dispatch* as editorial writer in 1923 to free lance, provided creative reporting of the scandal. He won not only the Pulitzer Prize for his reporting but also remembrance as "the last of the muckrakers." But Edward B. ("Ned") McLean, who had inherited the *Cincinnati Enquirer* and the *Washington Post,* played a shoddy role in trying to protect Fall from Senate disclosures.

Frederick L. Allen in his *Only Yesterday* reported, as a commentary on the political morality of the time, that at the outset condemnation by much of the press was reserved for the public officials responsible for bringing the facts to light. Still the impeccable press, as represented by the new American Society of

Newspaper Editors, was outraged, as the public around it became more indignant, at the behavior of Bonfils and Tammen. Certainly in the new professional society of editors, they seemed the bastards at the family reunion.

That organization to serve the improvement of the press and the status of its editors held its first full meeting in 1923. And ready for its adoption was the solemnly prepared code of ethics. All present knew that its prohibitions constituted practically a description of the things Tammen and Bonfils had done which nice newspapermen should not do. It was proposed that strong teeth be shown in the new code by expelling the Denver editors for blackmailing Sinclair and so selling out their readers. Righteousness was rampant, but calmer counsels prevailed. The expulsion failed on technical grounds: The deal had taken place before the code was adopted. Ethics evidently had just been invented.

Tammen died on July 19, 1924, while the appalling evidence on the oil corruption was still coming in. Bonfils lived and prospered ten years longer. He died just before he was to be interrogated in a libel suit he had brought against the *Rocky Mountain News*. In it he was called upon to answer questions on a "devastating" bill of forty-one counts against him. The questions were unanswered. He left a lot of money and a foundation for "the betterment of mankind."

Magee, whose editorial curiosity about Secretary Fall's sudden munificence helped uncover the Teapot Dome scandals, lived longer and is less well remembered. In 1925, in an encounter with the judge who had sent him to jail for contempt, Magee accidentally killed a good friend of his own. While Magee himself was recovering from injuries received in that battle in a hotel, his son died in an airplane crash. He was not through crusading. His *Tribune* was sold to the Scripps–Howard chain. When Scripps-Howard bought the *Rocky Mountain News* and moved into Denver to start a slugging, spending struggle for survival with the *Denver Post,* it was first planned to make Magee the fighting Scripps editor. Instead, he did his anticlimax crusading on the chain's *Oklahoma News.* He died at seventy-three in 1946, well-to-do and long-forgotten as an inventor of a parking meter. So far as national fame was concerned, he had overstayed his allotted time. That sometimes happens to crusaders, as to parkers.

The time of the crusading editor and personal journalism again seemed spent. Long before he died in 1921, Henry Watterson had announced with rhetorical finality, "The soul of Bombastes has departed, and journalism is no longer irradiated by the flash of arms." When Watterson himself departed, the equally often quoted William Allen White wrote sadly to the same effect of Watterson in the Emporia *Gazette*. White had watched the consolidation of many independent papers and the resulting unemployment, for a time at least, of many newspapermen. He had seen too much of a journalism "that floats complacently, securely, witlessly in the serene pool of our American finance-capital structure!" Watterson's death moved him to say that the newspaper business was developing no more individualistic editors like "Marse Henry," who sometimes seemed Bombastes himself.

Yet fortunately there were clear evidences that crusading editors were a durable breed, even in an age of change and the growth of newsvending as a commodity industry. Chain newspapers did not necessarily mean that a tactful pursuit of profit by pleasing everybody had made obsolete men ready with the editorial cat o' nine tails for those they regarded as malefactors. Though little remembered today and accorded only a couple of sentences in the standard history of American journalism, Don R. Mellett was a good example. He did not own his paper. Indeed, on *The News* in Canton, Ohio, he worked for the chain of newspapers built by James M. Cox, badly defeated Democratic candidate for the Presidency in 1920. Yet with freedom and force Mellett undertook a crusade to break the hold of gangsters on the government of his town. The World War I industrial boom created a need for more workers there. Manufacturers boosted their profits by importing cheap foreign labor, especially from Mexico and the Caribbean. In the new crowding and with the new opportunities for criminal profit provided by Prohibition, a notorious underworld developed. Few dared resist it. But Mellett struck out. His blows hit home. The old and recurring alliance of politics, profit, and crime was not safe in his editorial presence. On July 16, 1926, he was shot down and killed in his own dooryard by the hoodlums of the racketeer politicians. His death stirred the city to vigorous measures in civic sanitation which eliminated the major vice gangs. The prize for public service which Joseph Pulitzer had provided fifteen years before went to the Canton *News*. Mellett's murder was his monument. He seemed to safer editors a sort of Nathan Hale of a journalism presumably ready to risk all its lives for civic virtue. Around his martyrdom in pride (and comfort, too) the American press, prize-givers, newspaper organizations, schools of journalism could all take their stand for a crusading press.

But proud and comfortable remembrance can never be the measure of crusading editors. Most of those of the past would look awkward in bronze on marble pedestals. Though there are monuments to him, in his lifetime Horace Greeley's personal eccentricities embarrassed even many of his editorial contemporaries. William Lloyd Garrison was an irritant not only to slave-holders but to many fellow Abolitionists as well. Not all, of course, were virtuosos of verbal violence. Much of the uninterrupted impression of the press on American history has been made with sugar as well as vinegar. After all, there was William Rockwell Nelson, whose *Star* got Kansas City out of the mud, as well as Ochs, whose *Times* proved it possible to get the New York press out of the dirt. The crusade of Henry Grady of the Atlanta *Constitution*, more oratorical than editorial, was his effort to love the North and South together again after division. The range of crusade runs all the way from caress to cocklebur. Not the causes for which crusading editors fought but the vitality which they brought to their views has been the mark of the breed. Certainly the time-determined righteousness of their causes does not shape the pattern of the men.

Ben Edes of Revolutionary Boston helped make freedom ring, but he aroused Patriot mobs to behavior which can only be described as hoodlum. Edmund Ruffin of Virginia was as ready to be a martyr for slavery as Elijah P. Lovejoy for abolition in Illinois. It is beside the point that Albert Parsons was an anarchist or that John Reed died to be buried with Bolshevik honors. Pulitzer as well as Hearst was as much concerned about circulation as about Cuba. Possibly E. W. Scripps, who stoutly took the side of the "95 per cent," the common people, was aware that they could buy more penny papers. Yet the notion that the business office dulls the fighting edge of the press disregards the fact that the first little fighting editors were their own editorial and business departments at the same time. George Jones of *The New York Times*, who fought the Tweed Ring, was a publisher in the most modern sense of the term.

Much may have happened since the days when it was said that a man with a handkerchief full of type could set up a paper and array it against all the evil forces he saw in his world. Yet John Peter Zenger wanted more assurance than his few fonts of type when he ridiculed the royal governor. In his ink-stained apron Zenger would look odd at gatherings of either the American Society of Newspaper Editors or the American Newspaper Publishers Association. Fashions have changed swiftly in this century in the press as in everything else. Now newspapers are only items in the midst of media, often stumbling in their tasks over the cables of electronic competition. Even the press itself as industry, as big and costly business, has altered. That could not be made more clear than in the transition from regal William Randolph Hearst to diminutive Samuel I. Newhouse. As an opulent entrant into metropolitan journalism, Hearst paid $180,000 for the New York *Journal*. Newhouse, adding to a lengthy chain or collection, in 1963 paid more for the New Orleans papers than Thomas Jefferson did for the Louisiana Purchase.

The descent of Hearst on Park Row was almost a costumed crusade in itself. Newhouse seemed to rise almost secretly from the *Staten Island Advance*. And in the ownership of newspapers in all parts of the nation, Sam Newhouse remains almost secret. Hearst arrived at his properties in special trains with retinues in attendance. His editors everywhere attended his wishes and waited for his words.

Newhouse comes by commercial plane carrying a brief case. He seems to have no desire to impose his personality on his properties. Their increasing number, from Syracuse, to Portland, to Birmingham, to New Orleans, indicates that he understands profits. Even some publishers, who fear the growth of chains and monopolies as likely to turn political thinking to ideas of public regulation, have not been quite sure whether to regard the swiftly growing Newhouse as millionaire mouse or menace. He could be the embodiment of an impersonalized press. Yet under his ownership, crusade—under local direction—has gone on. His Portland *Oregonian,* which won a Pulitzer Prize for distinguished public service before he obtained it, went on in a costly crusade after Newhouse bought it to win another.

In modesty or self-effacement in self-interest, Newhouse has been a man buying big but appearing seldom and briefly on the scene of his expanding press power. Legends have already grown of subordinates in some cities asking who that man was who had turned up and was poking around. Neither his face nor his words have been familiar to the public in general even in the towns in which he controls all the newspapers. He could become the figure for the impersonal press, only in the Newhouse case his friends and subordinates speak of it as an institutionalized press. They could be the same thing. The arrival of Newhouse— or the Newhouses—in city after city could constitute the arrival of the long-predicted doom of the crusading editor.

"A great deal of twaddle" is still the best description for this notion now, as it was when Dana wrote after Greeley died.

There will always be crusading newspapers and editors. The weakest and strongest papers and editors are inescapably crusaders. Mediocrity gets its message across. Timidity can be taught, and in too many towns it is, now as in the past. *Afghanistanism,* editorship which thunders at distant dangers but is muted about municipal affairs, did not begin in our times. Back in the days after the Spanish War there was an editor of *The Greensboro Patriot* in North Carolina who never saw shenanigans in City Hall but gave unshirted hell to Aguinaldo, leader of the Philippine insurrectionists. His nickname became "Aguinaldo" the rest of his days. There have been such men in all the years since Gutenberg invented printing. There will be such if man ever settles with his need for news on the moon.

There will be crusading editors, too, so long as there is vitality, dissent, determination among literate men. The causes in which they enlist their pens, their typewriters, or their dictating machines do not determine their quality. They may fight great rogues or urge the planting of roses. Their positions may be radical or reactionary, and about matters great or small. The measure is their militancy.

William Allen White inadvertently called attention to the source of the best definition of such editors when, in 1896, he damned among other Populists a lady in Kansas, Mary Elizabeth (called Mary Ellen) Lease. White did not mention her name. He only referred to her in his editorial, "What's the Matter with Kansas?" as one of "three or four harpies out lecturing." But clearly his reference was to Mary Ellen, a woman nearly six feet tall, with no figure, a thick torso, and long legs—but with a golden voice. She could, said the Emporia editor, "recite the multiplication table and set a crowd hooting or hurrahing at her will." The great sentence recalled from her speaking irritated White then. It deserves remembrance now.

"It is time," cried Mary Ellen in her rich contralto, "for Kansas to raise less corn and more hell."

There always have been editors who have felt that it was time to raise hell—against the British Crown, the Federalists, the Jeffersonians, the Whigs, both Andrew Jackson and those who did not like him, against slavery and against emancipation, against Tammany and the trusts, against anarchists and communists, pacifists and militants, and against the Money Power, for and against Prohibition, against and for labor and capital, civil rights and civil righters, against crooks and against reformers.

The crusades in the past were diverse and collided often. They always will. And on every side there will always be men and women in editorial offices ready to raise hell about the causes which concern them. Not personal journalism but American vitality will have been exhausted when there are not such editors in cubbyholes or executive suites, in little independent Emporias, even in the maze of monopoly. And there will always be beside them others wringing their hands over the disappearance of crusading editors while new crusading editors are ringing alarm bells. Across all the years ahead, they will be heard!

Sources and Acknowledgments

This book was begun, I am sure, when as infant I contemplated my parentally gentle but editorially explosive father in his newspaper office which smelled so nicely of ink and paper, paste and Democrats.

He was Josephus Daniels, editor of *The News and Observer*, of Raleigh, North Carolina. He liked to call his paper "The Old Reliable" but was not distressed when a good many of his readers called it "The Nuisance and Disturber." Half-buried in exchanges, proofs, copy paper, and unfiled letters, he wrote with rushing pencil. But his editing was an almost surgical business in which his pencil was by turns everything from scalpel to meat ax. He cracked some high heads. Undoubtedly he spilled some innocent blood, but he missed few of the guilty. There was never any fighting anywhere around him in which he did not gladly stick up his head to take his chances on getting his share of the licks. He took some wallopers.

He survived without a scar. Never was there a more serene man in the art of indignation. His services as Cabinet Minister and Ambassador were only interludes in his editing. If he had become God he would still have considered himself something in the nature of editor of the world.

Let the paper always be "the tocsin," he said in his will, and I was left to sound that alarm bell. I would not want any other work, but being a public scold can sometimes be a lonely business in life. So I naturally sought the company of greater crusading editors in history. There are enough to eliminate the possibility of loneliness among them, though some make only curmudgeon company even in history.

I have only sought the congregation of a few such editors. To many of them I have been led by my daughter, Lucy Daniels Inman, who also was born with ink on her hands, but has used it to gentler, more gracious ends in her novels. Her researches provide the bone and sinew of this book. Others, newspapermen, librarians, historians, helped me. I only name a few of them when I say my thanks to Paul M. Angle, Francis Brown, G. A. Buchanan, Turner Catledge, René Cazenave, Lenoir Chambers, Thomas D. Clark, Julia L. Crawford, Virginius Dabney, Richard Bache Duane, Mrs. Sarah W. Flannery, Frank Gilbreth, Miss Margaret Hackett, Ambrose Hampton, Philip Hochstein, Roy Howard, Sexson E. Humphreys, Earl J. Johnson, Walter Johnson, Norval Neil Luxon, David Mearns, Mrs. Margaret Price, Stephen T. Riley, Arthur M. Schlesinger and Arthur M. Schlesinger, Jr., Miss Clyde Smith.

It was fun to seek the ink-stained ghosts of hellbent or, as they were sure, heavenbent editors. Some of them were hidden in obscurity and others were almost equally lost in the prolixity of their legends. Some are hardly visible now, for the politicians they pushed ahead took pompous places before them. But all put themselves on exhibition in their own pages.

Their pages are the best sources about them. But even in a microfilm age their pages run to miles. No such brief consideration as I have given the men in this book could be based on full reading of the writings of their lives. Fortunately, their friends and followers left memoirs. Scholars have searched for the details of their stories. Local histories place them in the parts they played in the national story. I have been much helped, of course, by *The Dictionary of American Biography* and that inexhaustible trove, the *American Guides* of the WPA. I list below some other books and sources which helped me much in trying to tell something of the kind of editors whose contemporary clamor shaped much of the directions and the destiny of America.

Abernethy, Thomas Perkins: *The Burr Conspiracy*, New York, 1954.

Abbeville, S. C., *Medium*, Feb. 9, 1876: *Memoir of Francis W. Dawson of The News and Courier*, published *News and Courier* Job Printing Office.

Adams, Charles Francis: *The Works of John Adams*, Boston, 1856.

Adams, Henry: *History of the United States during the Administration of Thomas Jefferson*, reprint, New York, 1930.

American Guide Series: California; Illinois; Kansas; Kentucky; Missouri; New York; Virginia.

Barrett, James W.: *THE WORLD The Flesh and Messrs. Pulitzer*, New York, 1931.

Beecher, Rev. Edward: *Narrative of the Riots at Alton*, Alton, Illinois, 1838.

Benton, Thomas Hart: *Thirty Years' View*, New York, 1856.

Berger, Meyer: *The Story of The New York Times 1851–1951*, New York, 1951.

Bergh, Albert (ed.): *The Writings of Thomas Jefferson*, Washington, D.C., 1907.

Bowers, Claude G.: *Jefferson and Hamilton—The Struggle for Democracy in America*, Boston and New York, 1925.

————*The Party Battles of the Jackson Period,* Boston and New York, 1922.

Brown, Francis: *Raymond of the Times,* New York, 1951.

Carmer, Carl: *The Hudson* (American Rivers Series), New York, 1939.

Cash, E. B. C.: *The Cash-Shannon Duel* (ed. by Bessie Cash Irby), Greenville, S.C., *The Daily News* Job Printing Office.

Christman, H. N. (ed.): *The Mind and Spirit of Peter Altgeld,* Univ. of Illinois Press, 1960.

Churchill, Allen: *Park Row,* New York, 1957.

————*The Improper Bohemians,* New York, 1959.

Clark, Allen C.: "William Duane" in *Records of the Columbia Historical Society,* Washington, D.C., IX (1906).

Clark, Thomas D.: *The Kentucky* (American Rivers Series), New York, 1942.

Clough, Frank C.: *William Allen White of Emporia,* New York, 1941.

Cobb, Irvin S.: *Exit Laughing,* New York, 1941.

Coblintz, Stanton A.: *Villains and Vigilantes: The Story of James King of William and Pioneer Justice in California,* New York, 1936.

Coit, Margaret L.: *Mr. Baruch,* Boston, 1957.

Craven, A. O.: *Edmund Ruffin, Southerner,* Durham, 1932.

Current Literature, Vol. XIX, No. 6 (June 1896).

Dawson, Captain Francis W.: *Reminiscences of Confederate Service 1861–1865,* Charleston, S.C., 1882.

Dawson, Sarah Morgan: *A Confederate Girl's Diary,* Indiana University Press, 1960.

Dickerson, O. M.: *Boston Under Military Rule as Revealed in a Journal of the Times,* Boston, 1935.

Drewry, John E. (ed.): *Post Biographies of Famous Journalists,* Athens, Georgia, 1942.

Duane, Richard B. (comp.): *The Descendents and Some of the Forebears of Hon. William John Duane and of his wife Deborah Bache Duane,* 1951.

Duffus, R. L.: *The Tower of Jewels—Memories of San Francisco,* New York, 1960.

Gonzales, N. G.: *In Darkest Cuba*, Columbia, S.C., 1922.

Gray, James: *The Illinois* (American Rivers Series), New York, 1940.

Gramling, Oliver: *AP—The Story of News*, New York, 1940.

Greeley, Horace: *The Autobiography of Horace Greeley*, New York, 1872.

Hale, William Harlan: *Horace Greeley—Voice of the People*, New York, 1950.

Heaton, John L.: *The Story of a Page*, New York, 1913.

Henley, S. W.: *The Cash Family of South Carolina*, Intelligencer print, Wadesboro, N.C., 1884.

Hooker, Richard: *The Story of an Independent Newspaper*, New York, 1924.

Hunt, Rockwell D., and Sanchez, Nellie Van De Grift: *A Short History of California*, New York, 1929.

Ickes, Harold L.: *Freedom of the Press Today*, New York, 1941.

Ireland, Alleyne: *Joseph Pulitzer—Reminiscences of a Secretary*, New York, 1914.

Irwin, Will, and others: *A History of the Union League Club of New York City*, New York, 1952.

James, Marquis: *Andrew Jackson—Portrait of a President*, Indianapolis, 1937.

Johnson, Gerald W.: *An Honorable Titan*, New York, 1946.

Johnson, Walter: *William Allen White's America*, New York, 1947.

Keating, Edward: *The Story of "Labor,"* Washington, D.C., 1953.

Kirschten, Ernest: *Catfish and Crystal*, New York, 1960.

Lewis, Lloyd: *Sherman—Fighting Prophet*, New York, 1932.

Logan, Frank S.: *Francis W. Dawson, 1840–1889: South Carolina Editor*, Master's thesis Duke University, 1947.

Lovejoy, Joseph C., and Owen: *Memoir of the Rev. Elijah P. Lovejoy*, New York, 1838.

Lyon, Peter: *Success Story: The Life and Times of S. S. Mc-Clure*, New York, 1936.

McElroy, Robert: *Jefferson Davis—The Unreal and the Real,* Two vols., New York, 1937.

McGrane, Reginald C. (ed.): *The Correspondence of Nicholas Biddle,* New York, 1919.

McPhaul, John J.: *Deadlines & Monkeyshines—The Fabled World of Chicago Journalism,* New York, 1962.

McRae, Milton A.: *Forty Years in Newspaperdom,* New York, 1924.

Madison, Charles A.: *Critics and Crusaders,* New York, 1947.

Marble, Annie Russell: *From 'Prentice to Patron: The Life Story of Isaiah Thomas,* New York, 1935.

Milton, George Fort: *The Age of Hate,* New York, 1930.

Morgan, James Morris: *Recollections of a Rebel Reefer,* Boston and New York, 1917.

Morris, Joe Alex: *Deadline Every Minute—The Story of the United Press,* New York, 1957.

Mott, Frank Luther: *American Journalism,* Revised edition, New York, 1950.

Nevins, Allan: *The Evening Post, A Century of Journalism,* New York, 1922.

Nixon, Raymond B.: *Henry W. Grady The Spokesman of the New South,* New York, 1943.

O'Connor, Richard: *The Scandalous Mr. Bennett,* New York, 1962.

———*Hell's Kitchen,* Philadelphia, 1958.

Parsons, Lucy E.: *Life of Albert R. Parsons—With Brief History of the Labor Movement in America,* Chicago, 1889.

Parton, James: *Life of Andrew Jackson,* New York, 1860.

Perkin, Robert L.: *The First Hundred Years—An Informal History of Denver and The Rocky Mountain News,* New York, 1959.

Pollack, Queena: *Peggy Eaton, Democracy's Mistress,* New York, 1931.

Pollard, James E.: *The Presidents and The Press,* New York, 1947.

Ravenel, Beatrice St. Julien (ed.): *Charleston Murders,* New York, 1957.

Reed, John: *Ten Days That Shook the World*, New York, 1919.

Rutherfurd, Livingston: *John Peter Zenger: His Press, His Trial, and a Bibliography of Zenger Imprints*, New York, 1904.

Sandburg, Carl: *Abraham Lincoln—The Prairie Years and The War Years*, One vol. ed., New York, 1954.

Sass, Herbert Ravenel, and others: *Outspoken*, University of South Carolina Press, 1953.

Schlesinger, Arthur M.: *Prelude to Independence—The Newspaper War on Britain 1764–1776*, New York, 1958.

——"The Colonial Newspapers and the Stamp Act", *The New England Quarterly*, Vol. VIII, No. 1 (March 1935).

Schlesinger, Arthur M., Jr.: *The Age of Jackson*, Boston, 1945.

Scripps, E. W.: *Damned Old Crank*, edited by Charles R. McCabe, New York, 1951.

Seaton, William Winston: *A Biographical Sketch* (editor unlisted), Boston, 1871.

Seitz, Don C.: *Horace Greeley, Founder of the New York Tribune*, New York, 1926.

——*Joseph Pulitzer, His Life and Letters*, New York, 1924.

Simkins, Francis Butler: *Pitchfork Ben Tillman*, Baton Rouge, 1944.

Smith, Margaret Bayard: *The First Forty Years of Washington Society* (ed. Gaillard Hunt), New York, 1906.

Steffens, Lincoln: *Autobiography of Lincoln Steffens*, New York, 1931.

——*The Shame of the Cities*, New York, 1904.

Stevenson, Elizabeth: *Lafcadio Hearn*, New York, 1961.

Stickney, William (ed.): *Autobiography of Amos Kendall*, New York, 1949.

Stone, Melville E.: *Fifty Years a Journalist*, New York, 1921.

Swanberg W. A.: *Citizen Hearst*, New York, 1961.

Tanner, Henry: *The Martyrdom of Lovejoy*, Chicago, 1881.

Tebbel, John: *The Life and Good Times of William Randolph Hearst*, New York, 1952.

Twain, Mark: *Sketches: New and Old*, New York, 1903.

Van Doren, Carl: *Benjamin Franklin*, New York, 1938.

Villard, Oswald Garrison: *John Brown*, New York, 1910.

——*Newspapers and Newspapermen*, New York, 1923.

Wainwright, Nicholas B.: *The History of The Philadelphia Inquirer*, Philadelphia, 1962.

Wall, Joseph Frazier: *Henry Watterson—Reconstructed Rebel*, New York, 1956.

Wells, William V.: *The Life and Public Services of Samuel Adams*, Boston, 1865.

Werner, M. R.: *Tammany Hall*, New York, 1928.

——and John Starr: *Teapot Dome*, New York, 1959.

White, Stewart Edward: *The Forty-Niners, A Chronicle of the California Trail and El Dorado*, New Haven, 1918.

White, William Allen: *Autobiography of William Allen White*, New York, 1946.

Williamson, Jefferson: *The American Hotel*, New York, 1930.

Wilson, Forrest: *Crusader in Crinoline, The Life of Harriet Beecher Stowe*, Philadelphia, 1941.

Wilson, James H.: *The Life of Charles A. Dana*, New York, 1907.

Index

331

About the Author. Jonathan Daniels started his journalism career as a cub reporter on *The News and Observer* in Raleigh, North Carolina, while he was attending the University of North Carolina. Now editor of that paper, he has also been a staff writer for *Fortune* magazine.

In 1942, Mr. Daniels was appointed Assistant Director of Civilian Defense and later became Administrative Assistant to the President. He was Presidential Press Secretary under President Roosevelt and has served in many other government positions since that time.

Mr. Daniels is the author of fourteen books, including *The Devil's Backbone,* one of McGraw-Hill's American Trails Series. His first book, which is a novel entitled *Clash of Angels,* won him a Guggenheim Fellowship in creative writing.

The father of four grown daughters, Mr. Daniels lives with his wife, Lucy, in Raleigh, North Carolina.

N.C.
071
D